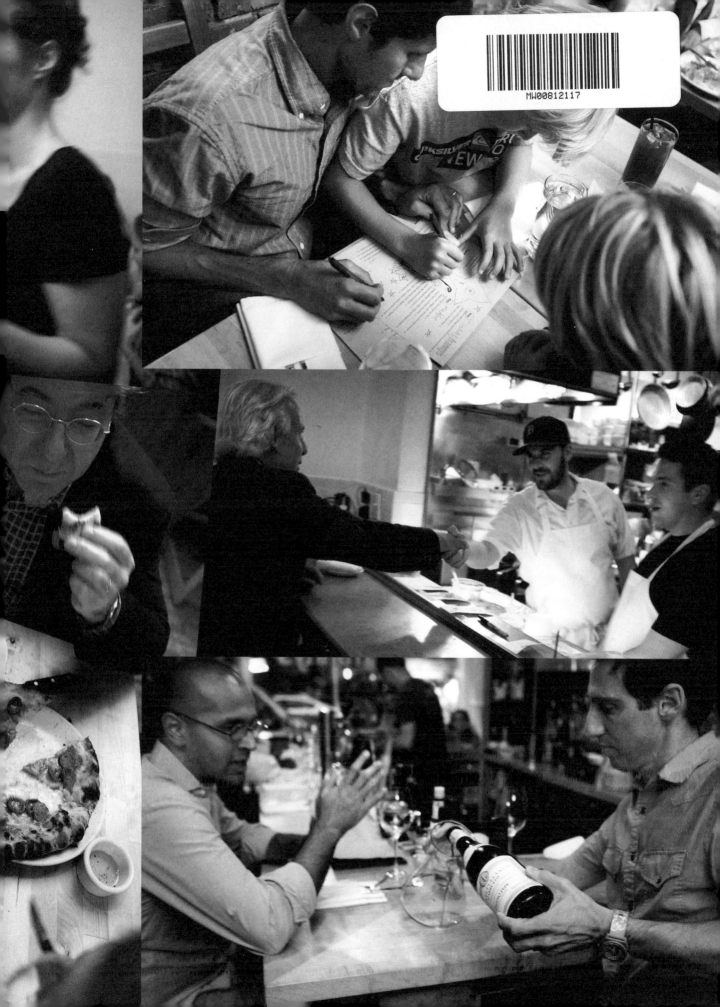

FRANNY'S

FRANNY'S

ANDREW FEINBERG

FRANCINE STEPHENS

MELISSA CLARK

ARTISAN

NEW YORK

Published by Artisan
A division of Workman Publishing Company, Inc.
225 Varick Street
New York, NY 10014-4381
artisanbooks.com

Published simultaneously in Canada by Thomas Allen & Son, Limited

———————————————————————————————

Library of Congress Cataloging-in-Publication Data
Feinberg, Andrew
  Franny's : simple seasonal Italian / Andrew Feinberg,
Francine Stephens, Melissa Clark.
     pages cm
  Includes index.
  ISBN 978-1-57965-464-1
 1. Cooking, Italian. 2. Cooking—New York (State)—Brooklyn.
I. Stephens, Francine. II. Clark, Melissa. III. Title.
  TX723.F43 2013
  641.5945—dc23   2012028954

———————————————————————————————

Design by air conditioned
Printed in China
First printing, April 2013

10 9 8 7 6 5 4 3 2 1

For our moms, Shelley Feinberg and Barbara Stephens

CONTENTS

FOREWORD

The thing that instantly struck me about Franny's was the aroma of the place. It's an almost synesthetic experience, so much more than just the smell of a typical wood-fired pizza: a golden sort of scent, of warmth and light and all things savory. Franny's just smells *good*—which is, sadly, not the case at many restaurants. But at Franny's there is the scent of fresh garlic, and really good olive oil, and the fire you see the moment you walk in the door. There is the intensification of all smells in the marriage of ingredients in the flames: blistered Romano beans with chili oil, fire-roasted broccoli, melting cheese, blackening crust. It is unforgettable.

Francine and Andrew's famous clam pizza was the first dish to woo me—to my knowledge, there is no other clam pizza like it. It is nearly naked, spread with a clam-broth-and-cream reduction and sprinkled with shelled clams, chili pepper, and fresh parsley leaves. Every element of the pizza is deftly calibrated so that the clams' real taste—their essential clamness—comes through. You can taste this harmony of ingredients in all Franny's pizzas, from the classic balance of buffalo mozzarella, San Marzano tomato sauce, and house-made fennel sausage on the sausage pizza to the radical simplicity of the pizza bianca: chewy, thin, charred crust; extra-virgin olive oil; and a generous scattering of Maldon sea salt. Where else can you find this? I believe there is no better pizza in all of New York.

When Franny's introduced pastas, it seemed impossible to imagine that you would ever want to eat one *instead* of their incredible pizza—and yet, unsurprisingly, it is some of the best pasta I have had outside of Rome. The beauty of each dish is in its simplicity: there's nothing eccentric or exotic here, just perfect al dente spaghetti, maccheroni, and penne, strewn with seasonal vegetables and herbs. And, indeed, the salads and vegetables here are as much the stars as the pizza and pasta. Francine writes that "great ingredients demand respect, and vegetables are as deserving as any"—and you can see this vegetable reverence in every dish. One spring I had the best fava bean crostini imaginable at Franny's: little garlicky toasts overflowing with fresh fava beans, torn mint leaves, and Pecorino cheese. (You can find the recipe—which is shockingly straightforward—on page 22.) And as you thumb through these pages, you start to absorb the easy grace with which meals are assembled at Franny's, taking in the idea of improvising with whatever happens to catch your eye at the farmers' market. This book shows you that with some good bread or dried pasta, some cheese, and a bunch of ripe vegetables, you can always make something delicious for your family.

Just as remarkable amid all this inspired cooking is the sense of community that the restaurant engenders. I love the way they list all their suppliers on every menu—all the farms, creameries, and orchards that grow or produce the ingredients that make these dishes possible. Andrew and Francine are part of a network of restaurateurs who are our kindred spirits, believing in the importance of provenance and seasonality and ripeness. And the community they have created within the walls of their restaurant is lovely to see: There are few things as magical as eating hot pizza in their back garden on a warm summer evening, in the glow of strings of small globe lights, the sky holding on to the blue color of twilight for hours. I love that they make room for families too, so that in those early dinner hours, the place is full of kids who are getting introduced, some of them for the very first time, to this wonderfully basic Italian food. It is so great to be able to come back to this restaurant, to be able to rely on something so straight-forward, without pretense. Thank goodness there is someone who is doing this! This book captures the beating heart of what makes Franny's so beautiful: its simplicity, its hospitality, its ability to make the ordinary surprising, and—above all—its celebration of honest everyday cooking.

—Alice Waters

INTRODUCTION

There are many ways to bring people together, but food is one of the most powerful. And for us at Franny's, that means pizza.

Opening a pizza restaurant wasn't always the plan. Creating a restaurant, specifically an Italian restaurant, yes—that we both knew we wanted almost from the moment we laid eyes on each other. The pizza part, however, came later.

Andrew and I met in early 2000. I had just gotten my very first bartending job, at Savoy, the groundbreaking locavore restaurant in SoHo. I kept my head down, focused on learning how to make a proper martini. Meanwhile, Andrew, a recent culinary school grad, was busy cleaning radishes and slicing garlic just a few feet away in the kitchen. I was dimly aware of him rushing past the bar several times a night on his way to the fireplace where he roasted meats and veggies. That went on for months, until one night, we both looked up. I don't know if it was love at first sight, but we noticed each other in a big way.

Right from that first glance, we bonded over food—Andrew cooking for me, gathering friends around it, exploring different flavors and dishes. Before I started at Savoy, I worked in the nonprofit sector of environmental advocacy and sustainable agriculture. That was a perfect fit with Andrew's cooking ethos, centered on the rich flavors of seasonal local ingredients.

The culture of food, and every step of the journey from farm to table, was a vital part of our connection from the start.

So when Andrew told me he wanted to open his own restaurant, something clicked for me too. The idea of uniting around Andrew's cooking thrilled me, and besides, I knew that if I was going

1

to be in a relationship with a chef, the only way I'd ever get to see him was if we worked together.

Andrew had loved Italian food ever since he was a kid growing up on Long Island. He said it was the only thing he could imagine cooking every day for the rest of his life. We daydreamed together about our perfect Italian restaurant and realized we had the passion and drive needed to make it happen, except for one crucial thing: neither of us had ever been to Italy.

It was March. We'd been dating—and dreaming about our restaurant—since October. It was time to get serious on both fronts. So we eloped to Italy.

We flew into Rome and got married on the Amalfi Coast. And we ate everywhere, seeking out street food and homestyle cooking whenever we could. We had some amazing high-end meals, but it was the rustic food, prepared in traditional, classic ways, that would eventually become the cornerstone of the menu at Franny's.

When we came back to New York, we settled in Brooklyn and started looking for spaces in Prospect Heights. What we wanted was our own little place that would become a part of the fabric of the neighborhood, somewhere the whole community would want to eat. And not just for special occasions, but over and over again.

That's when my brother-in-law suggested the obvious: pizza. Of course, he was right. Pizza is delicious, it's Italian, pretty much everyone loves it, and it would appeal to a neighborhood in flux. There were new families moving into brownstones, searching for more space; creative young folks spilling over from downtown Manhattan; and a vital, diverse group of residents who had been there for generations. Pizza would feed them all.

After much searching, we found a space on a gritty stretch of Flatbush Avenue. A former pet store, it was dark, forbidding, and a total mess, complete with desiccated fish skeletons lying in tanks. When I brought my mother in to look at it, she had to hold back tears. Our family and friends thought we were absolutely nuts.

But Andrew and I had our vision. We imagined a cozy neighborhood pizza restaurant with a focus on seasonal cooking. Where there was gloom, we saw soft yellow paint, exposed brick, and two rows of wooden tables filled with regulars. We imagined a cavernous wood-fired pizza oven and a little garden in back, a perfect spot for sipping Italian *rosato* in the summer, shaded by an apricot tree.

Of course, we didn't want to just sling around some pizza dough and then hang up a shingle. If we were going to serve pizza, it had to be the best pizza we could possibly make. We hired a slow-moving but highly knowledgeable Napolitano to build a brick pizza oven in the space, and while we waited, Andrew started experimenting with pizza dough at home (as well as curing his own sardines and perfecting his meatball recipe). It would be an understatement to say that it took a while to settle on the Franny's pizza formula. Towering piles of cookbooks and food science books filled our living room, while enormous bowls of dough slowly fermented in the fridge. It took over our lives, and our apartment—Franny's was truly invented in our home kitchen.

At last we opened. The pizza, to our great delight, found its way into the hearts of families in the community and beyond. Andrew steadily broadened his range, developing recipes for pastas, vegetables, soups, salads, and house-cured salumi. Aside from a handful of mainstays, nothing remains the same at Franny's; as the seasons change, so does our menu. It's food that's easy to love, and it's given Andrew the opportunity to continue pushing boundaries.

Our kids, Prue, born in 2006, and Marco, born in 2007, have grown up eating their daddy's house-cured-pancetta crostini and sausage pizza. And they're not alone—a good number of our regular customers are families with young children. We grew

with the tastes of the neighborhood. To make it easier to find the great ingredients that are the foundation for everything we cook in the restaurant as well as at home, in 2009 we opened a food market, Bklyn Larder, across the street from Franny's. Bklyn Larder soon settled into a successful rhythm, and we started looking for spaces for our next endeavor, a trattoria to be named after our son. A video store up the street had recently been vacated, and the space was completely unlike anything else in the neighborhood. Spacious and lofty, it had high ceilings and large windows that let in plenty of light. It had original period details like cast-iron columns and old mosaic tile floors under the worn carpeting. It was glorious, but not at all what we had in mind for an intimate trattoria—too big, too grand. Yet the space was calling us, and, not wanting to give it up, Andrew got the idea to move Franny's there and install Marco's where the old Franny's had been. In hindsight, it's completely obvious that Franny's had outgrown its original footprint. But it took us a while to see it.

Moving locations, however, didn't change what we were doing in the kitchen. It merely gave us more space in which to do it. Andrew, along with chefs Danny Amend and John Adler, is as enmeshed as ever in the craft of cooking fantastic pizza and rustic Italian food based on seasonal ingredients. Our more spacious new location simply allowed us to share that food with a much larger slice of the city we call home.

By writing a cookbook, we've taken this exchange even further, in what we hope will be an ongoing dialogue with people everywhere—not just in Brooklyn—who love to cook and eat. This is unequivocally a book for folks who want to make simple, hearty food with big flavors, not to mention some of the best, most home-oven-friendly pizzas imaginable.

Even better, all of the recipes are uncomplicated and straightforward. The brilliance of rustic Italian food is its simplicity, and you'll see examples of that in these pages again and again. The unexpected salty bite of a caper, the tang of aged Pecorino, or a final splash of tart, fresh lemon juice can be all it takes to make a dish sing. Our love affair with rustic Italian cooking is evident on every page, but it's Andrew's creativity in combining clean, vivid flavors that makes these recipes memorable—without making them difficult. That touch of pickled hot pepper in a citrus salad (see page 92), using lovage in salsa verde as a sauce for sautéed squid (see page 156), and adding Tuscan kale to crisp, golden zeppole (see page 60) all testify to this.

Along with the recipes, we've included ingredient and technique notes throughout the book that offer insights into many of the skills (crostini oiling, pasta saucing, pizza topping) that are fundamental to this style of cooking. The ideas presented in them are adaptable, and once you've learned them, they can easily be employed elsewhere in your kitchen. We've also provided a framework for using flavorful seasonings—such as lemon, garlic, capers, chilies, and anchovies—so that you'll be able to season these dishes to your own taste. And in keeping with our commitment to seasonal eating, we've arranged the recipes in each chapter in sequential seasonal order, starting with the first hardy bitter greens of early spring and moving through the year to juicy ripe tomatoes, sweet squashes, and dense, creamy sunchokes.

We believe that keeping the food fresh, simple, and whole is the secret to a successful dish. Food doesn't have to be complicated or elaborate to be spectacular. And if you start with high-quality ingredients—pastured meats, seasonal produce, well-crafted cheeses, artisan pastas, and other staples—you can make any good recipe even better. Cooking this kind of satisfying food is something Andrew and I have shared almost from that first moment we met. Running a restaurant together has allowed us to share this passion with an entire community. And writing this cookbook lets us share it with all of you. Cook from it and enjoy!

Cooking Notes

Great cooking is so much more than just following a recipe. Here are some tips and pointers that will make all your homemade meals—whether from this book or not—even better.

EAT SEASONALLY AND LOCALLY

The wonderful thing about eating seasonally is that without question, your food will be more flavorful. Cooking seasonally makes shopping easier, because you'll know that what you're getting is fresh. The cauliflower and kale that you can find in January are far better ingredients for your cooking in winter than pale, mealy tomatoes. Yet really ripe summer tomatoes are so remarkable that you need to do very little to them, and even a simple tomato salad (see page 79) can be extraordinary. The more local those tomatoes, the less distance they have had to travel and the riper they probably are. If you're lucky enough to have a farmers' market nearby, take advantage of it. It's hands down the best place to source seasonal, fresh, local ingredients. Plus, shopping at the farmers' market can be a rewarding experience—you can look your farmer in the eye, and you are directly subsidizing the people responsible for feeding you and your family (you don't get that kind of satisfaction in a supermarket).

Explore new produce that you may be unfamiliar with: farmers' markets and CSAs (community-supported agriculture) provide great avenues for experimentation. If you enjoy cucumbers, try a Tasty Jade or lemon cucumber instead of the Kirbys you usually buy. Tuscan black kale cooks just like its green cousin, but it has a slightly earthier flavor. Buying different heirloom varieties of vegetables that you might already be familiar with can be a great way to expand your cooking horizons.

Farmers' markets are fun, joyous places full of bounty and grateful shoppers, who themselves can be a resource. Don't be shy about asking folks around you about the things they're selling or the things they're buying. Talk to the farmers, and ask them what they do with the mizuna they're offering. Talk to other shoppers—ask the fellow in line ahead of you how he plans to cook those sunchokes. And, of course, there's always the Internet: if you don't know what to do with the gorgeous green garlic you lugged home, there's a website that will tell you.

USE HIGH-QUALITY INGREDIENTS

Many of the recipes in this book are very simple, with only a few ingredients, so it's important to make sure those ingredients are of the best quality you can find. Using real Parmigiano-Reggiano is a must—any other "Parmesan" just won't have the same flavor. A high-quality extra-virgin olive oil can make any recipe exceptional. Artisanally made dry pasta is vastly superior to most of the large-scale, industrially made pasta we're all familiar with. And good olive-oil-packed anchovies or Italian salt-cured anchovies are the only way to go. If you stock your pantry with great ingredients, you'll always have an excellent meal at the ready. Spaghetti with White Puttanesca (page 231) is a perfect example of a lovely, quick dinner that can be put together right out of your pantry. And while some of the products we recommend may be more expensive than what you're used to buying, they're absolutely worth it.

KEEP A WELL-STOCKED PANTRY

Build your pantry slowly, piece by piece, and be sure to restock your favorites. The essentials listed below will bring your cooking to another level. The Resources section (page 357) tells you where to purchase high-quality ingredients if you can't find them where you live.

- Extra-virgin olive oil, preferably a few different styles (such as a peppery Sicilian and a buttery Ligurian)
- High-quality olive-oil-packed anchovies
- Italian artisanal dry pasta, both short shapes and long (such as penne and spaghetti)
- Good dried chilies, preferably a few different types (such as chile de árbol and Controne)
- Dried beans, including cannellini and chickpeas

- Capers, both salt-packed and brined
- Canned D.O.P.-certified San Marzano tomatoes
- Vinegars: white wine, red wine, balsamic, and moscato
- High-quality unsweetened cocoa powder and chocolate
- Fresh shelled whole nuts such as walnuts, almonds, pistachios, and pine nuts (the oils in nuts are perishable, so buy from shops that have a high turnover and store the nuts in your refrigerator)
- King Arthur or other high-quality all-purpose flour
- Dried oregano, preferably Italian
- Fresh garlic
- Bread crumbs, preferably homemade (see page 353)
- A few different varieties of good olives, such as dark, briny Gaetas and fruity Castelvetranos

SIMPLE IS BETTER

With great basics on hand, you can simply add a few fresh ingredients—for example, sausage, cheese, and broccoli rabe—and create a spectacular bowl of pasta like Maccheroni with Pork Sausage and Broccoli Rabe (page 206) without a lot of kitchen prep. Once you have the best ingredients you can find, you won't need to do much to them. Keeping a dish simple means that you can really savor those little pops of sausage, the creamy sharpness of the cheese, and the bitter bite of the broccoli rabe.

Simplicity is one of the hallmarks of *cucina povera*, which inspired many of the recipes in this book. *Cucina povera* (literally "poverty cuisine") gets the most flavor possible out of a particular ingredient, and it also gets the most out of the ingredient, period. Many of us don't use up an entire loaf of good bread at one meal, but why let that heel go to waste? Turn it into bread crumbs or into rustic croutons to add to Squid Salad with Croutons, Cherry Tomatoes, Olives, and Capers (page 157). Or use your stale bread in Tomato Bread Soup (page 104), a *cucina povera* classic. If you've got the determination and time to make our luscious Pork Cheek and Beef Tongue Terrine (page 193), you'll be using cuts of meat that are more often than not discarded. And for our sweet and flavorful Broccoli Soup (page 108), we include the entire head of broccoli, stalks and all. Simplicity and economy go hand in hand, and it's truly gratifying to create a delicious meal following this philosophy.

BALANCING FLAVORS

Salty, sweet, sour, and bitter (and the "fifth taste," umami) are flavors that our palates experience distinctly. A dish that balances them in harmony is a beautiful thing. Beets with Pickled Hot Peppers, Walnuts, and Ricotta Salata (page 150) is a master class in balance: the sweet, earthy beets are set off by the salty, briny prickle of the hot peppers. The toasted walnuts provide a rich, nutty crunch against the softness of the vegetable, and mild ricotta salata adds a soothing, clean element. When you're cooking up something of your own, look for this same sort of equilibrium. Does your dish need a bit of additional salt? Add a handful of capers, olives, or some anchovies as a more complex seasoning agent. Does the dish need a bit more brightness? Give it a good squeeze of fresh lemon juice. Does it need a bit more texture? A generous showering of homemade bread crumbs should do the trick.

BUILDING A MEAL

The recipes in this book are flexible. You can build meals from the different chapters to suit your needs. If you just want a fresh, light, and satisfying summer lunch for two, the Marinated Mackerel with Capers, Croutons, and Herbs (page 158) is complex and lovely all on its own. When you're looking to build a larger, multicourse meal, pair recipes that balance one another. If you've decided to make rich, hearty Tomato, Mozzarella, and Sausage Pizza (page 269) for dinner, start off with a light, lovely plate of vegetables—maybe Sugar Snap Peas with Ricotta, Mint, and Lemon (page 128) if it's early summer, or Roasted Fennel with Lemon, Chilies, and Orange Zest (page 145) if it's early winter. If you're in the midst of the sweltering dog days of summer and turning your oven on is the last thing you want to do, Red Rice Salad with Cherry Tomatoes, Cucumbers, and Corn (page 80) can serve as a great, cool focal point for a meal, supplemented, perhaps, with Sautéed Squid with Garlic, Lemon, and Chili (page 168) and some simple crostini (see page 13).

Equipment

Most of the equipment you'll need to make the recipes in this book may already be in your kitchen. We love making pasta dishes in a very large (14-inch) skillet, and we're sure you'll use it elsewhere too. A food processor and a KitchenAid mixer will come in handy, and a sausage attachment for your KitchenAid will be necessary in order to make some of the recipes in the meat chapter. One piece of equipment that you might not have but that is of ultimate importance is a pizza stone. We've created a method of making pizzas at home that mimics our big wood-burning brick oven, but without a good pizza stone, it won't work nearly as well. A pizza stone is relatively inexpensive and an absolute breeze to use. Simply pop the stone into a very hot oven an hour or so before dinner, and you'll turn out beautifully blistered, authentic fresh pizza right in your own home. If you are in the market for some new kitchen equipment, do treat yourself to high-quality wares. Cooking and eating is something you'll be doing for the rest of your life, so you're investing in your future by buying equipment that will last. The equipment listed below should keep you primed to cook any of the recipes you'll find here.

- Pizza stone
- Kitchen scale
- Whisk
- 14-inch skillet or Dutch oven (for pasta dishes)
- Pasta pot
- Colander
- Tongs
- Chef's knife, paring knife
- Cutting board
- Rimmed baking sheets (aka sheet pans)
- Sausage stuffer
- Injection pump (also called a brining needle) for cured meats
- Mortar and pestle
- Mixing bowls (stainless steel ones are lightweight, heatproof, and sturdy)
- Citrus rasp (Microplanes are the best)
- Deep-frying thermometer (unless you have an electric deep fryer)
- Ice-cream maker

CROSTINI

Every meal deserves a great start—something small and delicious, a taste of food that explodes with flavor and gets you primed for what's to come. We like to start meals off with crostini, simple mouthfuls of grilled or toasted bread with all kinds of toppings. These intense little toasts set the tone for the whole meal. You know from the very first bite that you're going to be taken care of, that the meal will be satisfying and delicious.

You can put so many different things on crostini, from a simple drizzle of good olive oil to an herb butter topped with crisp pancetta to a pile of marinated vegetables. We vary our crostini with the seasons and with what's available at the greenmarket. Crostini should be a little unexpected and a little surprising, and an ever-changing selection ensures that no one ever gets bored.

Because crostini are small, their flavors should be intense. Layering ingredients such as good olive oil, coarse salt, freshly cracked black pepper, lemon juice, and sharp cheeses—both mixed into the topping and as a final garnish—helps the flavors pop when you take a bite. You can do this easily at home, creating your own crostini toppings with what you've got. Use the various cheeses in your fridge, some leftover or fresh vegetables, prosciutto or dried sausage (cooked meats don't work as well). Just put your ingredients onto good grilled or toasted bread, and garnish with the best olive oil you have, along with a sprinkle of salt and maybe a squeeze of lemon if the topping needs acid.

The one thing you *do* need is to start with really good bread. What that means can be a matter of debate. I like my crostini made with smaller, thinner pieces of bread, preferably rounds cut from a long Italian loaf. Andrew likes bigger slices of rough-textured country-style bread. So what we do is match each type of bread with a specific topping.

For vegetable-based crostini, we use a pagnotta made by Brooklyn's own Royal Crown Bakery. It's a rustic bread that's dark and crusty on the outside with a big, holey structure on the inside. We use it for larger, lighter crostini. Since it's a bigger portion, we top the slices with something you can easily eat a lot of: broccoli rabe, chickpeas, eggplant. To substitute for the pagnotta, try to find a good, thick country-style bread with a moist crumb, large air pockets, and a crisp crust. For heartier, meatier, more intense toppings, we use a smaller loaf. Crostini should be about starting a meal off, not filling up before the rest of the food arrives, and no one really wants a gigantic chunk of pancetta on a huge piece of bread. Royal Crown Bakery makes an Italian brick-oven long that's excellent for these smaller crostini. It looks like a French baguette, but the crumb is much denser, the exterior smoky and dark, and the flavor nice and mild. In a pinch, a baguette will do just fine in place of the Italian long.

Whatever you do, avoid sandwich bread when making crostini—you won't get the right crumb, texture, crust, or taste. Also, stick with a plain loaf, with no raisins or nuts to interfere with the flavors of the topping.

Crostini are great little appetizers for kids, and we serve them at home all the time. Our children love the salty, crunchy, oily bread, and we can usually get them to at least try whatever toppings we pile on top (though not always!). We have a big kitchen with an enormous table that takes up a large part of the room, and it is where we spend most of our time when we're at home. While Andrew cooks, the kids and I keep close by, and that proximity to Andrew's cooking holds our family together.

But no matter whom you are serving or where you are eating, crostini are about getting the meal off to a great start—a sign that the meal is going to get even better from here.

Extra-Virgin Olive Oil, Garlic, Sea Salt, and Black Pepper

This crostini was inspired by our last trip to Italy. We had just arrived in Rome and were all exhausted. The kids were crying, everyone was hungry, and we wound up eating at the closest place we could find. To our surprise, we had an amazing experience at that modest neighborhood *osteria*. It wasn't anything remotely fancy or trendy, just a place where they served homey, honest food to a local crowd. We drank the house wine and started our meal with a crostini that was so simple yet so delicious. It was just a piece of toasted bread topped with really good extra-virgin olive oil, a little garlic, plenty of salt, and—the thing that made it really special—a lot of freshly cracked black pepper. There was practically nothing to it, but it was so perfect that as soon as we got back home, we re-created it, and now we make it all the time.

SERVES 4

**Four ¾-inch-thick slices country-style bread
The best extra-virgin olive oil you can find
2 garlic cloves, halved lengthwise**

**Flaky sea salt, such as Maldon
Freshly cracked black pepper**

Preheat the broiler. Drizzle one side of the bread slices with olive oil. Toast, oiled side up, until golden and crisp, 1 to 2 minutes. Rub the toasted side of each slice of bread with a garlic clove half. Drizzle on a bit more olive oil and sprinkle with sea salt and a generous amount of pepper. Serve immediately.

Andrew's Note: You want to use a big olive oil here, something strong, peppery, and grassy–almost hot and spicy. The stronger the oil, the better the crostini. While there are some Tuscan oils that would work, I'd recommend something from Sicily: Frantoia and Olio Verde are great and widely distributed (see Resources, page 357).

CROSTINI

House-Cured Pancetta and Ramp Butter

You might think that pairing an aromatic compound butter and a slice of pancetta on a crostini would be too much—too rich and too intense—but it's actually a fantastic combination. The key is restraint: just a slick of butter and a thin slice of crispy pancetta, so that you can savor the tastes of both without being overwhelmed by either one.

If you want to go all out here, try making your own pancetta (see page 192). But what makes these crostini great is the compound butter. It carries all the flavors of the herbs and spices and gives the crostini a nice creamy richness that's different from the crisp fattiness of the pancetta, and the contrast between the two is what makes it so special. As the seasons vary, we switch the ingredients in the compound butter for what is available: ramps or green garlic in the spring, herb butter in the summer, fennel and chili in the fall and winter (see the Variations on page 16). No matter what time of year it is, these crostini are always delightful.

SERVES 6

FOR THE RAMP BUTTER
2⅔ cups thinly sliced ramp tops
  (from about 20 ramps, depending on size)
⅔ cup thinly sliced ramp bottoms
½ pound (2 sticks) unsalted butter,
  at room temperature

1 teaspoon chili flakes
1½ teaspoons kosher salt
3 thin slices pancetta
Six ½-inch-thick slices Italian long bread
Extra-virgin olive oil

Rinse the ramp tops and bottoms under cold running water to get rid of any grit; dry well. In a medium saucepan, melt 6 tablespoons of the butter over medium-low heat. Add half the ramp bottoms and cook until beginning to soften, 3 to 4 minutes. Add the chili flakes and stir until fragrant, then stir in the ramp tops and salt and cook over high heat until the greens are tender, 1 to 2 minutes. Remove from the heat, transfer to a bowl, and cool to room temperature.

In a food processor, blend the remaining ramp bottoms and cooked ramp mixture (it will not form a smooth puree). Transfer to a bowl and fold in the remaining 10 tablespoons butter. Spoon the ramp butter onto a large sheet of parchment or plastic wrap, roll into a log, twist the ends of the parchment to seal, and refrigerate or freeze until ready to use.

Coat a large skillet with a thin film of olive oil, then add the pancetta in one layer. Cook, turning once, until crisp and browned on both sides, about 2 minutes.

Preheat the broiler. Drizzle one side of the bread slices with olive oil. Toast, oiled side up, until golden and crisp, 1 to 2 minutes.

Spread 1 teaspoon of the ramp butter on the toasted side of each piece of bread and top each with a slice of pancetta. Serve immediately.

Andrew's Note: Leftover compound butter will keep for 1 week in the fridge, or you can freeze it for up to 3 months. It's great for finishing meat and fish, or just spread it on toasted bread for a simple but delicious crostini.

continued

CROSTINI

Variations

Chili Butter: Sauté 1 smashed and peeled garlic clove in 1 teaspoon olive oil until softened; let cool and finely chop. In a medium bowl, combine the garlic, 8 tablespoons (1 stick) room-temperature unsalted butter, 1½ teaspoons seeded and finely chopped jarred Calabrian chilies (see Resources, page 357), ¾ teaspoon of the oil from the jar, and ⅛ teaspoon kosher salt. Spoon the chili butter onto a large sheet of parchment or plastic wrap, roll into a log, twist the ends of the parchment to seal, and refrigerate or freeze until ready to use. Makes about ½ cup.

Herb Butter: In a small dry sauté pan, toast ¾ teaspoon fennel seeds until fragrant; let cool. Grind half the seeds in a spice grinder or mortar. Sauté 1 smashed and peeled garlic clove in 1 teaspoon olive oil until softened; let cool and finely chop.

In a medium bowl, combine the garlic, ground and whole fennel seeds, 1½ teaspoons chopped sage, 1¼ teaspoons chopped rosemary, ¼ teaspoon chili flakes, ⅛ teaspoon freshly cracked black pepper, ⅛ teaspoon kosher salt, and 8 tablespoons (1 stick) room-temperature unsalted butter. Spoon the herb butter onto a large sheet of parchment or plastic wrap, roll into a log, twist the ends of the parchment to seal, and refrigerate or freeze until ready to use. Makes about ½ cup.

Green Garlic Butter: Make a confit: Place the cloves from 2 heads of green garlic in a small pot, cover with 1 cup of olive oil, and cook over the lowest possible heat for 1 hour, or until very tender. Let cool.

In a large skillet, sauté the thinly sliced cloves from 4 more heads of green garlic in 4 tablespoons unsalted butter, with 3 chiles de árbol (or ¼ teaspoon chili flakes) and 2 teaspoons kosher salt; do not let the garlic burn. Cool, and discard the chili pods if necessary.

In a food processor, pulse together 1¼ pounds (5 sticks) room-temperature unsalted butter, the drained garlic confit, the sautéed garlic mixture, and ½ teaspoon freshly cracked black pepper. Spoon the garlic butter onto a large sheet of parchment or plastic wrap, roll into a log, twist the ends of the parchment to seal, and refrigerate or freeze until ready to use. Makes about 3 cups.

Fennel Butter: Toast 2½ teaspoons fennel seeds in a dry sauté pan until fragrant. Let cool, then grind half the seeds in a spice grinder or mortar. Sauté 5 smashed and peeled garlic cloves in 2 teaspoons olive oil until softened; let cool.

In a large skillet, sauté 1 chopped fennel bulb (reserve the fronds) in 4 tablespoons unsalted butter until soft. Season with ½ teaspoon kosher salt. Add ¼ cup finely chopped fennel fronds, and cook for 1 minute longer. Add the whole fennel seeds and 1½ teaspoons chili flakes and cook until fragrant, about 1 minute. Let cool.

In a food processor, pulse the sautéed garlic until finely chopped. Add the fennel mixture, 1 pound room-temperature unsalted butter, the ground fennel, 2 teaspoons kosher salt, 1 teaspoon fennel pollen, and 1 teaspoon cracked black pepper. Spoon the fennel butter onto a large sheet of parchment or plastic wrap, roll into a log, twist the ends of the parchment to seal, and refrigerate or freeze until ready to use. Makes about 2½ cups.

Rapini with Chilies and Garlic

In Italy, you'll see rapini, aka broccoli rabe, in pasta or on pizza, or as a side dish—it's a classic *contorno*. Here we put our own spin on the vegetable by using it for crostini. The rapini, with a little bit of garlic, chili, and ricotta salata, is just terrific on a piece of toasted bread, which soaks up all the pungent juices.

SERVES 4

1½ tablespoons plus 2 teaspoons extra-virgin olive oil, plus more for drizzling
2 large garlic cloves, smashed and peeled, plus 1 clove, peeled
¼ teaspoon chili flakes
8 ounces (1 small bunch) **broccoli rabe, tough ends trimmed**

¼ teaspoon kosher salt, plus a pinch
Juice of ¼ lemon
Freshly cracked black pepper
Four ¾-inch-thick slices country-style bread
½ cup grated ricotta salata

In a large skillet, warm 1½ tablespoons of the olive oil over medium heat. Add the smashed garlic and cook for 30 to 40 seconds, until fragrant but not browned. Add the chili flakes and cook for 10 seconds. Add a handful of the broccoli rabe and cook until wilted. Move the wilted rabe to one side, add the next batch, and cook until wilted; continue until all the rabe is wilted. Add the ¼ teaspoon salt and ⅓ cup water to the skillet. Bring to a boil, cover, and cook for 5 to 7 minutes, until the rabe is tender and most of the liquid is gone but some moisture remains. If the pan looks dry before the rabe is tender, add more water 1 tablespoon at a time as needed. Transfer the greens to a plate to let cool.

Chop the rabe, especially the large stems, into small pieces. Toss with the lemon juice, the 2 teaspoons olive oil, the pinch of salt, and a few turns of black pepper.

Preheat the broiler. Drizzle one side of the bread slices with olive oil. Toast, oiled side up, until golden and crisp, 1 to 2 minutes. Rub the oiled side of the toasts with the remaining garlic clove. Drizzle the toasts with a few drops of olive oil, top with the greens, sprinkle with the cheese, and grind on additional black pepper. Serve immediately.

Andrew's Note: Because these crostini are so simple, with only two basic elements, rapini and cheese, you want aggressive olive oil to bring out all the flavors. Use the spiciest, grassiest oil you can get; just a drizzle will make a huge difference in the taste. Also, while you can make this with supermarket broccoli rabe and it will be good, it becomes really special when you use a bunch from the farmers' market. It's both sweeter and more pungent, and sometimes there are yellow flowers still attached, which makes for an attractive presentation.

Ramps with Pine Nuts, Raisins, and Ricotta

Just a few years ago, no one knew what ramps were or how to cook them, but that's all changed, and now they're the hottest item at the farmers' market. I think people get excited about ramps because they symbolize the arrival of spring. You know it's finally here after a long, dreary winter—ramps are the first burst of green. Plus, the fact that ramps grow wild and can be foraged fascinates people. Years ago, when Andrew and I were living in Great Barrington, Massachusetts, we went for a hike just as the snow was melting, and the woods were filled with ramps. So we went home, got our gloves, and foraged some—it made us feel so resourceful.

Ramps are especially great when roasted; they caramelize beautifully, and the resulting sweetness is such a nice contrast against their pungent, garlicky flavor. That's how you'll find them here, on a bed of milky ricotta with raisins, pine nuts, and a touch of chili for heat.

SERVES 4

¾ **cup fresh ricotta**
¼ **cup golden raisins**
2 tablespoons moscato vinegar
  (see Resources, page 357)
2 tablespoons white wine vinegar
Kosher salt and freshly cracked
  black pepper

20 thin ramps with leaves (about 3 ounces;
  see Andrew's Note)
¼ **cup plus 4 teaspoons extra-virgin olive**
  oil, plus more for drizzling
4 teaspoons toasted pine nuts
½ **teaspoon chili flakes**
Four ¾-inch-thick slices country-style bread

Bundle the ricotta tightly in a piece of cheese-cloth. Place in a sieve set in a small bowl and refrigerate overnight.

Place the raisins in a small bowl and cover with the moscato and white wine vinegars. Cover tightly with plastic wrap and refrigerate overnight.

The next day, unwrap the ricotta and place in a small bowl (discard any water that has collected in the bottom of the bowl). Season with salt and pepper to taste, then use a whisk to whip the ricotta until light and fluffy. Set aside.

Trim the hairy roots from the ramps. Heat a large skillet over medium-high heat. Add ¼ cup of the olive oil and heat until hot. Add the ramps and cook, stirring, until the bottoms are golden and the tops are wilted, 1 to 2 minutes. Season with ½ teaspoon salt and continue to cook for another minute or so, until soft. Add the raisins, with

some vinegar still clinging to them (reserve the remaining vinegar), and scrape up any browned bits from the bottom of the pan, then cool to room temperature. Toss the ramp mixture with the pine nuts, the 4 teaspoons olive oil, reserved raisin vinegar, chili flakes, ¼ teaspoon black pepper, and salt to taste.

Preheat the broiler. Drizzle one side of the bread slices with olive oil. Toast, oiled side up, until golden and crisp, 1 to 2 minutes.

To serve, spread each toast with ricotta. Spoon the ramp mixture on top and drizzle with olive oil.

Andrew's Note: If your ramps are skinny, you can cook them whole. If they are more mature, you will need to slice the bottoms into small disks and slice the green tops into quarters.

Spring Onion Frittata

This is an unusual method for making a frittata. It solves the overcooked egg problem, which causes frittatas to be dry and a little granular instead of creamy and moist. Baking it in a low oven yields a delicate, custardy frittata. We serve it on top of toasted country-style bread as crostini, but it also makes a simple, nourishing supper on its own.

SERVES 8

3 spring onions, trimmed, plus 1 tablespoon slivered spring onion, including green parts

¼ cup extra-virgin olive oil, plus more for drizzling

¾ teaspoon kosher salt, plus more to taste

4 large eggs

⅛ teaspoon freshly cracked black pepper, plus more to taste

Juice of ½ lemon

1 tablespoon coarsely chopped flat-leaf parsley

2 teaspoons slivered mint leaves

Pinch of chili flakes

Eight ½-inch-thick slices Italian long bread

Preheat the oven to 425°F.

Cut the spring onions lengthwise in half (or into quarters if they are large). In a medium ovenproof skillet, heat 2 tablespoons of the olive oil over medium-high heat. Add the onions, cut side down, season with ¼ teaspoon of the salt, and sear for 10 seconds. Transfer the skillet to the oven, without moving the onions, and cook, turning once midway through cooking, until they are dark golden and tender, 8 to 12 minutes. Remove the onions from the oven and reduce the oven temperature to 250°F.

In a bowl, whisk together the eggs, the remaining ½ teaspoon salt, and the ⅛ teaspoon pepper. In an 8-inch ovenproof skillet, preferably nonstick, heat 1 tablespoon of the olive oil. Add the onions to the skillet and cook for 1 minute. Pour in the egg mixture and give the pan a quick shake so that the eggs cover the onions evenly. Transfer the skillet to the oven and cook until the eggs are just set, 18 to 20 minutes. Take it out when the top center, roughly the size of a quarter, still looks a bit undercooked. Let the frittata cool in the pan, then slide it out of the skillet onto a plate. (The

frittata can be made up to a day ahead; wrap tightly and refrigerate until ready to use.)

When ready to serve, slice the frittata into 2-inch-by-¼-inch-thick slices. Place in a bowl. Add the lemon juice, remaining 1 tablespoon olive oil, the slivered spring onion, parsley, mint, chili flakes, and salt and pepper to taste; gently toss to combine.

Preheat the broiler. Drizzle one side of the bread slices with olive oil. Toast, oiled side up, until golden and crisp, 1 to 2 minutes. Place the frittata slices on the toast and serve.

Andrew's Note: Spring onions are one of the first vegetables to appear after the winter. They are always sold with the green tops still attached, and you can use the tops as well as the bulbs. If you can't find spring onions, scallions are a better substitute than regular onions in this recipe, because you need the green tops. But scallions contain less sugar than spring onions. When you roast spring onions, they get really caramelized, and that sweetness comes through in the frittata.

Fava Beans and Pecorino

This is our take on the classic Ligurian *salsa maro*, which is made of crushed fava beans, mint, Pecorino, a little bit of garlic, and a squeeze of lemon to brighten the whole thing up. A mortar and pestle works beautifully here—you get a nice variation of texture, with some bigger pieces and smaller bits as well. If you just dump everything in a food processor and pulse it, you'll wind up with a more uniform consistency, which isn't quite as interesting to eat (see Andrew's Note).

SERVES 4

1 fat garlic clove, thinly sliced
¼ teaspoon kosher salt, plus a large pinch
1 cup peeled fava beans (see Andrew's Note, page 73)
12 mint leaves, torn
4 teaspoons coarsely grated Pecorino Romano

2½ tablespoons extra-virgin olive oil, plus more for drizzling
Freshly cracked black pepper
⅛ teaspoon fresh lemon juice
Eight ½-inch-thick slices Italian long bread

In a mortar, combine the garlic and a pinch of salt and pound together briefly with the pestle to break up the garlic. Add the fava beans and mint and pound until the mixture has a spreadable consistency. Stir in the Pecorino Romano and olive oil. Season with the ¼ teaspoon salt, pepper to taste, and the lemon juice.

Preheat the broiler. Drizzle one side of the bread slices with olive oil. Toast, oiled side up, until golden and crisp, 1 to 2 minutes.

Spread the hot toasts with the fava mixture. Drizzle with more olive oil and serve.

Andrew's Note: If you want to use the food processor for this, go ahead, but be careful and pulse the favas to get different-sized pieces.

CROSTINI

Crostini Techniques

1. Look for a dark-crusted country-style bread with large holes in a light crumb. This is the bread to use as the base for a vegetable-based topping that you can eat a lot of—broccoli rabe, chickpeas, eggplant.

2. Use smaller slices of bread from an Italian long loaf or a baguette for richer, meatier, and more intense toppings that you want only a few bites of: pancetta or chicken livers, for example.

3. Slice country-style bread into ¾-inch-thick slices and Italian long into ½-inch-thick slices.

4. Since the type and size of the bread you use may vary, we can't give you exact measurements for how much oil to use to coat the slices, but we can give you general guidelines. Basically, the surface of the bread should be moist with oil but not wet or dripping. When drizzling the oil on the bread, place your thumb over the spout to control the amount of oil leaving the bottle. (You can also brush the oil on with a pastry brush.)

5. For richer toppings, use less butter or oil. For example, you don't want to add too much compound butter to the pancetta crostini, because the pancetta is very rich on its own. You want just enough butter to enhance the flavor of the pancetta, not overpower it.

CROSTINI

6. For lighter, vegetable-based toppings, pile them onto the crostini so you get a good-sized portion, with lots of different textures.

Roasted Cherry Tomatoes with Ricotta

For these simple yet stunning crostini, roasted cherry tomatoes are paired with fresh, creamy ricotta, which also acts as an anchor for the tomatoes, keeping them from falling off the toast as you eat. Pile the tomatoes as high as you can for a truly spectacular summer snack. Make these crostini in August and September, when the tomatoes are really in season; in other months, tomatoes will not be exceptional.

SERVES 4

4 cups assorted cherry tomatoes
¼ cup extra-virgin olive oil, plus more
   for drizzling
¼ teaspoon kosher salt, plus more to taste
Four ¾-inch-thick slices country-style bread

1 fat garlic clove
¼ cup fresh ricotta
Freshly cracked black pepper
8 basil leaves
Flaky sea salt, such as Maldon

With a rack in the middle, preheat the oven to 250°F. Toss the tomatoes with the olive oil and salt. Spread out on a small baking sheet; the tomatoes should just fit on the baking sheet, without crowding. Roast for 2 hours.

Reduce the heat to 200°F and roast the tomatoes for 1½ hours longer, until shriveled and golden-edged. Cool the tomatoes completely on the baking sheet, then transfer, along with the oil from the pan, into a bowl.

Preheat the broiler. Drizzle one side of the bread slices with olive oil. Toast, oiled side up, until golden and crisp, 1 to 2 minutes. Rub the toasted side of the bread with the garlic.

Put the ricotta in a small bowl and season generously with salt and pepper. Spread 1 tablespoon of the ricotta on each toast. Lay 2 basil leaves on each one. Mound the tomatoes on the toasts. Season with sea salt and lots of pepper. Drizzle each toast with about 1 teaspoon of the roasted tomato oil and serve.

Andrew's Note: I prefer to use smaller cherry tomatoes—they tend to be sweeter and more intensely flavored. This recipe works with a variety of cherry tomatoes: Sun Golds, Sweet 100s, Mexican Midgets, currant tomatoes, or red wild ones. Try to get a mix of colors for the best presentation.

Zucchini, Cherry Tomato, and Pantaleo

This is a perfect summer crostini; it can be a staple when both tomatoes and zucchini are in their peak season because the flavors work beautifully together. The crostini was created by chef Danny Amend, who mixed slowly stewed zucchini with crushed ripe cherry tomatoes and chunks of Pantaleo, a hard goat's-milk cheese (if you can't find Pantaleo, substitute a four- to six-month-old Pecorino). A little fresh lemon juice finishes it off, and the whole thing is absolutely delicious!

SERVES 4

1 cup extra-virgin olive oil, plus more
  for drizzling
1 pound medium zucchini, trimmed and
  cut into 1-inch chunks
1 teaspoon kosher salt, or more to taste
6 garlic cloves, coarsely chopped, plus
  1 clove, smashed and peeled

1 cup basil leaves, plus 4 sprigs
¼ cup Pantaleo, cut into ½-inch dice
16 cherry tomatoes, smashed
Freshly cracked black pepper
Fresh lemon juice for drizzling (optional)
Four ¾-inch-thick slices country-style bread

In a large Dutch oven, heat ¾ cup of the olive oil over medium heat. Add the zucchini in a single layer. Cook gently, without letting it color, for several minutes, until softened. Sprinkle with the salt and chopped garlic, cover the pot, and cook over medium-low heat until the zucchini is tender, about 10 minutes. Stir in the basil sprigs and remove from the heat.

Let the zucchini stand, covered, for 10 minutes to allow the basil to perfume it, then remove and discard the basil sprigs and let the zucchini cool completely.

In a medium bowl, stir together the zucchini, Pantaleo, and tomatoes. Stir in the remaining ¼ cup olive oil and tear in the basil leaves. Season with pepper and with more salt if necessary. If the cherry tomatoes are very sweet, add a few drops of lemon juice to balance the flavors.

Preheat the broiler. Drizzle one side of the bread slices with olive oil. Toast, oiled side up, until golden and crisp, 1 to 2 minutes. Rub the toasted side of the bread with the remaining garlic clove.

Spoon the zucchini mixture over the toasts and serve.

Andrew's Note: I like to make this crostini with Romanesco zucchini, which has better flavor, is less watery, and has fewer seeds than regular zucchini. To me, it's the zucchini that tastes most like zucchini. Romanesco is usually smaller; it's paler in color and is ribbed. With regular zucchini, you have to be careful when you cook it, because it can fall apart and disintegrate. Romanesco stays firm and intact while cooking.

CROSTINI

Whipped Eggplant and Anchovy

This is one of our favorite crostini to make when we can find good Japanese eggplant. Andrew grills the eggplants whole on the barbecue, much as for baba ghanoush, until they collapse. Then he whips the smoky eggplant with olive oil, pepper, salt, and lemon juice, spreads it on the toasted bread, and tops it with great anchovy fillets.

Don't try this recipe with globe eggplants: they can be seedy, and the skin is far too tough. With Japanese eggplants, everything goes into the puree, smoky skin and all, and the flavor is much more pronounced.

SERVES 6

5 Japanese eggplants (about 12 ounces),
  stem ends trimmed
**½ cup plus 1 tablespoon extra-virgin olive
  oil, plus more for drizzling**
1 tablespoon kosher salt, plus more to taste
5 garlic cloves

Juice of 1 lemon
Freshly cracked black pepper
3 tablespoons chopped flat-leaf parsley
Six ¾-inch-thick slices country-style bread
6 anchovy fillets

CROSTINI

Preheat a charcoal or gas grill for medium-high indirect cooking, preferably using hardwood charcoal (if you have a gas grill, see Andrew's Note).

Toss the eggplants with ¼ cup of the olive oil and sprinkle with the salt. Transfer the eggplants to the unheated part of the grill and cook, covered, turning occasionally, until the skin is lightly charred and the flesh is soft, 10 to 15 minutes. (Alternatively, you can roast the eggplant in a 400°F oven until soft.) Cool completely.

Thinly slice 4 of the garlic cloves. In a small skillet, heat 2 tablespoons of the olive oil over medium heat. Add the sliced garlic and cook until fragrant and tender, about 2 minutes. Remove from the heat.

In a food processor, combine the cooled eggplant, the remaining 3 tablespoons olive oil, the lemon juice, garlic oil mixture, and salt and pepper to taste. Whip until smooth. Transfer the puree to a bowl and stir in the parsley.

Preheat the broiler. Drizzle one side of the bread slices with olive oil. Toast, oiled side up, until golden and crisp, 1 to 2 minutes.

Rub the toasted side of the bread with the remaining garlic clove. Spread the eggplant puree over the toasts. You want a nice thick layer. Drape an anchovy fillet over each crostini and serve.

Andrew's Note: If you have a gas grill, just be aware that you won't get as intense a smoky flavor unless you use some hardwood chips. To do this, take a metal pan, fill it with some chips and a little water, and place it over the fire before grilling the eggplants. The aim here is to have the water evaporate so the chips dry out and start smoking.

Roasted Peppers with Capers and Anchovies

Peppers are so important in classic Italian cuisine that it's too bad they are only in season in August and September here in New York. But in the short time that we have local peppers, we try to make the most of the harvest and to cook with them as much as we can until they disappear with the first frost. This is one of the easiest ways to use peppers—roasted, they become even sweeter and make a perfect topping for a crostini when marinated with herbs, garlic, and vinegar, and garnished with salty whole anchovies.

SERVES 4

FOR THE PEPPERS
1 red bell pepper
⅛ teaspoon kosher salt
Pinch of freshly cracked black pepper
1 garlic clove, thinly sliced
1 teaspoon salt-packed capers, rinsed, soaked, and drained (see Andrew's Note)
1 teaspoon chopped oregano

1 teaspoon red wine vinegar
2 to 3 tablespoons extra-virgin olive oil, or as needed

Eight ½-inch-thick slices Italian long bread
1 garlic clove
8 anchovy fillets
Basil leaves for garnish

If you have a gas stove, place the pepper over one of the burners, turn the flame up to high, and char the pepper, turning with tongs, until blackened all over. Or do this in your oven under the broiler, positioning the pepper 2 inches from the heat source. Place the pepper in a deep bowl, cover with aluminum foil, and let stand for 10 minutes.

Using your fingers or a paring knife, pull or scrape off the blackened skin from the pepper. Cut the pepper lengthwise into quarters and discard the seeds. Transfer the pepper to a bowl and season with the salt and pepper. Add the sliced garlic, capers, oregano, and red wine vinegar. Pour enough olive oil over the pepper quarters to cover them halfway. Cover with plastic wrap and refrigerate for at least 2 hours, or as long as overnight.

Preheat the broiler. Drizzle one side of the bread slices with olive oil. Toast, oiled side up, until golden and crisp, 1 to 2 minutes. Rub the toasted side of the bread with the garlic clove.

Thickly slice the pepper quarters and pile them on the crostini, with the herbs and capers clinging to them. Top each with an anchovy fillet and tear the basil leaves over the crostini. Drizzle with some of the pepper marinade and serve.

Andrew's Note: We use capers from Pantelleria (see Resources, page 357), which I think are the best available. They come packed in salt, so you need to rinse and then soak them before using.

Put them in a bowl, cover them with a lot of cold water, and let them soak for 3 to 5 hours, changing the water two or three times. In the end, they should taste seasoned but not overly salty. Once they are soaked, spread the capers on a clean cloth and let them dry out for a few hours. Then store them in a tightly covered container in the fridge for a week or two.

Fresh Cranberry Beans with Herbs and Garlic

You know summer is nearing its end when fresh shell beans show up at the greenmarket. We cook with beans year-round, but the fresh ones we get in late summer cook faster than their dried counterparts, and they don't need to be soaked. Shelling the fresh beans takes some work and time, but the difference in flavor is incredible: Dried beans are starchier, softer, earthier. Fresh beans are brighter in flavor and a little bit herbal.

You can make these crostini with any shell beans you find, but cranberry beans, which are the most common, work wonderfully. We make a puree out of some of the beans, and that puree anchors the whole beans that go on top. That way, you can eat your crostini and still feel graceful in the process, with no loose beans rolling around on the table.

SERVES 4

1½ pounds fresh cranberry beans, shelled (2 cups)
5½ tablespoons extra-virgin olive oil, plus more for drizzling
3 sage leaves, plus 2 teaspoons finely chopped sage
1 small rosemary sprig, plus 1 teaspoon finely chopped rosemary

4 garlic cloves
1½ teaspoons kosher salt, plus more to taste
¼ teaspoon freshly cracked black pepper, plus more to taste
Fresh lemon juice, for seasoning
Four ¾-inch-thick slices country-style bread

Place the beans and 3 cups water in a medium pot. Stir in 2 tablespoons of the olive oil, the sage leaves and rosemary sprigs, 2 of the garlic cloves, the salt, and the pepper. Bring to a simmer over medium-high heat, turn the heat down to low, and cook the beans until tender, 30 to 35 minutes. Cool the beans in their liquid, then drain, reserving 3 tablespoons of the liquid.

While the beans cook, coarsely chop the remaining 2 garlic cloves. In a small sauté pan, warm 2 tablespoons of the olive oil over low heat. Add the garlic and cook gently for several minutes, until soft and fragrant. Add the chopped herbs, remove the pan from the heat, and cool the oil to room temperature.

Transfer 1 cup of the beans to a food processor and add the reserved bean liquid. Puree the beans until smooth. With the motor running, add the remaining 1½ tablespoons olive oil and process just until the oil is mixed in. Season the puree with salt, pepper, and lemon juice. Stir the herb oil into the remaining whole beans and season with salt and pepper.

Preheat the broiler. Drizzle one side of the bread slices with olive oil. Toast, oiled side up, until golden and crisp, 1 to 2 minutes. Spread each toast with a layer of bean puree. Top with a layer of whole beans. Drizzle with olive oil and serve.

Hard-Boiled Egg with Bottarga di Muggine

This is, put simply, an Italian egg salad, but while it's unassuming, it's hardly commonplace. It is made from two types of eggs: chicken eggs and mullet bottarga, which is pressed salted, dried fish eggs. The hard-boiled eggs are creamy and luxurious, and the bottarga adds a refreshing briny taste.

SERVES 4

2 large eggs
⅛ teaspoon kosher salt
Freshly cracked black pepper
2 tablespoons extra-virgin olive oil, plus
  more for drizzling

Juice of ¼ lemon
Four ¾-inch-thick slices country-style bread
¼ cup grated bottarga (see Andrew's Note)

Place the eggs in a heavy 1-quart saucepan, cover with 3 cups cold water, and bring to a boil over high heat. Cover, lower the heat to a bare simmer, and cook for 8½ minutes. Remove the eggs and place in an ice bath until cold, about 10 minutes. Drain, crack, and shell the eggs.

Place the eggs in a small bowl and mash roughly with a fork, but don't break them up too much. Add the salt, pepper to taste, the olive oil, and the lemon juice.

Preheat the broiler. Drizzle one side of the bread slices with olive oil. Toast, oiled side up, until golden and crisp, 1 to 2 minutes.

Spoon some of the mashed eggs onto each toast and sprinkle generously with the grated bottarga. Drizzle with a little more olive oil, grind on some black pepper, and serve.

Andrew's Note: Bottarga is pressed salted fish roe. Look for mullet roe (*muggine*) rather than tuna (*tonno*) roe. Mullet roe is milder, tasting more subtly of the sea, without the slight bitterness of tuna bottarga. If you notice a thin waxy layer on top of the bottarga, use a paring knife to peel it off (it might get caught in your teeth if you leave it on).

| CROSTINI |

Ricotta with Olives and Pistachios

This crostini of olives and pistachios was inspired by the flavors of Sicily. The pistachio and ricotta combination reminds me of cannoli, though the olives put this firmly in the savory camp. You can also make this dish without the ricotta: just chop the olives and pistachios finer, almost like a pesto, and smear it onto the bread. It's important to use the proper olives here to make the whole thing come together. We like Castelvetrano olives from Sicily; if you can't find them, Cerignola olives make a decent, if not exact, substitute.

SERVES 4

¾ **cup ricotta**
¼ **cup coarsely chopped toasted pistachios**
¼ **cup Castelvetrano** (see Andrew's Note) **or Cerignola olives, pitted and chopped**
¼ **cup extra-virgin olive oil, preferably Sicilian, plus more for drizzling**
2 **tablespoons chopped flat-leaf parsley**
2 **anchovy fillets, minced**

Juice of ½ lemon
½ **teaspoon grated orange zest**
¼ **teaspoon kosher salt, plus more to taste**
Scant ¼ **teaspoon freshly cracked black pepper, plus more to taste**
Pinch of chili flakes
Four ¾-**inch-thick slices country-style bread**

Place the ricotta in a fine sieve and set the sieve over a bowl. Refrigerate overnight to drain the liquid from the cheese.

The next day, in a medium bowl, stir together the pistachios, olives, olive oil, parsley, anchovies, lemon juice, orange zest, salt, black pepper, and chili flakes.

In a small bowl, season the drained ricotta with salt and pepper to taste.

Preheat the broiler. Drizzle one side of the bread slices with olive oil. Toast, oiled side up, until golden and crisp, 1 to 2 minutes.

Spread each toast with about 3 tablespoons ricotta and top with the pistachio-olive mixture.

Andrew's Note: Castelvetrano olives from Sicily are big green olives that are extremely buttery, mild, and not too salty. But to keep them perfectly green, you need to leave them submerged in the brine until the last minute—otherwise, they'll turn brown. If you end up pitting more olives than you need, just drop them back into the brine.

Chickpeas and Olives

One of my pet peeves about crostini is that sometimes the topping falls off the bread, leaving me with just the toast. The biggest culprit tends to be chickpea crostini, as the chickpeas can roll off and run away. For this version, as for the cranberry bean crostini, we keep the chickpeas in place by first spreading the bread with a layer of chickpea puree. The pureed beans not only keep the whole chickpeas on top of the bread but also add a delicious, creamy texture.

SERVES 6

FOR THE CHICKPEAS
1 pound dried chickpeas
5 cups water
½ cup extra-virgin olive oil
2 tablespoons kosher salt
1 small onion (or ½ large), cut in half
3 large garlic cloves, smashed and peeled
1 bay leaf
1 small rosemary sprig

FOR THE PUREE
1¼ cups cooked chickpeas (from above)
⅓ cup reserved bean cooking liquid
1 tablespoon extra-virgin olive oil
¼ teaspoon kosher salt
Freshly cracked black pepper

FOR THE SALAD
⅔ cup cooked chickpeas (from at left)
4 spicy green olives, such as Calabrese, pitted and sliced
1 tablespoon chopped flat-leaf parsley
Juice of ¼ lemon
2 teaspoons extra-virgin olive oil
Pinch of chili flakes
Kosher salt and freshly cracked black pepper to taste

Six ¾-inch-thick slices country-style bread
Extra-virgin olive oil for drizzling
1 garlic clove

To make the chickpeas: Soak the chickpeas in a bowl of cool water to cover for at least 8 hours, or up to overnight.

Drain the chickpeas and place in a large saucepan. Cover with the 5 cups water and add the olive oil and salt.

Make a sachet by laying a triple layer of cheesecloth on a work surface. Place the onion, garlic, bay leaf, and rosemary in the center of the cheesecloth and tie the corners of the cheesecloth together to make a bundle. Place the sachet in the saucepan and bring to a boil over medium-high heat. Skim any foamy scum that comes to the surface. Reduce the heat to low to maintain a simmer, cover the pot, and cook the chickpeas until tender, 30 minutes to 1½ hours (depending on the freshness of the beans). Taste regularly to check the tenderness. Drain the chickpeas, reserving the cooking liquid.

To make the puree: Place the chickpeas, cooking liquid, olive oil, salt, and pepper to taste in the work bowl of a food processor. Process, scraping the sides down often, until the mixture is smooth.

To make the salad: In a small bowl, toss all the ingredients together.

Preheat the broiler. Drizzle one side of the bread slices with olive oil. Toast, oiled side up, until golden and crisp, 1 to 2 minutes.

Lightly rub the toasted side of the slices of bread with the garlic clove. Spread about a ¼-inch-thick layer of puree (about 2 tablespoons) on each toast and top with the chickpea salad.

Andrew's Note: You will have some chickpeas left over after making these crostini. They'll keep in the fridge for 5 or 6 days, and they make a great addition to soups and salads. Or you can mash them up with minced garlic, extra-virgin olive oil, some chopped flat-leaf parsley, lemon juice, coarse sea salt, and freshly cracked black pepper and turn them into a sandwich spread or dip. You can also use them as a substitute for the Controne beans in Seared Shrimp with White Beans, Olives, and Herbs on page 164.

Spuma di Tonno and Sal Secco Olives

This is what happens when a tuna sandwich goes upscale: it turns into a crostini. To make it, we whip the tuna with anchovies, capers, lemon, and butter until it turns into a creamy, salty, and utterly delicious mousse (*spuma* means foam), then spread it on the toasted bread. A few olives on top accentuate the tuna's brininess in a most compelling way.

SERVES 6

Two 5-ounce cans or jars Italian tuna packed in oil, drained
7 anchovy fillets
2 tablespoons salt-packed capers, rinsed, soaked, and drained (see Andrew's Note, page 30)
Finely grated zest of 2 lemons
12 tablespoons (1½ sticks) **unsalted butter, at room temperature**

1 tablespoon fresh lemon juice
¾ teaspoon freshly cracked black pepper
Six 1-inch-thick slices country-style bread
Extra-virgin olive oil for drizzling
6 sal secco (or other dry, salt-cured) **olives, pitted and chopped**

In the bowl of a food processor, combine the tuna, anchovies, capers, and lemon zest. Pulse several times to combine, then add the butter and process until well incorporated. Scrape down the bowl and pulse again until combined. Scrape the mixture into a bowl. Stir in the lemon juice and pepper.

Preheat the broiler. Drizzle one side of the bread slices with olive oil. Toast, oiled side up, until golden and crisp, 1 to 2 minutes.

Top the toasts with the tuna spread and olives. Drizzle with more olive oil and serve.

Chicken Liver and Pancetta

You'll see chicken liver crostini served in Italy, but not with pancetta on top. This crostini is one of my favorite dishes of all time; I love how it bridges the Jewish tradition with the Italian one.

Andrew combines the Jewish deli sandwich of chopped chicken liver and pastrami with the Italian flavors of capers, anchovies, and pancetta and turns the whole thing into a crostini. The pancetta is key; it takes the place of the pastrami and makes the flavors savory and delicious, while the creamy chicken liver acts almost like butter, anchoring the meat to the bread.

SERVES 8

8 ounces chicken livers
2 tablespoons plus 1 teaspoon extra-virgin olive oil, plus more for drizzling
¼ cup finely chopped Spanish onion
1 medium garlic clove, thinly sliced
2 anchovy fillets, minced
1 tablespoon salt-packed capers, rinsed, soaked, and drained (see Andrew's Note, page 30)

1 tablespoon chopped sage
1 teaspoon chopped rosemary
2 tablespoons dry vermouth
¾ teaspoon kosher salt
4 thin slices pancetta, unrolled and cut in half crosswise
Eight ½-inch-thick slices Italian long bread
Freshly cracked black pepper

Clean the chicken livers thoroughly, taking care to remove all the membranes and veins, and any pockets of green bile (but not the dark red or brown spots; those are fine). Keep the livers as whole and intact as possible, which is easier for cooking. Season the livers generously with salt and pepper on both sides.

Heat a large skillet over high heat until it just begins to smoke. Add 1 tablespoon of the olive oil and the livers (work in batches if necessary; be careful not to crowd the pan). Cook the livers until they begin to brown, 1 to 2 minutes per side. Transfer to a plate.

Add another tablespoon of olive oil and heat for 30 seconds. Add the onions to the pan and cook, stirring to pick up all the brown bits from the bottom of the pan, just until the onions are softened, 1 to 2 minutes. Use a slotted spoon to remove the onions and put them on top of the livers. Add the garlic and anchovies to the pan, reduce the heat to medium-low, and cook just until the anchovies dissolve and the garlic is slightly golden brown, about 1 minute. Add

the capers and chopped herbs and cook until fragrant, 30 to 40 seconds. Add the vermouth to the pan, stirring to deglaze, and cook until syrupy, about 1 minute. Scrape everything from the pan onto the livers and let cool.

Place the livers and other ingredients in the work bowl of a food processor and pulse until the mixture comes together but is still somewhat chunky. (The chicken liver can be made a few days ahead. Transfer to a bowl, press plastic wrap directly onto the surface, and refrigerate.)

In a large skillet, heat the remaining teaspoon of olive oil over medium-high heat. Cook the pancetta until golden brown and crispy, 1 to 2 minutes on each side. Remove from the heat.

Preheat the broiler. Drizzle one side of the bread slices with olive oil. Toast, oiled side up, until golden and crisp, 1 to 2 minutes.

Spread 1 tablespoon chopped liver on each toast, and top with a slice of pancetta. Top with olive oil and some black pepper. Serve immediately.

FRITTI

From the north to the south, Italians love fried food, and they prepare it very, very well. In every region that we've been lucky enough to visit, Andrew and I have always fallen for whatever *fritto* we encounter. In Milan, it's fried olives. On the Amalfi Coast, it's *bianchetti,* tiny little fish. Fried meatballs in Tuscany, *fritto misto* in Venice, fried cheese in Sicily . . . whatever the Italians fry, we are happy to savor.

Well-prepared fried food is incredibly tempting, and with good reason. When an ingredient is submerged in hot oil, its exterior turns golden and irresistibly crisp, while the center steams lightly without overcooking. A fried boiled potato emerges fluffy on the inside, a fried roasted artichoke is moist and succulent, fried zucchini softens without turning to mush. All the moisture in the vegetable's flesh is locked in place, along with its flavor and a lot of nutrients. It's a mistake to think that fried food is inherently unhealthy. If you are using the proper frying temperature, very little oil actually permeates the food itself. Sure, there may be some oil glistening in the browned nooks and crannies of our fried fingerling potatoes (see pages 62 and 63), but that's what makes them so delicious. Only deep-frying can create all the varying crunchy textures found in the recipes in this chapter. And, as you'll see, many of these recipes are all about experiencing the fullest and truest flavors possible—seasonal produce at its peak can be transcendent when fried.

Frying food at home can put some people off—many imagine a lot of mess, high heat, smell, and even a bit of danger. We say fried foods are worth the cleanup. And as for the danger element—the splattering—as long as you add your ingredients to the pot carefully, you'll be fine. It also helps to have the right tools, but the list is fairly basic: a heavy, preferably cast-iron, pot; a long deep-fry/candy thermometer that clips to the side of the pot; and a big jar for disposing of the spent oil. (That said, if you have an electric fryer, by all means pull it out and put it to good use here.)

When we were opening Franny's, our idea was to fry everything in a big cast-iron pot on the stove. Andrew had seen frying in cast-iron pots in New Orleans, and it stuck with him: We were on one of our first trips out of town as a couple, and we were eating at the fabulous Casamento's, famous for fried oysters and po'boys. In order to get to the restrooms, diners had to pass through the kitchen, and on his way through, Andrew spied a team of women cooks frying up everything to order in big black cauldrons. He loved the simplicity of this method and vowed to adopt it at the restaurant.

But, as things turned out, a big pot of frying oil on the stove in the middle of service just isn't practical. And our small kitchen couldn't handle the rush of orders that came in whenever we had something fried on the menu. Unlike the ladies in New Orleans, Andrew also had to tend to the rest of the menu, all those pizzas and salads. It was just too much. Back in those early days, our families were always coming in (supportive as they are), and one evening a big group of Andrew's relatives sat down for dinner. The kitchen got a ticket for eight orders of *carciofi alla giudía* (fried artichokes, Jewish-style), all from one table. It was a devastating blow to the busy kitchen—and Andrew realized it was for his family's table. That very night he decided to purchase a proper deep fryer.

Once he did, fried food came back on the menu with a vengeance. Now there's always something crispy and delicious on offer, even if it's as utterly unassuming (but addictive) as Potato Croquettes (page 58). These make for great bar food—when one half of a couple beats the other to the restaurant, that might be his or her reward while waiting, with a cocktail in hand.

Departing from finger food, Fried Eggplant with Parmigiano-Reggiano, Tomato, and Basil (page 54) is a more elaborate affair. Big gorgeous rounds of fried eggplant are plated with dollops of condensed cherry tomatoes and torn fresh basil, all in season and perfectly ripe at the same time. It's finished with shavings of Parmigiano-Reggiano, and you get a terrific combination of flavors and textures all in one bite.

Then there are our seasonal zeppole, which are hard to resist. These fabulous little fritters are crisp on the outside, pillowy in the center. We use the same batter for almost all our zeppole—a recipe adapted from Arthur Schwartz's *Naples at Table*. We loved the idea of a savory zeppole (all we'd ever known were the sweet New York City street-fair variety), and they quickly became a staple menu item, for more reasons than one. First, of course, they're delicious. And, like pizza dough, the batter is a great blank canvas for all matter of ingredients, a vehicle for whatever seasonal ingredient is perfect at the market *right now*. Zeppole are also forgiving—as long as you have the oil temperature right, they're almost impossible to screw up. And, while they're at their best steaming hot from the fryer, they are still appealing after they've cooled down a bit, which makes them adaptable enough to serve at home for a large party (though chances are they'll be devoured the second you bring them out). Plus, you can make the batter a day ahead, so other than the frying itself, there's not necessarily a lot of last-minute work.

In fact, many components of the recipes in this chapter can be prepared ahead. Some things can be breaded in advance and others boiled in advance, so that all you have to do when the time comes is drop your food into hot oil—from 350 to 375°F, depending on the ingredient. A great way to familiarize yourself with the frying process is to do a test: Drop a piece of whatever you are going to fry into your oil and see how it does. Does it brown too quickly, before the insides cook? Reduce the heat. Does it take too long to brown? Increase the heat. Keep an eye on your thermometer, keep your temperature constant, and don't overcrowd the pot, and you'll have delicious, golden results.

Another key to success is to use high-quality neutral oils such as safflower, canola, or grapeseed oil, which stand up well at higher temperatures. And, whatever you do, once you're done frying your batch of, say, Ramp Zeppole (page 43), and the oil has cooled, dispose of it. If you reuse it, whatever you fry in that oil will taste like ramps, and not in a good way.

When you retrieve your fried treasures from the cooking oil, season them immediately—the heat and slight gloss of oil helps the salt to cling. If your zucchini or green tomatoes or zeppole cool before you season them, the salt will simply fall off. And that finishing touch, while simple, is extremely important.

After salting, more often than not, Italians serve their *fritti* with little more than a wedge or two of lemon. And, indeed, that's how many of the dishes in this chapter are served—the crisp-tender, delectable mouthfuls don't need much else.

Zeppole Batter

We use this basic yeast-risen batter for almost all our zeppole. Because it has a fairly neutral flavor, it really takes on the character of whatever ingredient we add. It's also extremely flexible. You can use it immediately or make it a day ahead.

MAKES ABOUT 2¼ CUPS

½ **ounce fresh yeast** (2 tablespoons crumbled) **or 4 teaspoons active dry yeast**
1 **cup plus 2 tablespoons warm water**

½ **teaspoon kosher salt**
1½ **cups plus 2 tablespoons all-purpose flour**

In a large bowl, combine the yeast and water. Let the mixture stand for 5 minutes.

Whisk in the salt until it is dissolved. Whisk in the flour. Let the batter sit, covered, for 1 hour at room temperature. At this point, you can either use it or refrigerate it for up to 1 day. You don't need to let it come to room temperature before using it.

Andrew's Note: If you are using the batter the same day, use a lower temperature, about 365°F, when frying, because there are still fast-browning sugars in the flour. If using the batter the second day, heat the oil to 375°F so that the fritters brown more efficiently—the yeast has had time to eat the sugars, so it will take more heat and a slightly longer cooking time to brown them.

| FRITTI |

Ramp Zeppole

Ramps are so wonderfully distinctive, we use them whenever and however we can. During their short spring season, they show up in everything from cocktails to pasta to crostini. And they're great in zeppole. The verdant bits of pungent, oniony ramps are very compatible with the mild batter that envelops them. All we add is a little salty anchovy and a handful of capers to bring out the ramps' sweetness; that's all these wild beauties need.

MAKES ABOUT 1 DOZEN ZEPPOLE

3 ounces ramps
1 tablespoon drained brined capers,
  chopped
2 tablespoons pureed Garlic Confit
  (page 354)
1 teaspoon chili flakes

¾ teaspoon mashed anchovy
Zeppole Batter (page 42)
Safflower, canola, or grapeseed oil for
  deep-frying
Kosher salt

Rinse the ramps under cool running water and drain thoroughly. Trim away the hairy roots and discard them. Slice the dark green tops into long ¼-inch-wide ribbons (you should have about 2 packed cups). Thinly slice 1½ teaspoons of the bulbs; reserve the remaining bulbs for another use. Fold the ramps, capers, garlic confit, chili flakes, and anchovy into the batter.

In a deep fryer or heavy pot, heat at least 4 inches of oil to 365°F if you made the zeppole batter that day, 375°F if you made it the day before. Working in batches, drop large spoonfuls of the batter (about 3 tablespoons per zeppole) into the oil and cook, turning them occasionally, until evenly golden brown, 5 to 7 minutes. Transfer them to a paper-towel-lined plate to drain, then immediately sprinkle with salt and serve.

Andrew's Note: Don't overcrowd the pot when frying. If you add too much to the oil, it will bring the oil temperature down, which can make your fried food greasy. Always fry in small batches, and keep your eye on the thermometer to make sure the oil stays hot.

| FRITTI |

JOHN ADLER

FRANNY'S CHEF

Other than at Franny's, what is the best job you've ever had?

It's really hard for me to choose between Blue Hill at Stone Barns and Per Se, but I'd have to say Stone Barns. It was amazing to watch a piglet be born and then talk with the farmer about what he'd feed it based on what you wanted the meat to taste like. And then fifteen to eighteen months later, you'd be cooking that same pig, and find that the beets and melons and apples that the pig ate made the meat really sweet. That kind of opportunity to engage with the ingredient on such a personal level is second to none.

First memorable slice?

At Hartsdale Pizzeria, in my hometown up in Westchester County. We'd go there once a week, and I'd get a slice with onions and canned black olives. They also had little salads in those cheesy wooden bowls. It was heaven.

Has your relationship to pizza changed since you started working at Franny's?

Entirely. There's only one non-Franny's pizza I will eat: Pino's on Seventh Avenue in Park Slope has a great eggplant pie with tons of raw garlic and a really thin, crispy crust.

Favorite secret midshift snack?

Other than gelato, there's a snack we make in the kitchen once in a while that we jokingly call *saucisson en croûte.* We take a pork sausage, wrap it in pizza dough, and deep-fry it, then eat it with the pickled hot peppers. It's especially satisfying on a busy weekend double.

Spring Herb Zeppole

Of all our zeppole, this is probably my favorite. It's just what you want to be eating in late April or early May, or whenever winter finally thaws. As the spring sun comes out, so do soft spring herbs, and we use them here in abundance. Despite the fact that we use a profusion of them, the flavors of the herbs in this zeppole are distinct and special—you get bursts of each one. Assertive, earthy herbs such as oregano and sage mingle with anise-scented tarragon, grassy parsley, and sweet mint. And they're all undercut with the oniony notes of garlic chives. All told, there are nine different herbs, but if you can't find them all, feel free to bump up the quantities and use only four or five. Just be sure that they're all soft and tender.

MAKES ABOUT 1 DOZEN ZEPPOLE

2 tablespoons finely chopped spring onions
  or scallions
1½ tablespoons finely chopped flat-leaf
  parsley
1½ tablespoons finely chopped chive
  blossoms or chives
1 tablespoon finely chopped sage
1 tablespoon finely chopped fennel fronds
2 teaspoons finely chopped tarragon

2 teaspoons finely chopped garlic chives
1 teaspoon finely chopped thyme
1 teaspoon finely chopped mint
½ teaspoon finely chopped oregano
Zeppole Batter (page 42)
**Safflower, canola, or grapeseed oil for
  deep-frying**
Kosher salt

Fold the spring onions and all of the herbs into the zeppole batter.

In a deep fryer or heavy pot, heat at least 4 inches of oil to 365°F if you made the zeppole batter that day, 375°F if you made it the day before. Working in batches, drop large spoonfuls of the batter (about 3 tablespoons per zeppole) into the oil and cook, turning them occasionally, until evenly golden brown, 5 to 7 minutes. Transfer them to a paper-towel-lined plate to drain, then immediately sprinkle with salt and serve.

Spring Onion Zeppole

These zeppole might remind you of onion rings—really, really good onion rings—but these crunchy, irresistible fritters, filled with tender spring onions, are definitely more refined. To play up the sweetness of the juicy onion bulbs, we also add mild confited garlic, offset by the sharp boldness of chives and green onion tops. These nuanced fried treats are a delightful celebration of spring.

MAKES ABOUT 1 DOZEN ZEPPOLE

4 ounces spring onions
½ cup chives cut into ¾-inch lengths
Large pinch of chili flakes
1½ tablespoons pureed Garlic Confit
(page 354)

¼ teaspoon kosher salt, plus more
for sprinkling
Zeppole Batter (page 42)
Safflower, canola, or grapeseed oil for
deep-frying

Cut the dark green tops of the onions into ½-inch-wide slices. Thinly slice the white bulbs. Fold the onion greens and bulbs, chives, chili flakes, garlic confit, and salt into the batter.

In a deep fryer or heavy pot, heat at least 4 inches of oil to 365°F if you made the zeppole batter that day, 375°F if you made it the day before. Working in batches, drop large spoonfuls of the batter (about 3 tablespoons per zeppole) into the oil and cook, turning them occasionally, until evenly golden brown, 5 to 7 minutes. Transfer them to a paper-towel-lined plate to drain, then immediately sprinkle with salt and serve.

Roasted Corn and Pancetta Zeppole

Not all zeppole are alike. This batter includes cornmeal, which ends up producing something reminiscent of a hush puppy. But cornmeal is also an Italian staple (think polenta), and we play up that connection by adding pancetta and prickly hot peppers to the mix. This recipe is a terrific way to showcase corn at its peak.

MAKES ABOUT 1½ DOZEN ZEPPOLE

FOR THE BATTER
½ ounce fresh yeast (2 tablespoons crumbled)
  or 4 teaspoons active dry yeast
1 cup plus 1 tablespoon water
¾ plus ⅛ teaspoon kosher salt
¾ cup fine cornmeal
1¼ cups all-purpose flour

⅔ cup corn kernels (from 1 medium ear)
1 teaspoon extra-virgin olive oil
Kosher salt
⅛ teaspoon freshly cracked black pepper
4 ounces pancetta, cut into
  ⅜-inch-thick cubes
⅓ cup diced seeded hot peppers, such
  as jalapeño or hot wax
Safflower, canola, or grapeseed oil for
  deep-frying

To make the batter: In a medium bowl, stir the yeast into the water. Let stand for 5 minutes. Stir in the salt, then whisk in the cornmeal. Gently whisk in the flour until just combined (you don't want to overdevelop the gluten).

Preheat the oven to 500°F. Toss the corn with the olive oil, salt to taste, and the pepper and spread it in an even layer on a rimmed baking sheet. Roast until golden brown, 8 to 10 minutes. Don't stir; you want the kernels to brown on top and remain tender on the undersides. Cool completely.

Heat a medium skillet over medium-high heat. Add the pancetta and cook until most of the fat has rendered and the pancetta is beginning to brown, about 8 minutes. Transfer to a paper-towel-lined plate to drain and cool.

Fold the corn, pancetta, and hot peppers into the batter.

In a deep fryer or heavy pot, heat at least 4 inches of safflower oil to 365°F if you made the zeppole batter that day, 375°F if you made it the day before. Working in batches, drop large spoonfuls of the batter (about 3 tablespoons per zeppole) into the oil and cook, turning them occasionally, until evenly golden brown, 5 to 7 minutes. Transfer them to a paper-towel-lined plate to drain, then immediately sprinkle with salt and serve.

Fried Asparagus, Artichokes, and Spring Onions with Ramp Mayonnaise

As spring begins to hit its stride, some of the most wonderful vegetables start popping up at the markets. Asparagus and artichokes are both extraordinary on their own, but they are even better fried up together along with ultrasweet spring onions. Paired with an assertive tartar-sauce-like ramp mayonnaise, this lively spring mix is a fantastic riot of flavors and textures. But if you can't find all three vegetables, feel free to use two or even one. There's nothing wrong with serving a platter stacked high with crisp-fried asparagus spears or artichokes or spring onions, ready for dunking.

SERVES 6

FOR THE RAMP MAYONNAISE
Homemade Mayonnaise (page 354)
1 tablespoon finely chopped Pickled Ramps (page 353), **with some of their pickling vinegar clinging to them**
1 tablespoon minced chives
2 teaspoons drained brined capers, finely chopped
⅛ teaspoon freshly cracked black pepper
Fresh lemon juice (optional)
Kosher salt

FOR THE VEGETABLES
3 artichokes (about 1½ pounds)
3 tablespoons extra-virgin olive oil

Kosher salt and freshly cracked black pepper
4 ounces asparagus, trimmed
3 ounces thin spring onions or scallions, trimmed

FOR THE BATTER
½ cup cornstarch
½ cup all-purpose flour
1 cup club soda, plus more if needed

Safflower, canola, or grapeseed oil for deep-frying
Kosher salt

To make the ramp mayonnaise: In a bowl, stir together the mayonnaise, pickled ramps, chives, capers, and pepper. Taste and correct the seasonings, adding lemon juice and/or salt if needed. Refrigerate until needed. (The mayonnaise can be made up to 1 day ahead.)

Preheat the oven to 350°F. Trim the artichokes (see page 124) and halve them lengthwise.

Transfer the artichokes to a deep roasting pan. Sprinkle with the olive oil, 1 tablespoon water, and salt and pepper to taste. Cover the pan with foil and cook until the artichokes are tender, about 35 minutes. Let cool. Slice each artichoke half lengthwise in half. Set aside.

To make the batter: In a medium bowl, whisk together the cornstarch and flour. Whisk in the club soda. The mixture should have a consistency slightly thinner than that of pancake batter, similar to that of a crepe batter or buttermilk. Add more club soda if needed.

In a deep fryer or heavy pot, heat at least 4 inches of safflower oil to 375°F. Working in batches, dip the artichokes in the batter, then lower them gently into the oil and fry until they turn pale golden around the edges, 1 to 2 minutes; they won't get very brown. Use a slotted spoon to transfer them to a paper-towel-lined plate to drain, and sprinkle with salt while still warm. Repeat the battering and frying with the asparagus (1 to 2 minutes) and the onions (about 1 minute); drain and sprinkle with salt.

Serve the vegetables with the ramp mayonnaise for dipping.

| FRITTI |

Fried Zucchini with Parmigiano-Reggiano and Lemon

Fried zucchini is classic American pizzeria food. And even though much of what is out there is bland and heavily breaded and barely resembles the vegetable itself, most folks still love fried zucchini. At Franny's, whenever fried zucchini comes on the menu, it flies out of the kitchen at breakneck speed. We hit all the high notes: Long thick spears of summer-ripe zucchini are held in a fine, crisp shell, showered with curls of Parmigiano-Reggiano, and garnished with big golden wedges of lemon. It makes for a compelling sight—impossible not to order once it's been spotted.

Because fried zucchini is so adored, there's always a bit of a mourning period when zucchini falls out of season. But its departure gives us the opportunity to discuss sustainable, seasonal eating. It's always been fun to talk with our guests about the ever-changing menu—when they're sad to see ramps go, we remind them that zucchini is coming, and when they sadly say good-bye to fried zucchini, we reintroduce them to the wonders of fried potatoes. With seasonal eating, one door is always closing but another is always opening.

SERVES 4

1 pound slim zucchini, trimmed
1 teaspoon kosher salt, plus more for
  sprinkling

FOR THE BATTER
½ cup cornstarch
½ cup all-purpose flour
1 cup club soda

Safflower, canola, or grapeseed oil for
  deep-frying
Freshly cracked black pepper
Lemon wedges
Shaved or coarsely grated Parmigiano-
  Reggiano

Slice each zucchini lengthwise into quarters; if necessary, slice each quarter in half again to make ¾-inch-thick sticks. Cut out the seeds. Place the zucchini in a colander set over a bowl and toss with the salt. Let stand for 30 minutes.

To make the batter: In a medium bowl, whisk together the cornstarch and flour, then whisk in the club soda.

Pat the zucchini very dry with paper towels.

In a deep fryer or heavy pot, heat at least 2 inches of oil to 375°F. Working in batches, dip several zucchini sticks at a time into the batter, lower carefully into the oil, and fry until light golden, about 3 minutes. Using a slotted spoon,

transfer to a paper-towel-lined plate to drain, then season with salt and lots of pepper. Serve the zucchini with lemon wedges and shaved cheese.

Andrew's Note: Presalting the zucchini is very important. Letting the watery flesh of the vegetable absorb the salt for 30 minutes ensures a well-seasoned, flavorful result. And don't skimp on the black pepper—this dish needs that aggressive bite.

Fried Green Tomatoes with Anchovy Mayonnaise

These fried tomatoes are a nod to the American South. We pair the crunchy, golden rounds of juicy, firm, tart tomato with homemade anchovy mayonnaise. It puts the dish right over the top, and it also lends it a distinctly Italian flair. This is an impressive recipe to serve as a starter course at a dinner party, but you could easily serve a larger plate as a decadent summer meal, alongside a salad and a cool, bright glass of white wine.

SERVES 4 TO 6

FOR THE ANCHOVY MAYONNAISE
Homemade Mayonnaise (page 354)
6 anchovy fillets (see Andrew's Note),
   minced and mashed to a paste
Fresh lemon juice (optional)
Kosher salt (optional)

FOR THE FRIED GREEN TOMATOES
**Safflower, canola, or grapeseed oil for
   deep-frying**
½ cup all-purpose flour
2 large eggs, lightly beaten
**1 cup dried bread crumbs, preferably
   homemade** (see page 353)
12 ounces green tomatoes (about 2),
   sliced ¼ inch thick
Kosher salt

To make the anchovy mayonnaise: In a bowl, whisk together the mayonnaise and anchovies. Taste and correct the seasonings, adding lemon juice or a pinch of salt if needed. Refrigerate until needed. (The mayonnaise can be made up to 1 day ahead.)

In a deep fryer or deep skillet, heat at least 1 inch of oil to 350°F. Place the flour, eggs, and bread crumbs in three separate wide, shallow bowls. Dip each tomato slice in the flour, turning to coat, then in the eggs, and then coat evenly with bread crumbs. Fry the tomatoes in batches, until crisp, about 2 minutes. Transfer to a paper-towel-lined plate to drain and sprinkle with salt while still warm. Serve the tomatoes with the mayonnaise.

Andrew's Note: Because there's so little going on with this mayonnaise, it is imperative that you use high-quality anchovies. Look for Italian anchovies packed in olive oil or salt. You're better off leaving the anchovies out entirely if you can't find a good-quality option.

Fried Eggplant with Parmigiano-Reggiano, Tomato, and Basil

It could be said that this is Franny's version of that Italian-American standby, eggplant Parm. Most of the elements are here (minus the mozzarella), but I have to say, this elegant dish is a world away from the cheese-covered versions of my Long Island childhood. And apparently that's true for other folks as well: I've often heard guests exclaim upon tasting this that they "would have liked eggplant a lot sooner" if they'd known what it really tasted like. We don't do much to the plump, dark vegetable itself—it retains a lot of its meaty character, but it gets brightened up by the condensed sweetness of ripe tomatoes and fragrant basil in the sauce. Shavings of Parmigiano-Reggiano and a good drizzle of olive oil finish it off perfectly. Serve this to anyone who loves a good eggplant Parm or serve it to someone who is eggplant-averse—I bet both will be surprised and delighted.

SERVES 6

FOR THE FRIED EGGPLANT
1 small eggplant (12 ounces), **sliced into
¼-inch-thick rounds**
**1 teaspoon kosher salt, plus more
for sprinkling**
**Safflower, canola, or grapeseed oil for
deep-frying**
½ cup all-purpose flour
2 large eggs, lightly beaten
**1 cup dried bread crumbs, preferably
homemade** (see page 353)

FOR THE TOMATO SAUCE
1¾ pounds ripe tomatoes
**3 tablespoons extra-virgin olive oil, plus
more for drizzling**
1 garlic clove, smashed and peeled
¾ teaspoon kosher salt

1 bunch basil
**A 3-ounce chunk of Parmigiano-Reggiano
for shaving**

In a large colander, toss the eggplant slices with the salt. Set the colander in the sink or on a plate and let stand for 1 hour. Drain the eggplant and pat it dry.

To make the tomato sauce: Bring a large pot of water to a boil. Using a paring knife, make a small X in the base of each tomato. Lower the tomatoes into the boiling water and blanch for 20 seconds. Remove with a slotted spoon. Once the tomatoes are cool enough to handle, remove the skin, then core and dice the tomatoes (you should have about 3½ cups).

In a large skillet, warm the olive oil over medium-high heat. Add the garlic and cook until fragrant and lightly colored, 1 minute. Add the tomatoes and salt and cook until the tomatoes

break down and the juices begin to evaporate, 15 to 20 minutes.

Press the sauce through a food mill or a sieve into a bowl. Cover with foil and keep warm, or reheat gently before serving. (The tomato sauce can be made up to 3 days ahead and refrigerated.)

To cook the eggplant: In a deep fryer or medium pot, heat 2 inches of oil to 375°F. Place the flour, eggs, and bread crumbs in three separate wide shallow bowls. Dip each eggplant slice in the flour, turning to coat, then in the eggs, and then coat evenly with bread crumbs. Working in batches, fry the eggplant until golden and crisp, 2 to 3 minutes. Transfer to a paper-towel-lined plate to drain, and sprinkle with salt while still warm.

continued

To serve, spoon some warm sauce onto each serving plate. Tear 3 basil leaves over each plate. Arrange about 5 eggplant slices on top of the sauce and tear 3 more basil leaves over the eggplant. Use a vegetable peeler to shave the cheese over each plate, and drizzle with olive oil. Serve immediately.

Andrew's Note: You can prep your eggplant up to a day in advance. Salt the slices, bread them, and lay them on a baking sheet, separating the layers with parchment paper. Refrigerate for up to 24 hours. Just be sure to let the eggplant slices come to room temperature before frying, or they will lower the temperature of the hot oil.

| FRITTI |

Fennel Zeppole

This is a subtle and savory zeppole, and the fennel shows up here in several ways: fennel seeds, fennel pollen, and fennel fronds all make an appearance alongside minced tender fennel bulb. Zeppole can be rustic fare, but the many kinds of fennel in this particular iteration make it decidedly sophisticated. Fennel's anise-scented sweetness pairs beautifully with salty, nutty Parmigiano-Reggiano. Because fennel has a nice long growing season, from summer through the autumn, it's one of those vegetables that you can depend on—all the more reason to use it often.

MAKES ABOUT 1 DOZEN ZEPPOLE

3 tablespoons extra-virgin olive oil
2 large garlic cloves, finely chopped
2 ounces Parmigiano-Reggiano, finely grated (about ½ cup)
½ small fennel bulb, finely chopped (⅔ cup)
1 tablespoon plus 2 teaspoons fennel seeds
1 tablespoon fennel pollen

¼ teaspoon kosher salt, plus more for sprinkling
¼ teaspoon freshly cracked black pepper
Zeppole Batter (page 42)
Safflower, canola, or grapeseed oil for deep-frying
Lemon wedges for serving

In a small skillet, heat the olive oil over medium heat. Add the garlic and cook until just fragrant but not colored, about 30 seconds. Cool completely.

Fold the garlic-oil mixture, cheese, chopped fennel, fennel seeds, fennel pollen, salt, and pepper into the batter.

In a deep fryer or heavy pot, heat at least 4 inches of safflower oil to 365°F if you made the zeppole batter that day, 375°F if you made it the day before. Working in batches, drop large spoonfuls of the batter (about 3 tablespoons per zeppole) into the oil and cook, turning them occasionally, until evenly golden brown, 5 to 7 minutes. Transfer to a paper-towel-lined plate to drain, then immediately sprinkle with salt. Serve with lemon wedges.

Fried Olives

We eat these salty meat-stuffed olives often in Italy, where they show up as a little gift served with cocktails. Our version has a more complex flavor than what you usually find. We sauté ground pancetta in sweet butter, then season it with garlic, fresh herbs, and two kinds of tangy cheese—provolone and Parmigiano-Reggiano. Fried up and served hot, these go well with pretty much any cocktail or aperitif, or a chilled glass of crisp white wine or rosé.

MAKES 3½ DOZEN STUFFED OLIVES

3 ounces pancetta, diced and frozen
6 tablespoons unsalted butter
3 garlic cloves, finely chopped
2 teaspoons finely chopped rosemary
1 teaspoon dried oregano
⅛ teaspoon freshly grated nutmeg
2 large eggs
**2½ ounces Parmigiano-Reggiano,
  finely grated** (about ⅔ cup)

1½ ounces provolone, grated (about ⅓ cup)
3½ dozen Cerignola olives, pitted
3 tablespoons all-purpose flour
**¼ cup dried bread crumbs, preferably
  homemade** (see page 353)
**Safflower, canola, or grapeseed oil for
  deep-frying**

In a food processor, grind the pancetta to the consistency of ground meat.

In a large skillet, melt the butter over medium-high heat. Add the pancetta and cook, stirring, until golden brown, about 8 minutes. Reduce the heat to medium, add the garlic, and cook until soft but not browned, about 2 minutes. Stir in the rosemary, oregano, and nutmeg and cook until fragrant, 30 seconds. Remove from the heat and let cool.

In a medium bowl, beat 1 egg until frothy. Stir in the pancetta mixture, followed by the cheeses. Cover and chill until firm, at least 3 hours, or as long as overnight.

Stuff each olive with 1 teaspoon of the cold pancetta mixture.

Place the flour, the remaining egg, and the bread crumbs in three separate wide shallow bowls; lightly beat the egg. Dip each olive in the flour, turning to coat, then in the eggs, and then coat evenly with bread crumbs. Chill for at least 30 minutes, and (well covered) up to 2 days.

In a deep fryer or heavy pot, heat at least 2 inches of oil to 365°F. Working in batches, fry the olives, turning them occasionally, until evenly golden brown, about 2 minutes. Transfer them to a paper-towel-lined plate to drain. (Because the olives are salty, you don't need any additional salt.) Serve hot.

| FRITTI |

Potato Croquettes

We've experimented with many dishes from Naples, and these potato croquettes are a classic Neapolitan *fritto*. Andrew adapted the recipe, making it his own, by adding provolone piccante, an aged cheese with pronounced sharpness that also contributes some moisture to the croquettes. For a good part of her early life, our daughter, Prue, basically subsisted on these: they would arrive at the table piping hot, we'd cut them in half to release some of the steam, and Prue would wait expectantly for her nibbles of the creamy croquettes as Andrew and I said, "Hot-hot-hot." Kids love these unanimously, and so do adults. At the restaurant, we shower the croquettes with very finely grated Parmigiano-Reggiano. It's not necessary, but the effect is very pretty, like a snow-covered mountain. They're just a wonderfully simple yet polished little bite, and they'd make a superior snack for a cocktail party.

MAKES ABOUT 2 DOZEN CROQUETTES; SERVES 6 TO 8

FOR THE CROQUETTES
1 pound Yukon Gold potatoes, peeled
2 tablespoons plus ¼ teaspoon kosher salt
5 tablespoons unsalted butter, melted and still hot
3 ounces provolone piccante, finely grated (about ¾ cup)
¼ teaspoon freshly cracked black pepper
3 large eggs

½ cup all-purpose flour
1½ cups dried bread crumbs, preferably homemade (see page 353)
Safflower, canola, or grapeseed oil for deep-frying
Kosher salt and freshly cracked black pepper
2 ounces Parmigiano-Reggiano, finely grated (about ½ cup)

In a large pot, combine the potatoes, 8 cups water, and 2 tablespoons salt. Bring to a boil and boil until the potatoes are tender, 20 to 25 minutes. Drain.

Place the butter and provolone in a large bowl. Pass the hot potatoes through the medium plate of a food mill into the bowl. Season with the remaining ¼ teaspoon salt and the pepper. Stir in 1 of the eggs.

Spread the batter in an even layer on a rimmed baking sheet and cool completely. Cover tightly with plastic wrap and chill for at least 6 hours, and as long as overnight.

To make the croquettes: Place the flour, the remaining 2 eggs, and the bread crumbs in three separate wide shallow bowls; lightly beat the eggs. Roll the cold potato mixture into tablespoon-sized balls. Dip each ball in the flour,

turning to coat, then in the eggs, and then coat evenly with bread crumbs. (At this point, the croquettes can be refrigerated on a baking sheet tightly covered with plastic wrap for up to 3 days; bring to room temperature before frying.)

In a deep fryer or heavy pot, heat at least 2 inches of oil to 360°F. Working in batches, fry the croquettes until golden and crisp, 2 to 3 minutes. Transfer to a paper-towel-lined plate to drain. Toss with salt and pepper and the Parmigiano-Reggiano while still warm.

Andrew's Note: If you can't track down provolone piccante, use a combination of cheeses—about 25 percent Pecorino and 75 percent caciocavallo.

| FRITTI |

Kale Zeppole with Calabrian Chili Honey

We all know how compelling the flavor combination of salty and sweet can be—the pleasure centers in our brains are hardwired to respond with floods of feel-good endorphins whenever we eat the two together. But the beauty of these zeppole is that in addition to being totally addictive, they are chock-full of health-giving kale (kale is about as nutrient-dense a vegetable as you can find). Apart from in desserts, it's rare for Franny's to feature a "sweet" flavor as clearly as we do here, but the chili-spiked honey drizzled over the earthy fritters works beautifully. Tuscan kale fries up in a particularly appealing way—little bits of the near-black leaves inevitably rise from the batter in ragged pieces, creating a wonderfully brittle, crunchy bite against the soft, doughy interior.

MAKES ABOUT 1 DOZEN ZEPPOLE

FOR THE CHILI HONEY
3 tablespoons honey
2½ teaspoons fresh lemon juice
2 jarred Calabrian chilies (see Resources, page 357), **seeded and finely chopped**
1 teaspoon chili oil from the jar

FOR THE ZEPPOLE
¼ cup plus ½ teaspoon kosher salt, plus more for sprinkling
1¼ pounds Tuscan kale, center ribs removed

2½ tablespoons unsalted butter
2½ tablespoons extra-virgin olive oil
1 small onion, finely chopped
1 large garlic clove, finely chopped
2 small anchovy fillets, chopped into ¼-inch pieces
½ batch Zeppole Batter (page 42)
Safflower, canola, or grapeseed oil for deep-frying

To make the chili honey: In a small saucepan, heat the honey over low heat until it is just warm to the touch; do not bring it to a simmer. Whisk in the lemon juice. Remove the pan from the heat and whisk in the chilies and chili oil. Cool completely. (The honey can be made a week in advance and refrigerated. Bring to room temperature when ready to use.)

To make the zeppole: In a large pot, bring 4 quarts of water and the ¼ cup salt to a boil. Add the kale and cook until tender, 1 to 2 minutes. Drain well.

In a large skillet, melt the butter with the olive oil over medium-low heat. Add the onion, the remaining garlic, and ½ teaspoon salt and cook until the onion is translucent, about 5 minutes. Stir in the kale, cover, and cook over medium-high heat until the pot begins to steam. Remove the lid and cook until most of the liquid has evaporated, 5 to 7 minutes. Cool completely.

Finely chop two-thirds of the kale mixture; coarsely chop the remaining third. Gently fold the kale and anchovies into the batter. Chill for at least 30 minutes, and up to 3 hours.

In a deep fryer or heavy pot, heat at least 4 inches of safflower oil to 365°F if you made the zeppole batter that day, 375°F if you made it the day before. Working in batches, drop large spoonfuls of the batter (about 3 tablespoons per zeppole) into the safflower oil and cook, turning them occasionally, until evenly golden brown, 5 to 7 minutes. Transfer to a paper-towel-lined plate to drain, then immediately sprinkle with salt. Serve with the chili honey alongside for dipping.

Cauliflower Zeppole

This big, bold zeppole has assertive and pronounced flavors—well-browned cauliflower, briny anchovies, sweet garlic confit, and pickled capers join together to create a really satisfying fritter. Set off by the sunny freshness of lemon, these robust zeppole are great whenever you can get good cauliflower in season.

MAKES ABOUT 1½ DOZEN ZEPPOLE

½ **head cauliflower, cut into small florets**
2 tablespoons extra-virgin olive oil
Kosher salt and freshly cracked
   black pepper
2 tablespoons drained capers,
   coarsely chopped
4 anchovy fillets, finely chopped

2 large cloves Garlic Confit (page 354)
1½ teaspoons Garlic Confit oil (page 354)
Zeppole Batter (page 42)
Safflower, canola, or grapeseed oil for
   deep-frying
Lemon wedges, for serving

Preheat the oven to 500°F. Toss the cauliflower with the olive oil and season with salt and pepper. Spread in a single layer on a rimmed baking sheet (or two, if one baking sheet is crowded) and roast, tossing frequently, until the cauliflower is tender and golden, about 20 minutes. Cool completely.

Fold the cauliflower, capers, anchovies, garlic confit, garlic oil, and pepper into the batter.

In a deep fryer or heavy pot, heat at least 4 inches of safflower oil to 365°F if you made the zeppole batter that day, 375°F if you made it the day before. Working in batches, drop large spoonfuls of the batter (about 3 tablespoons per zeppole) into the oil and cook, turning them occasionally, until evenly golden brown, 5 to 7 minutes. Transfer to a paper-towel-lined plate to drain, then immediately sprinkle with salt. Serve with lemon wedges.

Fingerling Potatoes with Provolone Piccante, Scallions, and Capers

We based this recipe on a classic Neapolitan potato salad. Traditionally it's a cold salad in which small cubes of spicy provolone cheese, sliced scallions, and capers cling to tender boiled potatoes. It's simple and delicious. Here we tweak things a bit, serving the potatoes deep-fried and hot, with the provolone grated over the top so it melts and sticks to the crispy fingerlings. This is a lush, tangy, and unusual potato preparation that is excellent served alongside a perfectly seared steak or roasted chicken, or as a starter course in its own right.

SERVES 4

FOR THE FRIED POTATOES
8 ounces fingerling potatoes
1 bay leaf
1 garlic clove
1 small rosemary sprig
1 small sage sprig

Safflower, canola, or grapeseed oil for
   deep-frying
Kosher salt

FOR THE SCALLION-CAPER VINAIGRETTE
⅓ cup finely chopped scallions
1½ tablespoons salt-packed capers,
   soaked, rinsed, and drained
   (see Andrew's Note, page 30)
Juice of 1 lemon
2 tablespoons extra-virgin olive oil

2 ounces provolone piccante or
   caciocavallo, grated (about ½ cup)

To make the potatoes: Place the potatoes in a large pot of salted water. Tie the bay leaf, garlic, rosemary, and sage in a piece of cheesecloth and secure with kitchen twine. Drop the sachet into the water. Bring to a boil and cook the potatoes until just tender, about 20 minutes; drain.

While the potatoes are still warm, but cool enough to handle, smash them lightly with the palm of your hand. You can fry the potatoes now or chill them for up to 2 days (bring to room temperature before frying).

In a deep fryer or heavy pot, heat at least 3 inches of oil to 360°F. Working in batches, fry the potatoes until golden, 2 to 4 minutes. Use a slotted spoon to transfer them to a paper-towel-lined plate to drain, then sprinkle lightly with salt while still warm.

To make the vinaigrette: In a large bowl, whisk together the scallions, capers, and lemon juice. Whisk in the olive oil.

Toss the hot fried potatoes with the provolone and the dressing and serve.

Andrew's Note: Crushing the boiled potatoes creates additional texture. By releasing some of the flesh from the skins, you get a jagged, uneven surface to expose to the hot oil, and you'll get a much better crunch. There will inevitably be bits that break away, but they get really crisp and are delicious.

Fingerling Potatoes with Parmigiano-Reggiano and Mayonnaise

These fried fingerlings are like Italian french fries. In Europe, most people opt for mayonnaise with their fries instead of ketchup, and I've always loved that tradition. Here the crackling-hot potatoes are tossed with a garlicky lemon vinaigrette and plenty of grated Parmigiano-Reggiano so these flavors seep into the lovely crisp potato crevices, and are served with a generous amount of homemade mayonnaise. I can't really think of anything better. These fingerling potatoes are a rich, enticing accompaniment for simple roasted meats.

SERVES 6

FOR THE FRIED POTATOES
12 ounces fingerling potatoes
1 bay leaf
1 garlic clove
1 rosemary sprig
1 sage sprig

Safflower, canola, or grapeseed oil for deep-frying
Kosher salt

FOR THE LEMON VINAIGRETTE
½ teaspoon grated or minced garlic
Juice of 1½ lemons, or to taste
1 tablespoon extra-virgin olive oil

Kosher salt and freshly cracked black pepper
2 tablespoons finely grated Parmigiano-Reggiano

Double recipe of Homemade Mayonnaise (page 354)

To make the potatoes: Place the potatoes in a large pot of salted water. Tie the bay leaf, garlic, rosemary, and sage in a piece of cheesecloth and secure with kitchen twine. Drop the sachet into the water. Bring to a boil and cook the potatoes until just tender, about 20 minutes; drain.

While the potatoes are still warm, but cool enough to handle, smash them lightly with the palm of your hand. You can fry the potatoes now or chill them for up to 2 days (bring to room temperature before frying).

In a deep fryer or heavy pot, heat at least 3 inches of oil to 360°F. Working in batches, fry the potatoes until golden, 2 to 4 minutes. Use a slotted spoon to transfer them to a paper-towel-lined plate to drain, then sprinkle lightly with salt while still warm.

To make the vinaigrette: In a large bowl, whisk together the garlic and lemon juice. Whisk in the olive oil.

Toss the potatoes with the vinaigrette, salt and pepper to taste, and the cheese.

Smear ¼ cup of mayonnaise on each plate. Spoon the potatoes on top and dollop with additional mayo. Serve hot.

Andrew's Note: These boiled-then-smashed potatoes are great for other preparations as well, and they keep in the refrigerator for up to 2 days. Bring them to room temperature, toss them with extra-virgin olive oil or butter, and roast at very high heat (450°F) until golden.

SALADS

For most people, the word "salad" automatically conjures up an image of a big bowl of lettuce tossed with dressing. That, however, is only a small part of the story. Many fine salads combine a host of different vegetables, fruits, nuts, and/or cheeses, with lettuces and other greens staying quietly in the background. And some salads even leave out the greens altogether. Vegetables often appear raw in salads, but you'll also find them cooked. Most salads are eaten cold or at room temperature, but warm salads, such as the traditional spinach and bacon salad, or our Warm Controne Bean Salad with Radicchio and Pancetta (page 84), can be wonderful exceptions.

The beauty of a salad is that it can be any and all of these things. Ultimately, we've decided that what separates a salad from a vegetable *contorno* (side dish) is an inherent *saladness*. All of these salad recipes have a freshness, tartness, and lightness that primes you for the next course. The exact ingredients and techniques matter less than the overall flavor, texture, and feeling of the dish.

This is especially true of salads, which have to be adaptable to reflect what produce is at its peak. We like to use dandelion greens, arugula, and asparagus in the spring; tender lettuces, herbs, cucumbers, and tomatoes in the summer; radicchio, celery, and cabbages in the fall; and escarole, sunchokes, and citrus fruits in the dead of winter.

In the beginning at Franny's, this was somewhat confusing to customers who wondered why they couldn't get a plain green salad with dressing all year long. When we opened in April, we had some early lettuces that we mixed with fresh local parsley. I remember one woman sending hers back—she said it just wasn't correct to have that much parsley in a salad. But that doesn't happen anymore. Now people have opened up to the idea that salad can be a lot of different things. The possibilities run deep no matter what time of year it is.

We often take the American rather than the Italian approach, serving salads as a first course rather than at the end of the meal, or as a side dish, as they do in Italy. We want to awaken our diners' palates for more dishes to come, and a tangy fresh salad will do just that. At home, we generally don't have multicourse meals with our kids, but a salad usually finds a place on the table, even if it's only a simple bowl of fresh arugula tossed with just enough lemon juice, olive oil, and sea salt to complement the leaves' peppery green flavor. And sometimes a big salad becomes the meal, paired with good bread and rounded out with a little cheese and cured meat.

For all of salad's apparent simplicity, it can be one of the most difficult things to do well—especially when it comes to seasoning. You need to add the right amount of salt, the perfect touch of acid, and just enough good olive oil to bring out the flavors of the vegetables or other ingredients, without either obscuring them in too much dressing or leaving them almost naked and underseasoned.

Using a great olive oil makes a tremendous difference. Again and again, we turn

to Southern Italian extra-virgin olive oils. If you're like us and have an ever-changing selection of distinctive oils in your kitchen, make sure the collection includes one high-quality extra-virgin oil, preferably from Sicily, if you can find it. The olive oil from that region has loads of character, bite, and aggressive peppery notes that are beautifully suited for a wide range of salads.

As for the acid, most of the recipes here are spiked with red wine vinegar or fresh lemon juice, and we choose between them according to what kind of flavors we're after. Lemon juice is milder, sunnier, fruitier; red wine vinegar is more assertive and acidic. For salads with meat (bacon, pancetta, salami), we sprinkle on red wine vinegar because its sturdy acidity can stand up to the rich, oily meats. This relationship is played out in the Farro Salad with Favas, Sopressata, and Pecorino (page 73). But for something leaner, such as the Shaved Asparagus with Parmigiano-Reggiano, Lemon, and Black Pepper (page 71), lemon juice gives it an edge without overwhelming the vegetables; vinegar just wouldn't taste right here.

We very rarely use balsamic vinegar in salads. It's overdone; we've just seen it too many times. The one exception is the Red Cabbage with Hazelnuts, Balsamico, and Pancetta (page 87), where it lends the perfect winy, caramelized kick. With

balsamic, sourcing the best-quality vinegar made in a traditional manner, preferably from Modena, is essential. For the most part, though, when we want vinegar with a sweet, fruity note, we'll reach for moscato vinegar. It can be hard to find, but its honeyed character is worth the search. For sources and a cheater's substitute, see page 357.

And, finally, salt is critical in salads (and everywhere else), acting as the amplifier, the highlighter of all flavors. We especially love the crunch of sea salt against the juicy citrus fruits in the Citrus Salad with Pistachios, Olives, and Chilies (page 92).

When it comes to putting a salad together, instead of using tossers or tongs, try tossing your salad with your (clean) hands. You'll get a much better sense of the amount of dressing to use and of when the greens or vegetables are nicely coated. Add a little bit of dressing at a time, and taste, taste, taste until it tastes delicious to you. If it's not delicious, it probably needs a tiny bit more salt, or acidity, or maybe even olive oil. It's better to go lighter at first, because you can always add more, but once you've overdressed a salad or overseasoned it, it's impossible to go back. When it tastes just right, you'll know it.

Dandelion Greens with a Fried Egg, Croutons, and Anchovy Dressing

Here's our spin on Caesar salad. Instead of the usual mild romaine, we use robust, slightly bitter dandelion greens, which make for a heartier, more deeply flavored salad. The piquant cheese, anchovy, and peppery Sicilian extra-virgin olive oil balance the strong flavor of the leaves, and the egg yolk adds a lovely richness.

If you can't find good dandelion greens, try using escarole, frisée, chicory, or Treviso radicchio. You want something that's sturdy and slightly bitter. Avoid arugula and baby spinach—they are far too delicate for this dressing and will quickly wilt.

SERVES 6

FOR THE CROUTONS
3 cups torn chunks crusty bread
  (about 5 ounces)
2 tablespoons extra-virgin olive oil
¼ teaspoon kosher salt
Freshly cracked black pepper

1 small garlic clove, finely chopped

¼ teaspoon kosher salt
2 teaspoons red wine vinegar
2 anchovies, mashed to a paste (1 teaspoon)
6 tablespoons extra-virgin olive oil
6 large eggs
Freshly cracked black pepper
5 cups dandelion greens
Coarsely grated Parmigiano-Reggiano

To make the croutons: Preheat the oven to 400°F, with a rack positioned in the middle. Toss the bread with the olive oil, salt, and pepper. Spread the bread on a baking sheet and toast until the croutons are golden and crisp, about 10 minutes. Set aside.

Using a mortar and pestle or the side of a large knife, mash the garlic into a paste with a pinch of salt. Transfer to a small bowl. Whisk in the vinegar, anchovy, and salt. Whisk in 2 tablespoons of the olive oil.

In a large skillet, heat the remaining ¼ cup olive oil over medium-high heat until hot but not smoking. Crack the eggs into the skillet and season with salt and pepper. Reduce the heat to medium and cook the eggs until the whites are just set, about 5 minutes. Remove from the heat.

In a large bowl, toss the greens and croutons with the dressing. Divide the salad among six serving plates. Top each with an egg and garnish with grated cheese.

Andrew's Note: Always taste dandelion greens before buying them; sometimes they can be too bitter. Just tear off a tiny piece of a leaf (most vendors at the farmers' market will let you do this) and take a bite. The greens should have a hint of bitterness, but it shouldn't be overwhelming.

Arugula Salad with Pecorino and Lemon

If you have superb greens, some good olive oil, and a piece of delicious cheese, a great salad doesn't need to be complicated. The arugula that emerges in the early spring, with a delicate bite, is perfect here. It's tossed with an uncomplicated fresh lemon dressing, and the nutty, creamy curls of Pecorino Rosselino play off the spicy leaves.

Pecorino Rosselino is a semi-firm Italian sheep's-milk cheese aged for about three months. If you can't find it, don't be tempted to substitute Pecorino Romano—it's much too hard and salty for this salad. Instead, look for another semi-firm sheep's-milk cheese, even if it's not from Italy. A young Manchego or the French Ossau-Iraty would serve as a good substitute.

SERVES 4 TO 6

5 tablespoons extra-virgin olive oil
Juice of 1 lemon, plus more if needed
½ teaspoon salt
½ teaspoon freshly cracked black pepper

10 cups arugula
4 ounces Pecorino Rosselino
 (see Andrew's Note), **coarsely grated**

In a small bowl, combine the olive oil, lemon juice, salt, and pepper.

Place the arugula in a large bowl and add the dressing and cheese. Toss to combine. Add more lemon juice if needed and serve immediately.

Andrew's Note: Use a coarse Microplane grater (or even a vegetable peeler) to grate the cheese. This salad calls for big, coarse pieces of Pecorino.

Shaved Asparagus with Parmigiano-Reggiano, Lemon, and Black Pepper

Serve this salad with the first-of-spring crisp, thin asparagus. Early asparagus has a unique earthy taste, and we like to leave it raw, slicing it thinly on the bias. What you get on your plate is juicy, green, and grassy asparagus—a harbinger of spring's arrival and just the thing after so many months of hearty, wintry dishes. The dressing for the salad is minimalist: just lemon juice, olive oil, salt, and lots of black pepper. Because this dish is so elemental, don't try it unless you can get really great, extremely fresh, young asparagus. Anything old or out of season won't do it justice.

SERVES 4

1 pound thin young asparagus, trimmed
5 tablespoons extra-virgin olive oil,
  or more to taste
Juice of 1 lemon, or more to taste

½ teaspoon kosher salt, or more to taste
¼ teaspoon freshly cracked black pepper
4 ounces Parmigiano-Reggiano, coarsely
  grated (about 1 cup)

Thinly slice the asparagus on the bias (you should have about 4 cups). Transfer to a large bowl.

Add the olive oil, lemon juice, salt, and pepper. Toss in the cheese. Taste and add more lemon juice, olive oil, and/or salt if needed. Serve.

Andrew's Note: This salad is meant to be well-dressed, so don't skimp on the olive oil and use the best extra-virgin oil you've got. And be sure to be generous with the finish of black pepper.

Peas and Pea Shoots with Pecorino Romano and Mint

As soon as the first, smallest, sweetest peas pop up at the market in spring, we start making this salad. Andrew combines barely blanched peas with tiny pea shoots, which makes sense: the two share a similar fresh pea flavor, though the peas are sweeter and richer and the shoots fresher and more herbal. The contrasting textures are also really nice, with the smooth cooked peas softening the crisp raw shoots. A little Pecorino Romano adds a piquant flavor, and the lemon juice and mint brighten everything up.

SERVES 4

¾ cup shelled fresh peas
8 cups pea shoots
¾ cup freshly grated Pecorino
   Romano
½ cup mint leaves, torn in half

5 tablespoons extra-virgin olive oil, or
   more to taste
1½ tablespoons fresh lemon juice,
   or more to taste
Kosher salt to taste

Bring a pot of salted water to a boil. Add the peas and cook until just tender, 45 seconds to 1 minute. Drain well and plunge the peas into an ice bath to stop the cooking. Drain again, then spread the peas out on a dish towel and pat very gently to dry them.

Toss the peas and all the remaining ingredients together in a large bowl. Taste and adjust the seasonings if necessary.

Andrew's Note: Look for small, tender pea shoots that you can eat raw. The large ones are never as delicious. And always taste your peas before buying. They should be sweet and crunchy and not at all starchy, especially for this salad.

Farro Salad with Favas, Sopressata, and Pecorino

Pairing favas with Pecorino is classic in Tuscany, and you'll see it all over the region in springtime. This combination, with the addition of chunks of sopressata and nutty farro, becomes a very sustaining salad that you could serve for a light meal.

For the dressing, use a good-quality red wine vinegar. It has the right acidity to cut through the oiliness of the salami. And while shelling and peeling fresh favas can be time-consuming, you don't need a lot of them here, so it won't take all day.

Look for a sopressata that's seasoned with garlic and maybe a little wine but not much else. You want to taste the pork, not the flavorings. Feel free to use other types of salami here, as long as they don't contain fennel seeds, chilies, or other strong ingredients.

SERVES 4

1 cup semi-pearled farro
6 tablespoons peeled cooked fava beans
  (see Andrew's Notes)
2½ ounces sopressata, cut into ¼-inch
  cubes (6 tablespoons)
2 ounces Pecorino, cut into ¼-inch cubes
  (6 tablespoons)
6 tablespoons thinly sliced scallions

¾ teaspoon red wine vinegar,
  or more to taste
3 tablespoons extra-virgin olive oil,
  or more to taste
⅛ teaspoon kosher salt, or more to taste
⅛ teaspoon freshly cracked black pepper,
  or more to taste

| SALADS |

Preheat the oven to 350°F. Spread the farro out on a rimmed baking sheet and toast, stirring once after 10 minutes, until the grains darken and smell toasty, 15 to 20 minutes. Remove from the oven.

Bring a large pot of heavily salted water to a boil. Add the farro and boil until the grains are tender but still chewy, 25 to 30 minutes. Drain and transfer to a large bowl.

Stir the favas, sopressata, Pecorino, and scallions into the farro. Dress with the vinegar, olive oil, salt, and pepper. Taste and correct the seasonings if necessary.

Andrew's Notes: To prepare fava beans, shell about 1 pound of them in the pod. Cook in 8 cups boiling water seasoned with ¼ cup kosher salt until tender, 1 to 2 minutes, depending on the size. Drain and immediately plunge the favas into 4 cups of ice water seasoned with 2 tablespoons salt. Drain the beans. They should now slip easily from their skins. One pound of favas yields about ½ cup peeled cooked beans.

I like to toast farro before boiling it. It amplifies the grain's slightly nutty, earthy taste. After toasting, cook farro like pasta, in plenty of boiling salted water, until it's just al dente. Look for semi-pearled or pearled farro, which will cook in 20 to 25 minutes. Whole-grain farro is more like spelt or wheat berries and can take hours to soften.

Lettuce and Herb Salad with Moscato Vinegar

This salad is less about technique and more about shopping: you really need to use the most interesting mix of the freshest lettuces you can get your hands on. The farmers' market is your best bet here; most supermarket greens are pretty disappointing.

We based this salad on *misticanza*, a mix of different types of lettuces that you find at greenmarkets all over Rome. To mimic that, assemble diverse greens with different characteristics. Try to get as many varieties as you can. An ideal mix would contain something peppery, such as arugula; something soft, such as red oak lettuce; something crunchy, such as baby romaine; something spicy, such as radicchio or baby mustard greens; something bitter, such as chicory; and something delicate and fresh, such as Bibb lettuce. In addition to the greens, add plenty of fresh herbs, which you should tear rather than cut. Chopping bruises the leaves, and here you're aiming for large, rustic pieces.

The lettuces get the barest drizzle of slightly sweet moscato vinegar, a little salt, black pepper, and some good olive oil. That's all this simple, perfect salad needs.

SERVES 4

12 cups mixed lettuces (see the headnote), **torn into large pieces**
16 small basil leaves (or 8 or so big leaves torn in half)
16 mint leaves, torn
½ cup 1-inch pieces chives

Moscato vinegar (see Resources, page 357) **for drizzling**
Extra-virgin olive oil
Kosher salt and freshly cracked black pepper

In a large salad bowl, using your hands, gently toss together the lettuces and herbs. Sprinkle with a tiny bit of vinegar and drizzle with a bit of olive oil. Sprinkle with salt and pepper, toss, and taste. Add more salt, vinegar, and/or olive oil as needed. Serve immediately.

MARTIN GOBBEE

FRANNY'S DIRECTOR OF OPERATIONS

First job you had in the food industry?

It was at a little place in Nolita called Mexican Radio. It was such a small place that it was baptism by fire—it was truly a one-person show. We had to do everything: set up, bartend, serve, take delivery orders. But I would walk out with $400 in cash for a lunch shift in the late '90s.

First memorable slice?

At a mall in Waterbury, Connecticut. I was just old enough to get dropped off with my friends, and it was a real treat, this first taste of freedom. We'd go get a slice at this Italian pizza joint. They served just a really classic, great big cheese-dripping slice.

Has your relationship to pizza changed since you started working at Franny's?

Absolutely. I'm one of those people with realistic expectations. If I'm in a diner, I'm not going to order fish, I'm going to order french fries. With pizza, it's the same. When I go and get a slice somewhere, I know what I'm getting. But I know it won't hold a candle to what the kitchen at Franny's is doing.

Favorite dish on the menu, past or present?

The mushroom pizza. It makes for great leftovers the next day. I pop it in the toaster oven and put a fried egg on top of it.

Favorite secret midshift snack?

Candy—a gummy bear, or a mini Reese's peanut butter cup. Beyond that, I invoke my manager privilege of sticking a big spoon into whatever gelato is in the freezer—no double-dipping, of course, which is why the spoon is very, very full.

Cucumber Salad

The success of this salad depends upon what you can get at the farmers' market. Try to include at least two or three different kinds of cucumbers, such as Kirbys, English, Persian, and/or lemon cucumbers. They all have different textures and flavors, and it's the mix of them that makes this juicy, tangy salad really interesting.

Andrew briefly cures the cucumbers in salt and sugar before seasoning them very lightly with a mix of red and moscato vinegars, fresh herbs, onion, and olive oil. The flavors are pure and sweet and very summery.

SERVES 4 TO 6

1½ pounds mixed cucumbers, such as Kirby, Suyo Long, English, Tasty Jade, Persian, and lemon
2½ teaspoons kosher salt
2 teaspoons sugar
1 medium red onion, cut into ¼-inch-thick batons (about ½ cup)
2 teaspoons red wine vinegar

2 teaspoons moscato vinegar (see Resources, page 357), **plus more for drizzling**
2 tablespoons extra-virgin olive oil, plus more for drizzling
6 basil leaves, torn
4 mint leaves, torn
¼ cup coarsely chopped flat-leaf parsley

Using a vegetable peeler, remove half the skin from Kirby, Suyo Long, and other smaller cucumbers in long strips, creating a striped appearance. Slice them into ¼-inch-thick rounds. Stripe English, Tasty Jades, and other long cucumbers in the same way. Slice them lengthwise in half, scoop out the seeds, and cut them into 2-by-¼-inch batons. Stripe-peel the lemon cucumbers. Slice them in half, scoop out the seeds, and cut them into ¼-inch half-moons. (You should have about 3½ cups sliced cucumbers.)

In a bowl, combine the cucumbers, salt, and sugar. Let stand for 45 minutes. Drain the cucumbers, pat them dry, and refrigerate until cold.

In a medium bowl, toss the cucumbers with the onion, vinegars, olive oil, and herbs. Drizzle with additional moscato vinegar and olive oil and serve.

Andrew's Note: The most important technique here is the dry-brine—salting and sugaring the cucumbers. It's like making a very light, quick pickle; the dry brine draws out the moisture, firms up the cucumbers, and makes them crisp. And it seasons them at the same time.

TOMATOES

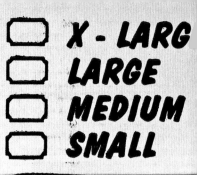
VT. 25 LBS.
.34 Kg.

PRODUCE OF U.S.A.

GROWN & PACKED BY:

NET WT. 25 LBS.
11.34 Kg.

☐ GROWN ON STAKES

MATOES

PLUM
TOMATOES

- X - LARGE
- LARGE
- MEDIUM
- SMALL

- ☐ BLUSH
- ☐ MORE COLOR
- ☐ RED

☐ GRO

TOMATOES

- ☐ X - LARGE
- ☐ LARGE
- ☐ MEDIUM
- ☐ SMALL

NEW
RSEY TOMATOES

NEW
JERSEY T

WT. 25 LBS.
11.34 Kg.

PRODUCE OF U.S.A.

NET WT. 25 LBS.
11.34 Kg.

TOMATOES

TOM

Tomato Salad with Burrata

This salad is the essence of summer, combining marinated heirloom tomatoes with a variety of different basils—opal, Thai, and regular green—and other herbs, and finishing them with dabs of milky, mild burrata cheese. It makes an ideal hot-weather lunch or light supper served with a loaf of good crusty bread.

SERVES 4

FOR THE MARINATED TOMATOES
2 medium heirloom tomatoes, cored and
    sliced into 6 wedges each
4 Yellow Rave or other small yellow
    heirloom tomatoes, cored and halved
¼ teaspoon kosher salt
⅛ teaspoon freshly cracked black pepper
1 tablespoon red wine vinegar
2 tablespoons extra-virgin olive oil

FOR THE SALAD
10 Sun Gold cherry tomatoes
10 red cherry tomatoes
1 sweet white onion, such as Vidalia, cut
    into ¼-inch-thick rings

½ cup basil leaves, torn into large pieces
½ cup opal basil leaves, torn into
    large pieces
½ cup Thai basil leaves, torn into
    large pieces
½ cup mint leaves, torn into large pieces
½ cup flat-leaf parsley leaves
½ teaspoon kosher salt
¼ teaspoon freshly cracked black pepper,
    plus more for sprinkling
1 tablespoon red wine vinegar
⅓ cup extra-virgin olive oil

8 ounces burrata
Flaky sea salt, such as Maldon

To make the marinated tomatoes: Spread the tomatoes in an even layer on a large platter or rimmed baking sheet. Sprinkle with the salt, pepper, vinegar, and olive oil. Let the tomatoes sit for 30 minutes.

To make the salad: In a large bowl, combine the cherry tomatoes, onion rings, basil, mint, and parsley. Season with the salt, pepper, vinegar, and olive oil.

Divide the marinated tomatoes among four dinner plates. Top them with the tomato salad, dividing it evenly. With a spoon, dab the burrata over and around the salads, 5 to 6 dabs per plate. Give a good crack of black pepper over the salad and a sprinkle of sea salt over the cheese and serve.

Red Rice Salad with Cherry Tomatoes, Cucumbers, and Corn

In Italy, whenever you walk into a store that sells salumi or prepared foods, you will inevitably see some kind of rice salad. It's as ubiquitous as coleslaw is in delis here, and these rice salads can be just as unimpressive—often a halfhearted mix of canned corn, sliced olives, lackluster ham, vegetables, and rice. Still, we've always liked the idea of a rice salad and so decided to come up with a fresher, livelier version, using summer vegetables at their peak—sweet corn, ripe cherry tomatoes, spicy radishes, cucumbers, and scallions, with herbs and caciocavallo cheese for complexity. But the biggest departure from the Italian standard is that instead of using the traditional white rice, we toss the vegetables with red rice from the Piedmont region. Red rice has a much deeper, earthier flavor than white rice and a firmer texture. If you can't find it, try using farro rather than substituting white or brown rice.

SERVES 4

1 cup Piedmont red rice
Kosher salt
2½ tablespoons red wine vinegar,
  or more to taste
5 tablespoons extra-virgin olive oil,
  plus more for drizzling
¾ cup mixed, halved red and gold cherry
  tomatoes (about 16)

½ cup corn kernels (about 1 ear)
4 ounces caciocavallo, diced (about ½ cup)
¼ cup diced cucumber
¼ cup diced radishes
¼ cup thinly sliced scallions
8 basil leaves, torn
4 teaspoons chopped flat-leaf parsley
Freshly cracked black pepper

Bring a large pot of unsalted water to a boil. Add the rice and boil until the grains begin to split, 15 to 18 minutes. Salt the water heavily and cook until the grains are tender, 5 to 10 minutes longer. Drain the rice very well and spread it out on a large rimmed baking sheet. Drizzle with the vinegar and 2½ tablespoons of the olive oil. Let cool.

Transfer the rice to a large bowl. Toss with the tomatoes, corn, cheese, cucumber, radishes, scallions, herbs, and the remaining 2½ tablespoons olive oil. Season with salt, pepper, and more vinegar if the salad needs a lift. Drizzle the salad with olive oil and serve.

Andrew's Note: When cooking red rice, don't add salt to the pot at the beginning. If you do, the rice won't get tender. Instead, salt it after the rice starts to split and is almost tender. That way, the salt won't impede the cooking, but the rice will still have time to absorb the salt.

Celery, Fennel, and Pear Salad with Pecorino and Walnuts

This autumnal salad spotlights the great celery we find at the farmers' market. It's got an intense, herbal flavor that is much richer than the pale supermarket variety you usually see. We add sweet, juicy pears; anise-scented, crunchy fennel; grassy celery leaves; and toasted walnuts to sliced celery stalks. Then, as a final garnish, the salad is covered with shaved Pecorino Ginepro, an aged hard but not too salty Pecorino cheese to add a creamy complexity. If you can't find it, use Parmigiano-Reggiano in its place—it works better than the saltier Pecorino Romano.

SERVES 4

¾ cup walnuts
2 small fennel bulbs, trimmed, quartered lengthwise, cored, and sliced crosswise ¼ inch thick (1 cup)
2 to 3 celery stalks, cut on the bias into ¼-inch-thick slices (1 cup)
1 large Bosc pear, quartered, cored, and cut lengthwise into ¼-inch-thick slices (1 cup)

2 tablespoons roughly chopped celery leaves
Juice of 1 lemon
Kosher salt and freshly cracked black pepper
2 tablespoons extra-virgin olive oil, plus more for drizzling
A 2-ounce chunk of Pecorino for shaving

Preheat the oven to 350°F. Spread the walnuts out on a rimmed baking sheet. Toast until fragrant and golden, about 8 minutes. Cool, then roughly chop.

In a large bowl, toss together the fennel, celery, pear, walnuts, and celery leaves. Season with the lemon juice, salt and pepper, and the olive oil.

Divide the salad among four serving plates. Use a vegetable peeler or a wide-bladed Microplane to shave the cheese over the salad. Finish with cracked pepper and a drizzle of olive oil.

Warm Controne Bean Salad with Radicchio and Pancetta

A winter salad should be filling and warm for those frigid, icy days. Warm salads can be hard to do well: most lettuces wilt as soon as they touch a warm, oily dressing, making a mess of everything. But here, radicchio—specifically Treviso radicchio—is sturdy enough to withstand the heat and retain its crunch. If you can't find Treviso, use regular radicchio or escarole instead.

It's worthwhile trying to find creamy, round Controne beans from Campagna, which have a fantastic, earthy flavor, for this salad (see Resources, page 357). But corona beans, large white beans, or cannellini beans will work too. We particularly love how the warm, crisp pancetta contrasts with the mild softness of the beans. Before you make this recipe, consider curing your own pancetta (see page 192); homemade pancetta will make a notable difference in the way this salad tastes. However, if charcuterie isn't your thing, get really good-quality pancetta at a specialty market. You could substitute bacon, but its smokiness would change the taste and mood of the salad.

SERVES 4

¼ cup plus 2 teaspoons extra virgin olive oil, or more to taste
5 ounces pancetta, diced into ½-inch pieces (1 cup)
4 cups thinly sliced Treviso radicchio
1⅓ cups cooked Controne beans

1 cup roughly chopped flat-leaf parsley
½ cup julienned red onion
4 teaspoons red wine vinegar, or more to taste
Kosher salt and freshly cracked black pepper

In a large skillet, warm the 2 teaspoons olive oil over medium heat until shimmering. Add the pancetta and cook, stirring occasionally, until golden brown and crispy, about 5 minutes. Transfer the pancetta to a paper-towel-lined plate to drain. Reserve the pancetta fat.

In a large bowl, combine the radicchio, beans, parsley, red onion, drained pancetta, the remaining ¼ cup olive oil, 4 teaspoons of the reserved pancetta fat, and the red wine vinegar. Toss well. Season to taste with salt and pepper, then add more vinegar and/or olive oil if needed. Serve.

Andrew's Note: The acidity in the dressing will seem more intense with a warm salad than with a room-temperature salad. So be judicious and more conservative with the vinegar than you normally would. You can always add more.

Red Cabbage with Hazelnuts, Balsamico, and Pancetta

In this complex salad, sweet red cabbage is combined with salty pancetta and a touch of balsamic vinegar. The cabbage is thinly sliced, just like you'd do for slaw (in fact, we always joke that this dish is a little bit like a fancy Italian slaw), then tossed with olive oil, red wine and balsamic vinegars, toasted hazelnuts, and crisp pancetta. We don't use balsamic often, but in this salad it really shines, adding a sharp sweetness that brings all the flavors together.

SERVES 4

¼ cup plus 1 teaspoon extra-virgin olive oil, plus more as needed
5 ounces pancetta, each slice unrolled and cut into 5 pieces
5 cups sliced red cabbage (about ½ head; approximately 1¼ pounds)
⅔ cup toasted, peeled, and roughly chopped hazelnuts

1½ tablespoons red wine vinegar, or more to taste
½ teaspoon kosher salt, or more to taste
¼ teaspoon freshly ground black pepper, or more to taste
Aged balsamic vinegar, for drizzling

In a large skillet, heat the teaspoon of olive oil over medium heat. Working in batches, and adding more oil as necessary, cook the pancetta until golden brown and crispy. Transfer to a paper-towel-lined plate to drain.

In a large bowl, combine the cabbage, hazelnuts, ¼ cup olive oil, red wine vinegar, salt, and pepper, toss with your hands to mix, squeezing the cabbage slightly while you toss. Taste and adjust the seasonings if necessary, adding more vinegar, salt, and/or pepper.

Place the cabbage mixture on a large serving plate. Arrange the pancetta on top, drizzle with the balsamic, and serve.

Andrew's Note: There are many great-quality balsamics that go through the traditional aging process. Invest in a small bottle of the best stuff you can find and use it sparingly; it will keep indefinitely. We use Riccardo Giusti Il Denso balsamic (see Resources, page 357), which is made from a combination of Trebbiano and Lambrusco grapes. After being reduced for sweetness and viscosity, it goes through the traditional aging process, moved through successively smaller wooden barrels over the course of ten to twelve years.

Escarole with Meyer Lemon, Parmigiano-Reggiano, and Black Pepper

This robust salad has a creaminess that's similar to that of a Caesar salad (thanks to all the Parmigiano-Reggiano), but with a brighter and spicier flavor from the Meyer lemon zest and plenty of cracked black pepper. It's on the lighter side of winter salads, hinting that spring just might be around the corner, and the escarole's crunch is a nice reprieve from all that heavy winter food.

Buy more heads of escarole than you think you'll need—at least three. Then only use the inner leaves that are white and yellow—they are the tastiest. (You can use the outer leaves for soups and braised dishes.) If you can't get good escarole, substitute romaine lettuce or endive. Boston Bibb and green leaf lettuces are too delicate and would wilt under the assertive dressing.

SERVES 4 TO 6

Grated zest of 3 Meyer lemons
⅓ cup fresh Meyer lemon juice
  (3 to 4 lemons)
**4 ounces Parmigiano-Reggiano,
  coarsely grated** (about 1 cup)
1 tablespoon Dijon mustard

¼ teaspoon kosher salt, or more to taste
**½ teaspoon freshly cracked black pepper,
  or more to taste**
½ cup extra-virgin olive oil
4 quarts (16 cups) **escarole, washed, dried,
  and torn into rough pieces**

In a food processor or blender, combine the lemon zest, juice, ½ cup of the Parmigiano-Reggiano, the mustard, salt, and pepper and blend for 1 minute. With the motor running, slowly drizzle in the olive oil.

In a large bowl, toss the escarole with about two-thirds of the dressing until well coated. Season with additional salt and pepper if necessary and sprinkle with the remaining Parmigiano-Reggiano. Taste and add more dressing, if you like. (Leftover dressing can be refrigerated for up to 1 week.) Serve.

Barley Salad with Sunchokes, Carrots, Almonds, Pecorino, and Pickled Fennel

Sunchokes, also called Jerusalem artichokes, are one of the few local vegetables available in winter in the Northeast. Shaved raw into a salad, they add a welcome crunchy juiciness. Here they are roasted until their sweet earthiness becomes even more pronounced and their texture softens. Then we mix them with caramelized roasted carrots, nutty toasted barley, and Pecorino. But what really brings everything together is the pickled fennel. You get this nice burst of tart pickle in your mouth along with the starchiness of the barley and the sunchokes.

If you don't want to take on making the pickled fennel stems, you can substitute any firm pickled vegetable: onions, carrots, peppers, even Italian giardiniera. As long as there's something crunchy and acidic mixed into the salad for a contrast, it will still be delicious.

SERVES 4

1 cup pearled barley
5 tablespoons extra-virgin olive oil, or more to taste
2 medium carrots, peeled and diced
6 ounces sunchokes, scrubbed and cut into ½-inch dice (about 1 cup)
Kosher salt and freshly cracked black pepper
½ cup coarsely chopped roasted skin-on almonds

2 ounces Pecorino, cut into ¼-inch cubes (about ½ cup)
¼ cup thinly sliced red onion
¼ cup chopped flat-leaf parsley
2 tablespoons Fennel Conserva (page 351) or chopped other firm pickled vegetable
1 tablespoon red wine vinegar, or more to taste

Preheat the oven to 400°F. Bring a large pot of salted water to a boil.

Toss the barley with 1 tablespoon of the olive oil and spread out on a baking sheet. Toast until dark golden brown and caramel in color, 10 to 12 minutes—the color will be uneven.

Add the toasted barley to the boiling water (leave the oven on), reduce the heat to medium, and cook, covered, until the barley is tender, about 30 minutes. Drain well and let cool to room temperature, then place in a large bowl and set aside.

Meanwhile, in a medium bowl, toss the carrots and sunchokes with 2 tablespoons olive oil. Season with salt and pepper. Spread in a single layer on a rimmed baking sheet and roast until lightly browned and tender, 30 to 40 minutes. Let cool to room temperature.

Add the roasted vegetables, almonds, cheese, onion, parsley, Fennel Conserva, vinegar, and the remaining 2 tablespoons olive oil to the barley and toss to combine. Season to taste with salt and pepper and add more vinegar and/or olive oil if needed. Serve.

Escarole Salad with Pine Nut Dressing and Ricotta Salata

This crunchy salad shows how familiar ingredients can take on new roles. The salad is all about the dressing, made by toasting pine nuts until they have a rich, caramel flavor, then blending them into a smooth nut butter before whisking in oil and vinegar. The dressing is tossed with crisp leaves of escarole, thinly sliced red onion, and salty crumbles of ricotta salata. This simple, unusual recipe is a great example of how good things can happen when traditional Italian ingredients are combined untraditionally.

SERVES 6

2 cups pine nuts
1 cup plus 1 teaspoon extra-virgin olive oil
¼ cup red wine vinegar
1½ teaspoons kosher salt, or more to taste
½ teaspoon freshly ground black pepper,
or more to taste

4 small heads escarole, outer leaves
removed
1 small red onion
6 ounces ricotta salata

In a large skillet, toast the pine nuts over medium-low heat, stirring occasionally, until light golden, 5 to 7 minutes. Pour the pine nuts onto a plate and let cool.

Add the pine nuts to a food processor, along with the 1 teaspoon olive oil, and blend, stopping occasionally to scrape down the sides, until you get a coarse paste.

Scrape the paste into a small bowl. Whisk in the vinegar, salt, and pepper. Slowly whisk in the remaining 1 cup olive oil. Taste and correct the seasoning if necessary.

Separate the escarole leaves and drop into a large bowl.

Using a mandoline or a very sharp knife, shave 6 paper-thin slices of red onion. Separate the slices into individual rings and add them to the lettuce.

Gradually add just enough of the vinaigrette to the salad, tossing the lettuce, to lightly coat. Use a vegetable peeler to shave the ricotta salata over the salad and serve.

Citrus Salad with Pistachios, Olives, and Chilies

If you like to keep a variety of fragrant citrus fruits on hand in winter, this is an ideal way to turn them into a juicy and satisfying last-minute lunch. Feel free to vary the types of citrus, letting the recipe evolve throughout their winter season: satsumas, Minneolas, tangerines, Cara Caras, blood oranges, and grapefruit can all make an appearance as they show up in your local market. The mix of colorful citrus, pistachios, briny olives, and pickled hot peppers is a surprisingly bright and piquant combination—especially in the winter, when flavors tend to be more muted and our tastes run toward richer food.

SERVES 4

2 small pink grapefruits
2 blood oranges
2 navel or Cara Cara oranges
2 tangerines
Scant ¼ teaspoon flaky sea salt, such as Maldon, plus a pinch
Pinch of freshly cracked black pepper
2 tablespoons red wine vinegar
2 tablespoons extra-virgin olive oil, plus more for drizzling

¼ cup Castelvetrano or other mild, meaty, green olives, pitted and sliced
1½ tablespoons minced red onion
2 tablespoons chopped fresh flat-leaf parsley
¾ teaspoon Pickled Hot Peppers (page 352)
3 tablespoons plus 1 teaspoon toasted pistachios

Slice the ends from the grapefruit and stand each one upright on a flat surface. Use a sharp knife to cut away the rind and white pith in strips from top to bottom, following the contour of the fruit. Cut the fruit into ¼-inch-thick wheels. Pick out and discard the seeds.

Peel the oranges. Remove any remaining white pith and slice the oranges into ¼-inch-thick wheels. Pick out and discard the seeds. Peel the tangerines, remove any remaining white pith, and separate the tangerines into segments. Remove any seeds with a paring knife.

Arrange the citrus on a large plate, mixing the colors and shapes. Sprinkle with the pinch of sea salt (this will bring out and intensify the flavor of the fruit without making it salty). Season with the pepper.

In a small bowl, stir together the vinegar, olive oil, olives, red onion, parsley, hot peppers, pistachios, and the remaining scant ¼ teaspoon salt.

Spoon the dressing over the citrus. Drizzle generously with olive oil and serve.

Puntarelle alla Romana

The first time we tasted puntarelle, a type of wild chicory, was when we were in Rome on our honeymoon. (Actually, it wasn't technically our honeymoon yet—we flew into Rome, then rented a car and drove down the coast to Amalfi, where the mayor of the town married us in the medieval cathedral.) We had dinner at a restaurant called Osteria dell'Angelo, where they had puntarelle on the menu. We were so excited to try it, and it was amazing—bitter, crisp, juicy, vibrant, and intense. A single puntarelle stalk offers many different textures. The edge of the leaf is celery-like, while farther down, the stalk is very crunchy. We thought it was one of the best things we'd ever tasted.

The traditional Roman dressing for puntarelle is a pungent mix of raw garlic, anchovy, olive oil, and red wine vinegar. We like to add a little lemon juice to brighten the salad. Use the best-quality anchovies you can find.

SERVES 4

1 head puntarelle, trimmed and sliced
¼ inch thick (see Andrew's Note)
4 anchovy fillets, mashed to a paste
(about 2 teaspoons)
½ teaspoon minced garlic
2 tablespoons fresh lemon juice, plus more
to taste

2 tablespoons extra-virgin olive oil
½ teaspoon kosher salt, or more to taste
½ teaspoon freshly cracked black pepper,
or more to taste

Soak the puntarelle for 2 hours in about 4 cups ice water; this reduces the bitterness and makes the puntarelle more juicy and crunchy.

Drain the puntarelle and dry well in a salad spinner.

In a small bowl, mix together the anchovy paste, garlic, lemon juice, olive oil, salt, and pepper. Toss the puntarelle with the dressing until well coated. Season with more lemon, salt, and pepper to taste if needed and serve.

Andrew's Note: Puntarelle can be hard to find. Start looking for it in winter at specialty produce markets and Italian groceries. To prepare it, first trim off the root end, then separate the leaves from the finger-like stems. Thinly slice the stems lengthwise. Soak them in ice water until they curl, about 2 hours (you can leave them in the water for several hours).

SOUP

Soup season at Franny's begins in late September. As soon as summer is winding down and there's a pronounced chill in the air at night, we think about putting soups on the menu, and we start craving them in our kitchen at home. Our soups are warming, hearty, and fortifying, and so we tend to enjoy hot soups more in the colder months than at other times of the year. Plus, when you forgo soup in summer, it gives you a chance to really anticipate its return in the fall.

The first recipes to turn to as soup season descends make use of the last of the late-summer produce. Zucchini, tomatoes, and basil are short-lived once the temperature drops, and perfect for the soup pot. Zucchini Soup with Parmigiano-Reggiano and Basil (page 103), Tomato and Cranberry Bean Soup with Pumpkin, Escarole, and Parmigiano-Reggiano (page 106), and Late-Summer Minestrone (page 100) all take full advantage of the bounty of harvest-season produce.

As fresh produce wanes and the frost arrives, soups become richer and more filling. Deep winter is the time to simmer up dried bean soups, brightened with hardy local greens or enriched with meat, grains, or pasta (or a combination). These chunky, fortifying soups are made for blustery nights, perfect warming recipes to keep the chill at bay. Andrew likes to make his bean and grain soups on the thicker side, pureeing half the ingredients and leaving the other half intact. This gives them a luxurious, creamy consistency, with a silky mouthfeel—particularly satisfying when it's harsh and cold outside and you want something soothing.

These soups can be either a starter or a main course, depending upon the size of your appetite and your soup bowl. In winter, we eat soup for dinner at home about once a week. Our five-year-old son, Marco, especially loves soup in all its forms, possibly because it was one of the first things he could eat all by himself. He can easily polish off an entire bowl, for which I am truly grateful. Soup can be a spectacular vehicle to get all kinds of seasonal, homemade, and nutritious food into our kids.

Many of the recipes in this book are based on traditional soups you'll find all over Italy: Pasta e Fagioli (page 112), Tomato Bread Soup (page 104), and Lentil, Farro, and Controne Bean Soup with Pancetta (page 117), to name a few. We stray from tradition in two noteworthy places: Our Broccoli Soup (page 108) and Zucchini Soup with Parmigiano-Reggiano and Basil (page 103) take advantage of good seasonal produce that we don't do too much to. We came up with these recipes when we wanted a couple of deep-flavored, vegetarian soups, and they've become steadfast favorites among our customers—whether they eat meat or not.

With the exception of our Chicken Brodo with Parmigiano-Reggiano, Maltagliati, Parsley, and Lemon (page 114), we use water as a base for all of our soups. Using water instead of stock allows the flavor of the ingredients to shine. Broccoli soup tastes deeply of broccoli, without any other distractions. Bean soup is earthy and rich. Soups made with water can be much cleaner and brighter, with articulated flavors that speak of the main ingredients that went into the pot, intensifying as they simmer. A stock can obscure the purity of flavors, which is an important part of

what we're after when we cook up a big pot of soup.

This is especially true with bean soups, such as the Cannellini Bean and Escarole Soup (page 109), Chickpea and Kale Soup (page 111), and Pasta e Fagioli (page 112). Beans simmered with aromatics and seasonings create their own heady, sublime broth. By the time the beans have softened, their broth is delicious and thoroughly developed. It offers the vital and fundamental essence of the thing you're cooking.

To add flavor and depth to soups made with water, Andrew has a few tricks that are easy to replicate at home. One is adding a chunk of Parmigiano-Reggiano rind to the bubbling mix. Another is tossing in prosciutto trimmings. In a way, these work like instant (but subtle) bouillon cubes, bumping up and accentuating the flavors already in the pot. You can usually get both of them from specialty stores or even large supermarkets with deli counters—anyplace that sells prosciutto and Parmigiano-Reggiano will likely have rinds and trimming to give you or sell at a nominal cost. Or just save the rinds from your Parmigiano-Reggiano whenever you buy a hunk. That's what we do at home, freezing them until we're ready to use them.

Because soup is such an essential, universal food, it's intensely personal, and there is

quite a range as to how people like it. What we might find comforting can be quite different from what others do. Some people like their soup really thick, almost like a stew, while others prefer it brothier. I like mine brothy, while Andrew appreciates all styles and is skilled at creating a whole range of textures in his soups. He lets his soup cool for a few minutes before eating it, but I like to eat my soup while it's still piping hot. Some people dunk bread in soup to sop up every last bit of broth; others leave that work to the spoon.

But no matter how you like to eat your soup, a good bowl of it demands a proper garnish. In Italy, soups are often finished with a generous drizzle of olive oil, a sprinkling of grated cheese, or a few drops of lemon juice. It might seem like an insignificant detail, but the addition of one or more of these final touches raises a soup to new heights—from good to sublime. It's amazing how this last step, which takes mere seconds, makes all the difference.

Late-Summer Minestrone

You'll find a version of minestrone in every region of Italy. The basic blueprint involves beans of some sort, an abundance of vegetables, and, frequently, pasta; we skip the pasta in ours. With so many other elements, we feel that pasta ultimately weighs the soup down. Instead, this minestrone is about the bounty of produce—chard, zucchini, tomatoes, green beans, fingerling potatoes—all at its peak in the harvest season.

To make the soup especially flavorful, we sauté the vegetables before adding them to the pot with the beans. Not only does this help maintain their color, it also allows the salt to penetrate and season the vegetables thoroughly, until they taste just right. If you just cook all the vegetables together in the soup pot along with the beans, the flavors of the vegetables will be diminished, since most of them will leach out into the broth. Additionally, seasoning the vegetables while sautéing helps keep them nice and firm, because the salt draws out the moisture. It may be slightly more work than your average minestrone recipe, but the results are well worth it.

SERVES 6 TO 8

1¼ pounds ripe tomatoes
10 tablespoons plus 2 teaspoons extra-
   virgin olive oil, plus more for drizzling
2 medium Spanish onions, finely chopped
   (about 3 cups)
3 tablespoons chopped garlic, plus 1 clove
1 sage sprig
5 ounces Parmigiano-Reggiano rinds,
   scraped (see Andrew's Note)
1½ pounds fresh cranberry beans, shelled
   (about 2 cups)

6 cups water
2 teaspoons kosher salt, plus more to taste
Freshly cracked black pepper
12 ounces fingerling potatoes, cut into
   ¼-inch-thick rounds (about 2 cups)
2 bunches Swiss chard
3 medium zucchini, preferably Romanesco,
   cut into ½-inch pieces (about 3 cups)
2 cups green beans cut into ¾-inch pieces
20 basil leaves, torn
Finely grated Parmigiano-Reggiano

Bring a large pot of water to a boil. Using a paring knife, cut a small X in the base of each tomato. Blanch the tomatoes in the boiling water for 30 seconds. Remove from the pot and let cool until you can handle the tomatoes comfortably, then peel away the skin with your fingers or a paring knife. Coarsely chop the tomatoes.

In a large Dutch oven, heat 5 tablespoons of the olive oil over medium heat. Add the onions and chopped garlic and cook until soft, about 10 minutes. Add the sage and chopped tomatoes and cook for about 5 minutes.

Wrap the cheese rinds in a square of cheesecloth and knot it. Stir the cheese rinds, cranberry beans, and water into the pot, then stir in the salt and 5 or 6 turns of black pepper and cook until the beans are about halfway cooked, 15 to 20 minutes.

Add the potatoes and cook until both beans and potatoes are tender, about 20 minutes more.

Meanwhile, separate the chard leaves from the stems. Cut the stems into ½-inch pieces (about 2 cups). Coarsely chop half the leaves (about 4 cups; keep the remaining leaves for another use).

continued

In a large skillet, heat 5 tablespoons olive oil over medium-high heat. Add the chard stems and sauté for 2 minutes until tender; season with salt. Add the zucchini and sauté for another 2 minutes; season with salt. Add the green beans and sauté for another 2 minutes; season with salt. Finally, add the chard leaves, season with salt, and cook until the greens have just wilted.

Scoop out the sage sprig and the cheese rind sachet from the beans and discard them. Scrape the vegetable mixture into the pot. Season the soup with salt and pepper to taste.

In a mortar with a pestle, pound the garlic clove with the basil and the remaining 2 teaspoons oil.

Ladle the soup into bowls. Garnish each serving with a drizzle of the garlic-herb oil and a sprinkle of Parmigiano-Reggiano. Finish with a drizzle of olive oil and 1 or 2 turns of black pepper and serve.

Andrew's Note: When you add cheese rinds to a soup, make sure to scrape the waxy residue off the rinds first; you don't want the wax to end up in your soup. Use a chef's knife or a paring knife (not serrated), and you'll see it come right off. Then wrap the rinds in a square of cheesecloth, knot it, and use the sachet to add rich flavor to your broth. When the soup is done, just fish the sachet out and discard it.

If you don't have rinds but want to impart a cheesy flavor, you can, of course, just use a hunk of cheese. This, however, will cost you more than rinds, so it won't exactly be *cucina povera*. But it will taste good.

Zucchini Soup with Parmigiano-Reggiano and Basil

This lovely vegetable soup shows off two sides of zucchini—the sweet, fresh flavor of the lightly cooked vegetable and the intense, caramelized taste of zucchini that's been fried. We make it using the same technique as for our Broccoli Soup (page 108)—that is, cooking the vegetable on only one side until it turns mahogany and leaving the other side pale green and delicate. It's a perfect soup to simmer up in late September, when it first starts to get cool, with the last of the season's zucchini from the farmers' market. Since zucchini tends to be fairly mild, we give it some help flavorwise by adding handfuls of basil, parsley, scallions, and onion. A generous showering of Parmigiano-Reggiano brings it all together.

SERVES 4 TO 6

½ cup plus 2 tablespoons extra-virgin olive oil, plus more for drizzling
8 medium zucchini, trimmed and cut into 1-inch chunks (about 8 cups)
1 cup finely chopped Spanish onion
½ cup thinly sliced scallions
½ cup finely chopped flat-leaf parsley
3 garlic cloves, finely chopped

1¼ teaspoons kosher salt, plus more to taste
¾ teaspoon freshly cracked black pepper, plus more to taste
2 cups water
2 tablespoons chopped basil, plus torn leaves for garnish
Finely grated Parmigiano-Reggiano

In a Dutch oven, heat ¼ cup of the olive oil over high heat. Working in batches to avoid overcrowding the pot, cook the zucchini on one cut side until golden and caramelized. As soon as the squash has browned on one side, transfer it to a large plate.

Add the remaining 6 tablespoons olive oil to the pot. Add the onion, scallions, parsley, and garlic and season with ¼ teaspoon each of the salt and pepper. Cover and cook over medium heat until the vegetables become soft and translucent, about 10 minutes.

Return the zucchini to the pot and season with the remaining 1 teaspoon salt and ½ teaspoon pepper. Stir in the water. The water will not completely cover the squash. Bring to a simmer, then reduce the heat to low, taste for seasoning, and add salt if needed. Cover the pot and simmer until the squash is soft but not falling apart, about 20 minutes. Stir in the basil.

Use an immersion blender to puree the soup, but leave some texture; it should not be completely smooth. Lingering morsels of zucchini are welcome. Or transfer three-quarters of the soup to a food processor and pulse to a coarse puree, then stir back into the pot. Adjust the seasoning if necessary.

Ladle the soup into bowls and garnish with torn basil leaves, cheese, and a drizzle of olive oil.

Tomato Bread Soup

In simple, pure-tasting recipes such as this one, the quality of the ingredients becomes all the more important. Make this with dead-ripe tomatoes, and you'll be rewarded with a memorable, intense soup. You'll also need slices of good artisanal bread, which expand in the liquid like a sponge and give the soup a lovely body.

Besides ripe tomatoes and good bread, the soup has a secret weapon—Parmigiano-Reggiano cheese rinds. The rinds impart a dense and savory backbone to the soup. Finished with a kick of cracked black pepper, the soup will have you looking forward to tomato season every year.

SERVES 4 TO 6

4 pounds ripe tomatoes
2 medium white onions
½ cup extra-virgin olive oil, plus
  more for drizzling
5 garlic cloves, roughly chopped
2 cups water
¾ cup basil leaves, plus torn leaves
  for garnish

½ teaspoon kosher salt, or more to taste
6 ounces Parmigiano-Reggiano rinds,
  scraped (see Andrew's Note, page 00)
8 ounces day-old pagnotta or other country-
  style bread, crusts removed
Finely grated Parmigiano-Reggiano
Freshly cracked black pepper

Bring a large pot of water to a boil. Using a paring knife, score the bottom of each tomato with a small X. Blanch the tomatoes for 30 seconds. Remove from the pot and let cool until you can handle them comfortably, then peel off the skins with your fingers or a paring knife. Coarsely chop the tomatoes.

Slice the onions in half through the root, then thinly slice each half crosswise. (You should have about 3 cups.)

In a Dutch oven or a large pot, warm the olive oil over medium heat. Add the onions and garlic and cook, stirring to prevent browning, until soft and translucent, 7 to 10 minutes. Add the tomatoes, water, basil leaves, and salt. Tie the cheese rinds in a square of cheesecloth and drop into the pot. Cover the pot and simmer over low heat for 45 minutes.

Tear the bread into bite-sized pieces and stir them into the soup. Cover the pot again and continue simmering for 20 minutes longer. Remove and discard the cheese rinds. Add salt to taste if necessary.

Ladle the soup into bowls. Finish each serving with grated cheese, a drizzle of olive oil, cracked black pepper, and a sprinkling of torn basil leaves.

MORGAN REIS
FRANNY'S SERVER

Other than at Franny's, what is the best job you've ever had?

That's a hard one, but I'd have to say it was an incredible highlight to work with the playwright Adam Rapp at the Flea Theater. I played a gay, militant, theater-obsessed guerrilla leader. It was super real.

First memorable slice?

Joe's on Sixth Avenue in the city. It's just delicious. I still love it. It's fast and hot and crispy, the sauce is right, and it's not too greasy. I order a mozz slice and usually eat it standing up at one of those tables outside.

Has your relationship to pizza changed since you started working at Franny's?

Profoundly. I think Franny's has just raised my food bar in every way—so much so that it's challenging for me to dine out now, especially for pizza.

Favorite dish on the menu, past or present?

I was kind of a mushroom hater until the mushroom pizza rolled around. But I have to say my all-time favorite is the wood-roasted pork sausage. It's just unstoppable. I probably eat it once a week. It's so juicy and flavorful and delicious. I grew up in Ohio, so at heart I'm really a meat-and-potatoes girl.

Favorite secret midshift snack?

Sometimes I'll steal a spoonful of gelato out of the freezer (ideally fior di latte) and act like nothing ever happened. But I know I'm not the only one. . . .

Tomato and Cranberry Bean Soup with Pumpkin, Escarole, and Parmigiano-Reggiano

A brothy, autumnal soup embodies the transition from summer to fall, with the last of the season's tomatoes and cranberry beans and the first showing of pumpkin and escarole. Here the beans are cooked in water with Parmesan cheese rinds, creating the rich broth, and then we add pieces of roasted pumpkin, fresh tomato chunks, and escarole. The pumpkin provides some sweetness, the cranberry beans add satisfying little pops of richness, and the tomatoes at their peak of ripeness do what they do best—all set off by the bitter bite of escarole.

There is just a brief window at the greenmarket when all of these vegetables overlap, so when you start seeing pumpkins but can still get tomatoes and winter squashes, seize the moment. This soup is the sort of dish that makes you stop and appreciate the here and now.

SERVES 4 TO 6

4 medium-ripe tomatoes
¼ cup extra-virgin olive oil, plus more
  for drizzling
1 cup finely diced white onion
½ cup finely diced fennel bulb
½ cup finely diced celery
4 garlic cloves, chopped
1 pound Parmigiano-Reggiano rinds,
  scraped (see Andrew's Note)
1 large sage sprig

1 large rosemary sprig
1½ cups shelled fresh cranberry beans
  (from about 1 pound whole beans)
5½ cups water
1½ tablespoons kosher salt
2 cups peeled and diced
  (about ¾-inch pieces) **pumpkin**
6 cups chopped escarole
Freshly cracked black pepper

Bring a large pot of water to a boil. Using a paring knife, score the bottom of each tomato with a small X. Blanch the tomatoes for 30 seconds. Remove and let cool until you can handle the tomatoes comfortably, then peel off the tomato skins with your fingers or a paring knife. Coarsely chop the tomatoes.

In a large pot, heat the olive oil over medium heat. Add the onion, fennel, celery, and garlic and cook until tender. Add the tomatoes and cook until most of their juices are released (the liquid should be about level with the tomatoes). Lower the heat to a simmer.

Cut the cheese rinds into small pieces, to maximize the surface area exposed to the cooking liquid. Tie up the cheese rinds, sage, and rosemary in a square of cheesecloth. Add the sachet, the beans, water, and salt to the pot

and bring to a simmer, then reduce the heat to low. Cover the pot and cook until the beans are tender, about 45 minutes.

Stir in the pumpkin, cover the pot, and cook until the pumpkin is tender, about 20 minutes longer. Turn off the heat.

Add the escarole to the pot, cover, and stir every few minutes until the escarole is wilted. Remove the sachet and squeeze it over the pot to release any remaining flavor into the soup.

Ladle the soup into bowls and serve, drizzled with olive oil and finished with a few turns of pepper.

Andrew's Note: If you don't have Parmigiano-Reggiano rinds on hand but do have other hard cheese rinds lying around, like Grana Padano, provolone, or caciocavallo, they will also work well here.

Broccoli Soup

This remarkable soup is yet another example of just how rewarding the clarity of flavor resulting from using a limited number of ingredients can be. Andrew first made this soup at home; he had been thinking about making a broccoli soup, but he wanted to steer clear of anything heavy or cream-laden. He thought about roasting the broccoli to amplify its rustic sweetness, but he didn't want to lose its wonderful verdant grassiness. So he settled on a half-and-half method of cooking it: he sears and browns the broccoli on one side only, leaving the other side bright green. And he uses water as the base of the soup, so there's no chicken stock to muddle the vegetable's flavor. Finished with fresh lemon juice and a drizzle of olive oil, it's a pretty dazzling yet comforting soup.

SERVES 4 TO 6

¾ cup plus 3 tablespoons olive oil,
   plus more for drizzling
9 cups broccoli florets (from 2 large heads),
   plus the stems peeled and diced into
   ¾-inch pieces
2½ teaspoons kosher salt
2 tablespoons unsalted butter

3 tablespoons coarsely chopped garlic
1½ cups finely diced white onions
3 cups water
¾ teaspoons freshly cracked black pepper
5 teaspoons fresh lemon juice
Finely grated Parmigiano-Reggiano

In a Dutch oven, heat 3 tablespoons of the olive oil over high heat. Add about a quarter of the broccoli, just enough to cover the bottom of the pot in a single layer without crowding (which would cause it to steam rather than brown) and cook, without moving it, for 3 to 4 minutes, or until it's richly, darkly browned on one side only. Transfer to a big bowl and repeat with the remaining broccoli, adding 3 more tablespoons olive oil for each batch. When all of the broccoli has been browned (do not scrape out the brown bits from the pot), season it with 1 teaspoon of the salt and set aside.

Reduce the heat to medium-low, add the butter and the remaining 3 tablespoons olive oil to the pot, and let the butter melt. Add the garlic and cook for 1 to 2 minutes. Add the onions, season with ¾ teaspoon salt, cover, and cook until soft and translucent, about 4 minutes. Add the broccoli back to the pot, along with the water. Season with the remaining ¾ teaspoon salt, bring to a simmer, and cook for 5 minutes.

Using an immersion blender or a food processor, coarsely puree about half the broccoli, and add back to the soup. Stir in the pepper and lemon juice. Ladle into bowls and finish with grated Parmigiano-Reggiano and a drizzle of olive oil.

Andrew's Note: While your broccoli is browning, refrain from moving the pieces around: let them brown undisturbed for a few minutes—otherwise, instead of browning, they will steam.

Cannellini Bean and Escarole Soup

This classic white bean and escarole soup is similar to what you see all over Campania. Italians excel at marrying contrasting flavors—sweet with sour, nutty with fruity, and, as in this soup, mild with bitter. Cannellini beans are wonderful with many kinds of bitter greens, particularly escarole. The buttery beans and the sharp greens are a delicious pairing, and this soup is really all about their union, heightened with Parmigiano-Reggiano and a drizzle of good olive oil.

SERVES 10 TO 12

2½ cups dried cannelini beans (1 pound)
½ cup plus 1 tablespoon extra-virgin olive oil, plus more for drizzling
6 medium garlic cloves, minced
¼ teaspoon chili flakes
¼ cup tightly packed chopped flat-leaf parsley
1 cup minced yellow onion
1 cup minced celery
1 cup drained canned San Marzano tomatoes, coarsely chopped

2 ounces Parmigiano-Reggiano rinds, scraped (see Andrew's Note, page 102)
3 quarts water
Kosher salt
1 head escarole, cored and chopped into 2-inch pieces
Freshly cracked black pepper
Finely grated Parmigiano-Reggiano

Place the beans in a large bowl and pick through them, removing any stones or debris. Cover with cool water and let sit for at least 8 hours, or overnight. Drain.

In a Dutch oven, warm the olive oil over medium heat. Add the garlic. Once it begins to sizzle and become fragrant, add the chili flakes and cook for 30 seconds, then add the parsley and cook for 1 minute. Do not allow anything to brown. Add the onion and celery and stir to combine. Cover the pot, reduce the heat to low, and cook for 10 minutes. Add the tomatoes and cook for 5 minutes.

Cut the cheese rinds into small pieces, to maximize the surface area exposed to the cooking liquid, and tie up in a small square of cheesecloth. Add this sachet, the beans, and the water to the pot and bring to a simmer. Skim any foam that comes to the surface and stir in salt to taste. Reduce the heat to maintain a gentle simmer and cook the beans until tender, 30 to 45 minutes. (Cooking time will vary, depending upon the age of the beans.)

Add the escarole and cook until tender and wilted, 10 minutes. Season the soup with more salt and pepper to taste.

Ladle the soup into warmed bowls and finish with grated Parmigiano-Reggiano and a drizzle of olive oil.

Chickpea and Kale Soup

As far as we know, there's no classic Italian soup made with chickpeas and kale. This was born out of our love for the combination of Tuscan kale and chickpeas, which work beautifully together. Andrew came up with the recipe one day when he noticed that the broth left from cooking chickpeas was so delicious it was practically begging to be made into soup. So he did just that, adding fresh kale to the pot and letting it simmer until soft and silky. With its bright, deeply green color, this soup is as beautiful as it is delicious.

SERVES 8 TO 10

2 cups dried chickpeas
1 carrot, peeled and cut into large chunks
1 celery stalk, cut into large chunks
1 onion, halved
11 garlic cloves
5 strips lemon peel
1 rosemary sprig
1 tablespoon kosher salt, or more to taste

3½ quarts water
1½ cups plus 2 tablespoons extra-virgin olive oil, plus more for drizzling
¼ teaspoon chili flakes
2 bunches Tuscan kale
Freshly cracked black pepper
Lemon wedges
Finely grated Parmigiano-Reggiano

Place the chickpeas in a large bowl and cover with plenty of water. Let soak for 8 hours or overnight; drain.

Wrap the carrot, celery, onion, 3 garlic cloves, the lemon peel, and rosemary in a large square of cheesecloth and secure with kitchen twine or a tight knot.

In a large pot, combine the sachet of vegetables, the chickpeas, salt, water, and 1 cup of the olive oil. Bring to a boil over high heat, then reduce the heat to medium-low and simmer until the chickpeas are tender, about 1 hour.

Meanwhile, finely chop the remaining 8 garlic cloves. In a small skillet, heat 3 tablespoons olive oil over medium heat. Add the garlic and chili flakes and cook until the garlic is fragrant but not golden, about 1 minute. Remove from the heat.

Remove the center ribs from the kale and coarsely chop the leaves (you should have about 16 cups). In a large skillet, heat the remaining 7 tablespoons olive oil over medium-high heat. Add the kale in batches and cook, tossing occasionally, until tender, about 3 minutes. Remove from the heat.

When the chickpeas are cooked, combine the kale, garlic oil, 2 cups of the chickpeas, and 1 cup of the cooking liquid in a food processor and puree until smooth. Return the puree to the pot and cook over medium-high heat until hot. Season with salt and pepper to taste.

Ladle the soup into bowls. Finish with a squeeze of lemon, some grated Parmigiano-Reggiano, and a drizzle of olive oil.

Pasta e Fagioli

You'll find pasta e fagioli all over Italy, but it varies from region to region, town to town, even house to house. Some people like it thick and chunky; others prefer it thinner and brothier. You'll find versions that go really heavy on the tomato, and some without much tomato at all. This one splits the difference. It's a stick-to-your-ribs soup, with a deep, sweet tomato flavor from both tomato paste and San Marzanos that melds nicely with the meaty pancetta. This hearty, wintry soup can easily serve as a satisfying meal all on its own.

SERVES 6

FOR THE BEANS
2½ cups dried borlotti or cranberry beans
  (about 1 pound)
3 tablespoons extra-virgin olive oil
1½ teaspoons kosher salt
3 ounces Parmigiano-Reggiano rinds
2½ ounces prosciutto trimmings or
  prosciutto
½ onion
5 garlic cloves
1 sage sprig
1 rosemary sprig

FOR THE SOUP
1 cup finely chopped pancetta (5 ounces)
1 cup finely chopped onion
¼ cup finely chopped carrot
¼ cup finely chopped celery
5 garlic cloves, finely chopped
2 teaspoons finely chopped sage
1 teaspoon finely chopped rosemary
1 tablespoon plus 2 teaspoons
  tomato paste
⅓ cup canned San Marzano tomatoes,
  chopped
¾ cup ditalini or other small dried pasta
Kosher salt
Finely grated Pamigiano-Reggiano
Extra-virgin olive oil

To make the beans: Place them in a large bowl with plenty of cold water to cover and let stand for 8 hours or overnight.

Drain the beans and place in a large pot. Cover with 6 cups water. Stir in the olive oil and salt. Wrap the Parmigiano rinds, prosciutto, onion, garlic cloves, sage, and rosemary in a large square of cheesecloth and secure with kitchen twine or a tight knot. Drop into the pot of beans. Bring the water to a boil over high heat; then reduce the heat to medium-low and simmer the beans until tender and creamy, 45 minutes to 1 hour; add more water as needed to keep the beans fully covered. Remove from the heat and discard the sachet.

To make the soup: In a large skillet, cook the pancetta over medium-high heat until it is crisp and most of the fat has rendered, about 7 minutes. Reduce the heat to medium, add the onion, carrot, celery, garlic, sage, and rosemary, and cook, stirring, until the vegetables are soft, about 10 minutes.

Add the tomato paste and cook for about 2 minutes. Stir in the tomatoes and cook over medium-high heat until the vegetables are very soft and the tomatoes' juices have mostly evaporated, 3 to 5 minutes. Remove from the heat.

Transfer the vegetables and half the beans and their liquid to a food processor, working in batches if necessary. Puree until smooth. Return the mixture to the pot of beans and cook over medium heat until warmed through; add water if needed to reach the desired consistency. Keep warm.

In a large pot of boiling salted water, cook the pasta until al dente; drain.

Spoon the pasta into individual serving bowls. Ladle the hot soup over the pasta. Finish with grated Parmigiano-Reggiano, salt to taste, and a drizzle of olive oil.

Andrew's Note: When making this soup, don't combine the pasta (cooked separately) and soup until the last minute. If you cook the pasta in your soup, the soup will become too thick from the starch the pasta will release. Even worse, if you leave the pasta in the soup overnight, the pasta will be gummy and sticky the next day. Also be mindful of the shape of the pasta—small-cut pastas like ditalini, bite-sized shells, or macaroni are perfect here, or, alternatively, any pasta you have that you can break into pieces.

Chicken Brodo with Parmigiano-Reggiano, Maltagliati, Parsley, and Lemon

This heady soup is all about the broth, packed with flavor from all the best things you could want in your soup: chicken bones, cheese rinds, prosciutto trimmings, lemon juice, and olive oil. The trick here is to deeply roast the chicken bones to deepen their flavor. It's a luscious, intense soup that's elegant, refined, and altogether different from the chicken noodle you usually see.

Because the only thing that gives the soup some texture is the noodles, their shape is critical for the proper mouthfeel. You'll need a flat pasta, preferably homemade, such as our maltagliati. If you don't want to make it from scratch, substitute something like fresh pappardelle, or torn-up fresh or dried lasagna.

SERVES 6

FOR THE STOCK
5½ pounds chicken bones
  (see Andrew's Notes)
3 tablespoons extra-virgin olive oil
5½ quarts water
4 cups sliced white onions
2 cups roughly chopped celery
2½ cups roughly chopped carrots
1½ heads garlic, split horizontally
2 bay leaves

FOR THE BRODO
8 cups Chicken Stock (see left)
8 ounces Parmigiano-Reggiano rinds
  (see Andrew's Note, page 102)
2 ounces prosciutto trimmings
  (see Andrew's Notes)

Kosher salt if needed
6 ounces Maltagliati (recipe follows) **or
  broken lasagna noodles or other flat
  pasta** (see the headnote)
½ cup finely chopped flat-leaf parsley
Juice of 1 lemon, or to taste
6 tablespoons finely grated Parmigiano-
  Reggiano
Extra-virgin olive oil

To make the stock: Preheat the oven to 425°F. Chop the bones into 4- to 5-inch pieces, to maximize the browning surface area (you can have your butcher do this). Toss the bones with the olive oil and spread them out on two large rimmed baking sheets. Roast, uncovered, until the bones are golden, 40 to 45 minutes.

Transfer the bones to a large pot, cover with the water, and bring to a boil; skim off any foam that rises to the surface. Add the onions, celery, carrots, garlic, and bay leaves, reduce the heat to a low simmer, and cook for 2½ hours.

Strain the stock through a colander and then a fine-mesh sieve into a bowl or container, pressing down on the solids with the back of a spoon. If not using immediately, refrigerate for up to 3 days.

To make the brodo: In a medium pot, bring the 8 cups stock to a gentle simmer. (Reserve any remaining stock for another use.) Skim off any foam that rises to the surface. Gently simmer the stock, skimming frequently, until all of the impurities have been removed, about 15 minutes.

continued

SOUP

Wrap the cheese rinds and prosciutto trimmings in a piece of cheesecloth and tie it with kitchen twine or a knot. Lower the sachet into the stock and gently simmer until the stock has reduced by one-fifth (to about 4½ cups), about 1 hour.

Remove the cheesecloth sachet and press on it to release the excess moisture (and flavor) into the stock. Taste and season with salt if needed. Strain the brodo through a fine-mesh sieve into a bowl set over a larger bowl filled with ice water. Once the brodo has cooled, remove any residual fat that has solidified on the surface. (Alternatively, if you have time, let the brodo cool, chill it for at least several hours, or overnight, then skim the fat from the surface.)

When ready to serve, in a large pot of heavily salted boiling water, cook the pasta until 1 minute from al dente (which is about 3 minutes for the maltagliati; if you're using dried pasta, check the package directions); drain.

Meanwhile, return the brodo to the pot and bring to a simmer over medium heat.

Stir the pasta into the stock, then remove from the heat and stir in the parsley and lemon juice to taste. Ladle into serving bowls and finish with the grated cheese and a drizzle of olive oil.

Andrew's Notes: You'll notice that there's no chicken meat in the actual soup. Because of that, I don't recommend using a whole chicken carcass to make the stock—save it for a more noble pursuit. Instead use bones, wings, and backs. You can also make the stock using just wings and backs, or just wings—they're immensely flavorful.

You can usually get prosciutto trimmings at any deli that sells prosciutto. Just ask. You could use a chunk of prosciutto, but it's more expensive.

Maltagliati

MAKES 1 POUND

2⅔ cups durum flour
  (see Resources, page 357)
1 cup "00" flour (see Resources)
4 large eggs
2½ tablespoons water

In a bowl, combine the flours, eggs, and water. Knead until the dough comes together. Cover loosely with a dish towel and let rest for 30 minutes.

Set the rollers of a pasta machine to the widest setting. Divide the dough into 4 pieces. Run one piece of dough through the machine (keep the remaining dough covered while you work). Adjust the rollers to the next setting and run the dough through again.

Repeat with the next narrowest setting, and finish with the next narrowest. Transfer the dough to a lightly floured cutting board and cut it into irregular 2- to 3-inch triangles. Transfer to a flour-dusted baking sheet, and repeat with the remaining dough.

Lentil, Farro, and Controne Bean Soup with Pancetta

A warming soup is comforting in the dead of winter. What's special here is the distinct interplay among different textures—the pillowy Controne beans, toothsome farro, and soft lentils, all flavored with pancetta, herbs, and chili flakes. Add a bright but wintry salad—maybe the Citrus Salad with Pistachios, Olives, and Chilies (page 92)—and you have a satisfying supper.

SERVES 8 TO 10

1½ cups dried Controne or cannellini beans
8 garlic cloves, 4 crushed and peeled,
  4 finely chopped
2 bay leaves
2 rosemary sprigs, plus ¾ teaspoon
  chopped rosemary
2 sage sprigs, plus 1½ teaspoons
  chopped sage
½ cup plus 2 to 4 tablespoons extra-virgin
  olive oil, plus more for drizzling
9½ cups water

1 tablespoon kosher salt, plus more to taste
1 cup farro
5 ounces pancetta, finely diced
⅛ teaspoon chili flakes
½ cup chopped flat-leaf parsley
2 large carrots, peeled and cut into
  small dice
2 celery stalks, cut into small dice
1 onion, finely chopped
2 cups green lentils
Freshly cracked black pepper

Place the beans in a large bowl and pick through, removing any stones. Cover with cold water and let soak for at least 8 hours, or overnight; drain.

Wrap 2 of the crushed garlic cloves, 1 bay leaf, 1 rosemary sprig, and 1 sage sprig in a square of cheesecloth and knot. Place in a medium pot, add the drained beans, ½ cup of the olive oil, and 2½ cups of the water, and bring to a simmer over medium heat. Skim any foam on the top and stir in the salt. Cover, reduce the heat to medium-low, and simmer until the beans are tender, 45 to 60 minutes. Uncover and remove from the heat.

Meanwhile, wrap the remaining 2 crushed garlic cloves, bay leaf, rosemary sprig, and sage sprig in another square of cheesecloth and knot. Bring a pot of salted water to a boil. Add the sachet of aromatics and the farro, reduce the heat to medium-low, and simmer, uncovered, until the farro is tender, about 25 minutes. Drain.

In a large pot, heat 2 tablespoons olive oil over medium-high heat. Add the pancetta, reduce the heat to medium, and cook, stirring, until the pancetta is golden and most of the fat has

rendered, about 5 minutes. Stir in the chopped garlic, chili flakes, parsley, chopped rosemary, and chopped sage and cook for 2 minutes. Stir in the carrots, celery, and onion and cook over low heat until the vegetables are soft, starting to brown around the edges, and translucent, about 10 minutes; add up to 2 tablespoons more olive oil to the pot if it seems dry. Stir in the lentils and 4 cups water and bring to a simmer. Cover the pot and simmer the lentils until tender, about 45 minutes. Remove from the heat.

Transfer 2 cups of the lentil mixture to a food processor and puree until smooth. Return to the pot. Stir in the beans and their cooking liquid and the farro. Add the remaining 3 cups water, or additional if necessary, bring to a simmer, and cook for 10 minutes longer. Season with salt and pepper.

Ladle the soup into warm bowls and serve, drizzled generously with olive oil.

Andrew's Note: Take time when sautéing your vegetables for this recipe, letting them soften, brown, and develop flavors before you add the liquid. It really adds dimension to this soup.

VEGETABLES

When people learn that we own a restaurant, the simple answer to that inevitable first question is, "A brick-oven pizza place." But, as anyone who has eaten at Franny's knows, taking advantage of the amazing seasonal vegetables we're able to source is our not-so-secret other obsession.

Great ingredients demand respect, and vegetables are as deserving as any. High-quality vegetables don't necessarily need much, and the trick to cooking them well is knowing when to go all out with seasonings (garlic, chilies, lemon, olive oil) and when to hold back. Sometimes all a perfectly ripe vegetable needs is a bit of coaxing to bring out its character—maybe a gentle blanching and a minimal finish of olive oil and sea salt, or a quick sauté with a little butter and garlic. When you want to add richness, it can be as simple as grating some cheese over the dish, or adding a sprinkle of chopped nuts, which will also lend crunch. If you want to include a little something briny, toss in some capers, anchovies, or olives, or all three.

Vegetables often change over the course of their season, and it's fascinating to pay attention to the nuances. For example, when zucchini make their first appearance, they're slim and tender—all they need is a little acid, some fresh herbs, and a touch of chili, as in our Marinated Zucchini with Mint, Garlic, and Chili (page 130). As the heat of the summer wears on, those same zucchini grow plump and dense, which makes them ideal for cooking low and slow. Stewed Zucchini with Mint, Olives, and Tomatoes (page 131) is a great example of this. The same can be said for asparagus. The first tender stalks are wonderful lightly battered and briefly fried (see Fried Asparagus, Artichokes, and Spring Onions with Ramp Mayonnaise, page 48), or even shaved and eaten raw (see Shaved Asparagus with

Parmigiano-Reggiano, Lemon, and Black Pepper, page 71). As they grow thicker and heartier, roasting them until they caramelize softens their intense grassy flavor. There's a wide and wonderful wealth of variety in the vegetable world—all you need to do is explore.

Eating seasonal produce can be incredibly rewarding. When the first tart dandelion greens start showing up at the market in early spring, I'm always ready for their slightly bitter freshness to break up the starchy monotony of winter's potatoes and sunchokes. That perfectly crunchy green bean in July is everything it should be and tastes better than a green bean ever could in January, especially when sautéed with a pinch of Controne pepper and a squeeze of lemon (see page 133). And the sweet, dense squashes that come into season in October fortify us for the chill of winter.

The best place to find great seasonal produce is, of course, your local farmers' market. If you can make it a part of your weekly routine, you'll really be able to witness the seasons unfold and change from week to week. It can be both exhilarating and heartbreaking—one week you might be able to score the first, most tender ramps, only to find they've completely disappeared two weeks later, when you've finally figured out exactly how you love to cook them. On the flip side, as much as we adore kale and carrots and parsnips, they can get monotonous by February, when they're still the only things around. But embracing the rhythm is part of the thrill.

For years, Andrew and I did all the greenmarket shopping for Franny's ourselves. On Mondays we'd go to Union Square in Manhattan; I'd sit in the car so we wouldn't get a ticket, and Andrew would blitz through, collecting everything we'd need for that night. On Tuesdays and Thursdays, we went to the Borough Hall Market in Brooklyn. On Wednesdays, we'd schlep up to Dag Hammarskjold Plaza (across from the United Nations) to see one of our main suppliers, Bill Maxwell—it was almost like a weekly pilgrimage to our veggie guru. I'll never forget one trip in particular: I'd just given birth to our

daughter, Prue, and so there I was with her waiting for Andrew in the back of the car, the day after I'd left the hospital.

These days, our chefs do the shopping for the restaurants and we only have to buy produce for our family, which has freed us up to enjoy the farmers' market in a whole new way. We make a day of it. We take the kids to Grand Army Plaza in Brooklyn and wind our way through all the vendors' stalls. Marco finds the sight of the apple-cider doughnuts irresistible, while the flowers pull Prue with an almost gravitational force. They're both totally fascinated by the big whole fish at the fish stand, and they always love visiting with Bill Maxwell (for a while, they thought Bill was The Only Farmer, period). And Andrew and I can just buy what we want to feed the family for that week, without worrying about sourcing enough delicata squash to roast for an entire restaurant.

Needless to say, the farmers' market, with all its sights and sounds, provides us with a fabulous avenue to get our kids curious about vegetables. And every so often, even Andrew and I discover something new. Greenmarkets are great places to broaden your vegetable horizons, but a CSA, your town's food co-op, or even a supermarket can yield seasonal goodies. A little mindfulness is all you need to track them down.

Slow-Cooked Leeks with a Fried Egg and Pecorino Sardo

Among the very first local springtime vegetables to appear in New York are overwintered leeks. Planted in July, the leeks sit in the ground all winter long. When the ground finally thaws in the early spring and the leeks are pulled, they have an incredible concentrated sweetness. Leeks are often in the background, but this dish lets them shine. After a quick blanching, they are roasted in the oven, where they lose most of their moisture, caramelizing and intensifying the flavor. Salty shavings of sharp sheep's-milk cheese and the runny sunny-side-up eggs make this a hearty first course. But it could also serve as a perfect vegetarian lunch, or a spectacular brunch dish.

SERVES 4

2 pounds medium leeks (about 5)
Kosher salt
1½ tablespoons plus 2 teaspoons extra-virgin olive oil, plus more for drizzling
¾ teaspoon freshly cracked black pepper, plus more as needed

4 large eggs
Flaky sea salt, such as Maldon
Fresh lemon juice
1-ounce chunk Pecorino Sardo or Parmigiano-Reggiano, shaved, for serving

Preheat the oven to 325°F with a rack in the middle of the oven. Trim the hairy ends of the leeks and remove the dark green tops. Without cutting all the way through the root end, split the leeks lengthwise in half. Rinse each leek under lukewarm running water, fanning it apart to get to any grit between the layers.

Bring a large pot of heavily salted water to a boil. Add the leeks and cook until tender but not limp, 6 to 7 minutes. Drain well and pat dry. Split the leeks completely through the root end.

Arrange the leek halves on a rimmed baking sheet in 2 rows, with the thicker bulbous ends facing outward (these will most benefit from the sides of the oven, where the heat is strongest). Drizzle the leeks with 2 teaspoons of the olive oil and season with the pepper. Roast until light golden brown, about 30 minutes.

Carefully flip the leeks and continue to cook until golden on top, about 25 minutes more. Remove from the oven and keep warm.

In a large skillet, heat the remaining 1½ tablespoons olive oil over medium heat. Crack the eggs into the skillet and season with salt and pepper. Reduce the heat to medium-low and cook gently until the whites are set, about 6 minutes.

Divide the leeks among individual plates. Sprinkle lightly with sea salt, pepper, and lemon juice. Top each plate with an egg and shower with shaved cheese. Drizzle with olive oil and serve.

Andrew's Note: Leaving the leeks partially attached when boiling them keeps them from falling apart. So, while you might be tempted to cut them all the way through for cleaning, don't do it.

Marinated Artichokes

When we serve this dish at Franny's, it literally flies off the menu. Someone only has to see it on a nearby table to want it for themselves. Artichokes are so extraordinary that eating them feels like a special occasion.

But there's no reason not to make them yourself at home—we do, often and for as long as the season lasts. Yes, trimming them can be a little time-consuming, but there is nothing like the sweet, umami flavor of a fresh artichoke.

This is a brighter take on the usual marinated artichokes you see on antipasti plates. Most store-bought marinated artichokes are pretty mediocre. But here the sweet thistle's flavor is rounded out with classic Italian ingredients: wine, lemon, chili, and garlic. Tossed with fresh parsley and mint, these artichokes are complex, pungent, and addictive.

SERVES 4 TO 6

Juice of 2 lemons
4 medium artichokes

FOR THE COOKING LIQUID
½ cup extra-virgin olive oil
6 garlic cloves, halved
5 tablespoons chopped flat-leaf parsley
½ teaspoon chili flakes
2 cups dry white wine
3 cups water
1 tablespoon plus 2 teaspoons kosher salt

FOR THE DRESSING
¼ teaspoon kosher salt
¼ teaspoon freshly cracked black pepper
¼ teaspoon finely grated lemon zest
Juice of 1 lemon
¼ cup extra-virgin olive oil, plus more
  for drizzling
¼ cup chopped flat-leaf parsley
2 tablespoons chopped mint

To make the artichokes: Fill a large bowl with cold water and add the lemon juice. As you trim the artichokes, dip them occasionally into the lemon water to prevent browning.

Pull off and discard the outer leaves of each artichoke until you reach the pale green leaves at the center. Using a paring knife, trim away the dark green skin from the base. Slice off the very tip of the stem: you will see a pale green core in the stem, surrounded by a layer of darker green; use a paring knife to trim away as much of the dark green layer as possible; the white part of the stem is as tasty as the heart. Slice off the top third of the artichoke at the place where the dark green tops fade to pale green. Using a teaspoon (a serrated grapefruit spoon is perfect for this

task), scoop out the hairy choke in the center of the artichoke, pulling out any pointed purple leaves with your fingers as well. The center of the artichoke should be completely clean. Drop the artichoke into the lemon water.

To make the cooking liquid: In a large saucepan, warm the olive oil over medium-high heat. Add the garlic and cook for 1 minute. Stir in the parsley and chili flakes and cook for 30 seconds more. Pour in the wine, bring to a boil, and cook for 1 minute. Pour in the water and add the salt. Add the artichokes (the liquid should almost but not quite cover them; if necessary, add more water). Bring to a simmer, then cover and simmer over medium-low heat until the artichokes are tender, 25 to 30 minutes. Check for tenderness

continued

124

by sticking a paring knife through the base of an artichoke; it should slide through easily.

Remove the artichokes from the liquid; reserve the liquid if you plan to store the artichokes before serving them. Let the artichokes (and liquid) cool completely (if you cool the artichokes in the liquid, they will continue to cook). If storing, combine the artichokes and cooled liquid in an airtight container and refrigerate for up to 1 week.

To serve, slice the cooled artichokes lengthwise in half and place in a large bowl. Season with the salt and pepper. Add the lemon zest and juice, then add the olive oil, parsley, and mint and toss gently, so that the artichokes don't fall apart. Serve drizzled with additional olive oil.

Andrew's Notes: Raw artichokes impart a bitter flavor to whatever they come in contact with, so give your cutting board a good scrub when you're finished prepping them.

To store the marinated artichokes, after tossing with the marinade, loosely pack the artichokes into a jar or other container and cover with more olive oil. Make sure the artichokes are completely submerged in the oil. They will keep for at least 1 week.

Sautéed Dandelion Greens with Anchovy, Chilies, and Butter

Sautéed dandelion greens is a classic *contorno* (side dish) you'd see in a trattoria in Southern Italy. Wilted bitter greens are spectacular with all sorts of big, bold meats, and they make for a healthy addition to any meal. If you've never cooked dandelion greens before, it might seem a little odd to be sautéing something you usually think about pulling out of your lawn. But dandelions can be incredibly delicious, especially when sautéed with pungent anchovy and garlic, then mellowed with sweet, creamy butter.

SERVES 4

¼ cup extra-virgin olive oil
8 garlic cloves, smashed and peeled
4 anchovy fillets
¼ to ½ teaspoon chili flakes

5 tablespoons unsalted butter
2 pounds dandelion greens, trimmed
½ teaspoon kosher salt

In a large skillet, warm the olive oil over medium-high heat. Add the garlic and anchovies and cook, stirring to break up the anchovies, until the garlic is golden, 1 to 2 minutes. Add the chili flakes and cook until fragrant, about 30 seconds. Stir in the butter. Let it melt and turn a bit brown, then add the dandelion greens. Cook the greens until they are just wilted, then season them with the salt and cook until tender, 2 to 3 minutes. Serve immediately.

Andrew's Note: The best dandelion greens are available in the spring. Small and tender, they are also the least bitter at this point. I prefer a dandelion variety that's dark green tipped with red—it almost looks like wild arugula—but it can be hard to find. If you can't find any dandelion greens, you could substitute Swiss chard here, though you won't get the same bitter character. This recipe would also work with mature (not baby) spinach.

VEGETABLES

Sugar Snap Peas with Ricotta, Mint, and Lemon

This springtime dish is crisp and sweet from the sugar snap peas, creamy from a layer of seasoned ricotta, and bright and fresh from a dressing of fragrant mint leaves, scallions, and parsley. It's almost like a very elegant crudité, and who doesn't love dipping crunchy vegetables into creamy dip? My kids certainly do, and this recipe is a great way to turn little ones on to the joys of green things. The sugar snap peas are intrinsically sweet, and they're ideal finger-food–size for little hands.

SERVES 4

½ cup whole-milk ricotta
¼ cup extra-virgin olive oil, plus more
  for drizzling
Kosher salt
¼ teaspoon freshly cracked black pepper,
  plus more to taste
2 cups sugar snap peas (½ pound)

2 tablespoons thinly sliced scallions
2 tablespoons coarsely chopped
  flat-leaf parsley
3 tablespoons coarsely chopped mint
2 tablespoons fresh lemon juice
Flaky sea salt, such as Maldon

Line a fine-mesh sieve with cheesecloth or a clean dish towel, set over a bowl, and add the ricotta. Refrigerate overnight; the ricotta will lose much of its water content and thicken.

In a small bowl, whisk the drained ricotta with 2 tablespoons of the olive oil until smooth. Whisk in salt and pepper to taste. Continue to whisk until the ricotta is fluffy and creamy. Set aside.

Bring a large pot of salted water to a boil. Fill a large bowl with ice water and salt it generously. Blanch the peas in the boiling water for 30 to 40 seconds, until bright green. Drain, immediately transfer to the ice water, and let stand until thoroughly chilled. Drain the peas and spread them out on a clean dish towel to dry.

In a large bowl, toss the peas with the scallions, parsley, mint, the ¼ teaspoon pepper, and the lemon juice. Stir in the remaining 2 tablespoons olive oil.

Smear 2 tablespoons of the ricotta in the center of each of four plates. Mound ½ cup of the peas on each plate. Finish with a drizzle of olive oil and a sprinkle of sea salt.

Andrew's Note: To get perfectly seasoned snap peas (and other dense vegetables, for that matter), blanch them in boiling salted water, drain them, and then cool them in salted ice water. Don't overcook sugar snap peas; they should literally be in and out of a pot of boiling water—just 30 to 40 seconds—then plunged directly into an ice bath. Any longer, and you risk losing their crisp texture.

Marinated Zucchini with Mint, Garlic, and Chili

When zucchini first start showing up in the markets, they're slim, dense-fleshed little marvels that taste more like zucchini than they ever will again. They're perfectly suited for searing and a quick soak with good olive oil, vinegar, chilies, and mint.

It's a good idea to salt sliced zucchini liberally ahead of time if you can. This gives the vegetable a chance to really absorb the seasoning all the way through. Then simply sauté the slices until they're deeply golden but still crunchy. Here chopped toasted pine nuts are a surprising and delicious addition.

SERVES 4

4 cups 1-inch-thick rounds zucchini
  (2 to 3 small zucchini)
1½ teaspoons kosher salt
1 tablespoon pine nuts
½ cup plus 2 tablespoons extra-virgin
  olive oil

2 tablespoons white wine vinegar
6 garlic cloves, thinly sliced
¼ teaspoon chili flakes
6 mint leaves, torn
Flaky sea salt, such as Maldon

Preheat the oven to 325°F.

Place the zucchini in a colander and toss with the salt. Let stand for 20 minutes.

Meanwhile, toast the pine nuts in a small baking pan, turning once, until they are golden brown in spots and smell rich and nutty, 5 to 8 minutes. Pour the nuts onto a plate to cool, then coarsely chop.

Pat the zucchini dry with paper towels. Heat a large skillet over high heat, then add ¼ cup of the olive oil and heat for 30 seconds. Add the zucchini and sear on both sides, without moving the slices too much, until deep golden, 7 to 10 minutes; they should still be somewhat al dente, not too soft. Transfer the zucchini to a bowl and toss with the vinegar and the remaining 6 tablespoons olive oil.

Return the skillet to medium heat, add the garlic, and cook until golden, about 1 minute. Add the chili flakes and cook for 30 seconds. Scrape the mixture into the bowl with the zucchini. Stir in the mint leaves and pine nuts.

To serve, use a slotted spoon to transfer the zucchini to plates. Drizzle with some of the marinade and sprinkle with sea salt.

Stewed Zucchini with Mint, Olives, and Tomatoes

As the summer wears on, zucchini just keep getting bigger. I may be imagining this, but I could swear I've seen zucchini grow overnight in my garden. Once the summer heat really sets in, they grow and grow and grow if they have enough space and water. So, what do you do with those big dog-days-of-summer zucchini? They're full of water, and they're blander than their early-season counterparts, but they're great on the grill, and they're fabulous slowly simmered with the big, full flavors of tomatoes and olives. Serve this dish with crusty bread, and perhaps some burrata or mozzarella. It's a perfect summer side for a family meal in your backyard or a casual gathering with friends.

SERVES 4 TO 6

2 pounds green or yellow zucchini, trimmed
1 tablespoon kosher salt plus a large pinch
About 7½ tablespoons extra-virgin olive oil
½ cup chopped flat-leaf parsley
1 tablespoon chopped oregano
1 tablespoon finely chopped garlic

¼ teaspoon chili flakes
1½ cups **Basic Tomato Sauce** (see page 349)
3 tablespoons chopped pitted
   Calabrese olives
10 mint leaves, roughly torn, plus additional
   torn leaves for garnish

Slice the zucchini into ¾-inch-thick lengths. Transfer to a colander set over a bowl and toss with the 1 tablespoon salt. Let stand for 20 minutes.

Preheat the oven to 325°F. Pat the zucchini very dry with paper towels.

In a large Dutch oven, heat 1½ tablespoons of the olive oil over high heat. Add a third of the zucchini and cook, without moving it much, until golden, about 3 minutes per side. Transfer to a paper-towel-lined plate. Repeat with the remaining zucchini in 2 batches, using about 1½ tablespoons more oil per batch.

Reduce the heat to medium-low and add the remaining 3 tablespoons olive oil. Stir in the parsley, oregano, garlic, and chili and cook, stirring, until fragrant, about 30 seconds. Increase the heat to medium. Stir in the tomato sauce and olives. Cook the sauce until it breaks and begins to release its oil, 2 to 3 minutes.

Return the zucchini to the pot and season with the large pinch of salt. Cover the pot and bake for 1 hour.

Stir the mint leaves into the zucchini and serve topped with additional mint.

Eggplant with Ricotta Salata, Pine Nuts, and Mint

To get the most out of this lovely dish, you need to use purple-skinned Japanese eggplants. If you can find them, the variety called Orient Express is just terrific—mild, tender, and not at all bitter—despite its politically incorrect name. These eggplants have a beautiful even shape, fewer seeds than other varieties, and a sweet, creamy texture. But you can use any fresh Japanese eggplants. Look for those that are taut, smooth-skinned, and shining, without any blemishes. As they age, the eggplants start to soften and turn brown in spots.

At Franny's, we have the luxury of being able to roast eggplant in our wood-burning oven, but a home oven cranked up high works great. The finish of mild ricotta salata pulls all the bright, spicy flavors together.

SERVES 4

8 Japanese eggplants (about 1¼ pounds), **ends trimmed**
2¼ teaspoons kosher salt, plus more to taste
½ cup plus 2 tablespoons extra-virgin olive oil
¼ cup pine nuts

¼ teaspoon chili flakes
Juice of 2 lemons
Freshly cracked black pepper
1 cup mint leaves, torn in half
A 1½-ounce chunk of ricotta salata for shaving

Slice each eggplant in half and score the flesh, making sure not to cut through the skin. Sprinkle the cut side of each half with ⅛ teaspoon salt. Place the eggplant in a colander set over a plate and let stand for 1 hour.

Preheat the oven to 450°F. Pat the eggplant halves dry and toss them with 4½ tablespoons of the olive oil. Arrange flesh side up on a rimmed baking sheet. Roast until golden brown and tender, 15 to 20 minutes. Cool completely.

Heat a small skillet over medium heat, then add the pine nuts to the dry skillet. Toast, tossing or stirring them, until they are golden brown in spots and smell rich and nutty, about 2 minutes. Pour the nuts onto a plate to cool.

Toss the cooled eggplant with 2½ tablespoons olive oil, the chili flakes, half the lemon juice, and pepper to taste. Divide among four serving plates.

In a small bowl, whisk together the remaining 3 tablespoons olive oil, remaining lemon juice, ¼ teaspoon salt, and pepper to taste. Whisk in the mint and pine nuts.

Using a vegetable peeler, shave 3 slices of ricotta salata over each serving. Spoon the dressing over the eggplant and serve.

Andrew's Note: When you roast the eggplant, make sure to cook it all the way—you don't want al dente eggplant. Any eggplant that isn't fully cooked just isn't pleasant.

Pole Beans with Garlic, Controne Chili, and Lemon

"Pole beans" is sort of an umbrella term—pole beans are any variety of bean that needs a trellis (or pole) to climb, including green beans and wax beans. We like to use a mix of those two, but either one alone will work in this recipe.

There aren't a lot of components to the dish: just spectacularly crisp summer-ripe beans, fresh garlic, lemon juice, and some Controne chili. Controne chili is extremely earthy and smoky, and we absolutely love it. It's made from a pepper indigenous to Southern Italy and is named for Controne, a small town at the foot of the Alburni mountain range near the border of Basilicata. There's really no equivalent and it is well worth the search, though in a pinch you could substitute crushed dried chili. The dish will still be excellent, if not quite as nuanced.

SERVES 4

6 tablespoons extra-virgin olive oil
1 pound mixed yellow wax and green beans
½ teaspoon kosher salt, or more to taste
2 garlic cloves, chopped

½ teaspoon crushed dried Controne chili (see Resources, page 357) or other crushed chili flakes
Juice of 1 lemon
Freshly cracked black pepper

In a large skillet, heat 5 tablespoons of the olive oil over medium heat. Add the beans and the salt. Once the beans take on some color, turn the heat to low and cover; the beans should be cooked in 3 to 5 minutes.

Remove the pan from the heat and add the remaining tablespoon of olive oil and the garlic. Once the garlic is fragrant, stir in the chili pepper and lemon juice and toss together. Taste and add more salt if necessary, season with black pepper, and serve.

Andrew's Note: In this recipe, the beans go into the skillet raw, so even when they take on some color and some char, they still retain some crunch and bite. That's the secret to their great flavor and texture.

Pole Beans and Potatoes with Olives, Anchovies, and Egg

In Southern Italy, you'd probably find a similar dish served in restaurants as an antipasto. But it also makes an excellent lunch or even a light dinner at the end of a hot summer day, rounded out with some crusty bread.

No matter when you eat it, it's a lovely way to enjoy fresh, crisp green beans. Andrew adds mild soft potatoes and creamy hard-cooked eggs as a textural contrast, and the olives and anchovies provide delicious salty-savory notes.

Even better, you can prepare the potatoes ahead of time. Fish the potatoes out of the pot with a slotted spoon and reserve all the cooking water. After peeling and slicing the potatoes, instead of dressing them, simply place them in a container and pour over enough cooking water to cover. They'll store beautifully in your refrigerator overnight.

SERVES 4

8 ounces fingerling potatoes
2 teaspoons red wine vinegar
1 teaspoon kosher salt
½ teaspoon freshly cracked black pepper, plus more to taste
6 tablespoons extra-virgin olive oil, plus more for drizzling
4 ounces green beans, trimmed
2 tablespoons thinly sliced red onion

2 tablespoons plus 2 teaspoons Nocellara olives, pitted and roughly chopped
2½ teaspoons salt-packed capers, soaked, rinsed, and drained (see Andrew's Note, page 30)
1½ teaspoons chopped oregano
2 tablespoons chopped flat-leaf parsley
4 hard-boiled eggs (see page 32), peeled and sliced
Flaky sea salt, such as Maldon
4 anchovy fillets

Add the potatoes to a large pot of boiling heavily salted water and cook until tender, 20 to 25 minutes. Drain.

When the potatoes are cool enough to handle, but still warm, peel them with a paring knife. Slice crosswise into ½-inch-thick rounds. Spread the potatoes on a large platter and sprinkle with 1 teaspoon of the vinegar, ½ teaspoon of the salt, and the pepper. Drizzle with ¼ cup of the olive oil. Cover the potatoes and let them stand for at least 1 hour, and up to 6 hours, at room temperature, or refrigerate for as long as overnight.

Bring a large pot of salted water to a boil. Prepare a large bowl of salted ice water. Add the beans to the boiling water and cook for 2 minutes. Drain and transfer to the ice water to cool, then drain.

Slice the beans in half crosswise. Transfer to a bowl and toss with the red onion, olives, capers, oregano, and the remaining 1 teaspoon vinegar and 2 tablespoons olive oil. Season with the remaining ½ teaspoon salt and pepper to taste.

Sprinkle the potatoes with the parsley and scatter the slices of egg over them. Season the egg with a pinch each of salt and pepper. Drizzle with olive oil. Spoon the bean mixture over the potatoes, top with the anchovies, and drizzle with olive oil.

Andrew's Note: Don't overcook the egg for this recipe. You want an egg yolk that still has a slight degree of softness, and plenty of golden yellow color. Overcooked egg yolks can be chalky.

DANNY AMEND
FRANNY'S CHEF

How did you get started cooking?

I've been cooking since I was six or seven. I grew up in Santa Rosa, California, and my parents had a pretty big garden. Every year there'd be an explosion of vegetables, and I grew up cooking out of that garden. I was a chubby kid who loved to eat. I bugged my mom enough times about what was for dinner that she finally said, "Why don't you just make something for yourself." That started it all.

What are your résumé highlights?

Per Se and Alain Ducasse. I worked a lot with fine French cuisine. But by the time I was leaving Per Se, I realized that style of cooking wasn't why I got into food. The aesthetic at Franny's is similar to my original style of cooking as a kid—out of the garden, and using up everything.

First memorable meal?

The first time I made gnocchi, when I was nine or ten. I was watching the Frugal Gourmet, and he had an article in the local paper about making russet potato gnocchi (I still have the newspaper clipping). My mom and I tried out the recipe, and I blended the potatoes in an old Cuisinart. They were the gummiest, most disgusting gnocchi I've ever had, but the next time I made them right.

First memorable slice?

The first time I came to the city, I stayed with a friend in Harlem and went to Slice of Harlem. I'd never had just a slice of pizza. It's not something we do out in California. I got one and then another and then another. It was a novel idea not to have to get a whole pizza.

Roasted Romano Beans with Calabrese Olives

It's unusual to see a recipe for roasted Romano beans, but roasting is a terrific way to cook these lovely, brawny beans, allowing them to collapse in the oven and caramelize around the edges. This recipe works particularly well toward the end of the summer, when the beans tend to get tougher and thicker-skinned. The key is to roast them at the hottest temperature you can—high heat brings out all their best qualities, and it also opens them up to absorb the seasonings of sweet tomato paste and dark, salty olives. Serve with a whole roasted fish or simple grilled meat.

SERVES 4

1¼ pounds Romano beans
½ cup plus 2 tablespoons extra-virgin
  olive oil
¼ teaspoon kosher salt, plus more to taste
¼ teaspoon freshly cracked black pepper,
  plus more to taste
1 cup finely chopped red onion

2 tablespoons chopped garlic
3 tablespoons tomato paste
¼ teaspoon chili flakes
¼ cup chopped, pitted Nocellara or
  Calabrese olives
½ teaspoon red wine vinegar
3 tablespoons torn basil leaves

Preheat the oven to 500°F. Toss the beans with 2 tablespoons of the olive oil and the salt and pepper. Spread on a large rimmed baking sheet and roast until they are completely soft and limp with some dark brown spots, about 20 minutes.

While the beans are roasting, make a soffrito: In a large skillet, warm the remaining ½ cup olive oil over medium heat. Add the onion and garlic and cook until they are very soft but with very little color, about 10 minutes. Stir in the tomato paste and chili flakes, increase the heat to medium-high, and sauté for 2 to 3 minutes.

Stir the roasted beans and olives into the soffrito and cook, covered, over low heat for 10 minutes. Remove the beans from the heat and sprinkle with the red wine vinegar and torn basil. Season with salt and pepper to taste and serve.

Sunchokes with Almonds, Pickled Fennel, and Pecorino

There are a few vegetables that really benefit from being overwintered, and sunchokes are one of them. The shock of our Northeast cold converts the sunchoke's starches into sugar, and when the overwintered crop starts showing up in the first weeks of March, they are just marvelous.

The limited local produce during a New York winter forces us to be inventive with what is available. Pickling fennel stems is a brilliant way of brightening up a sturdy winter vegetable, and here the little bites of tangy, licoricey crunch are delicious against the nutty sunchokes, toasty almonds, and sharp cheese.

SERVES 4

1 pound sunchokes, scrubbed and cut into ½-inch cubes
2 tablespoons plus 4 teaspoons extra-virgin olive oil
¼ teaspoon kosher salt, plus more to taste
¼ teaspoon freshly cracked black pepper, plus more to taste

2 tablespoons Pickled Fennel Stem, with its liquid (page 352)
2 tablespoons fresh lemon juice
6 tablespoons ¼-inch chunks Pecorino
¼ cup coarsely chopped toasted almonds

Preheat the oven to 400°F, with a rack positioned in the middle. Toss the sunchokes with 2 tablespoons of the olive oil and season with the salt and pepper. Spread in a single layer on a rimmed baking sheet and roast until lightly browned and tender, 30 to 40 minutes.

In a medium bowl, stir together the roasted sunchokes, pickled fennel, lemon juice, and the remaining 4 teaspoons olive oil. Season with salt and pepper to taste and let sit for at least 20 minutes, and up to 4 hours, before serving.

Just before serving, add the cheese and almonds and toss to combine.

Roasted Broccoli with Garlic, Chilies, and Colatura di Alici

We once went through a summer where we ate at Sripraphai, a famed Thai restaurant in Queens, at least once a week. (We still love it and have held some staff parties there.) The bright, fresh qualities of the food have always spoken to us, and for a while Andrew was obsessed with trying to translate Thai flavors into his Italian-based cooking. One of the bridges that connected the two is fish sauce: *nam pla* in Thailand, *colatura* in Italy. These are very similar pantry items—basically distilled, concentrated fish essences used to add savory notes to just about anything. Here Andrew pairs colatura with sturdy roasted broccoli, which can hold its own against the salty condiment.

We serve this cool rather than warm. Finished with lemon juice and some fiery chilies, it's a gutsy dish that quickly becomes addictive.

SERVES 4

2 pounds broccoli (about 2 large bunches)
5 tablespoons plus 1 teaspoon extra-virgin olive oil
½ teaspoon kosher salt, plus more to taste
¼ teaspoon freshly cracked black pepper, plus more to taste
Juice of 1 lemon

1 tablespoon colatura di alici (see Resources, page 357)
1½ teaspoons finely chopped jarred Calabrian chilies (see Resources)
1½ teaspoons finely chopped garlic
½ red onion, sliced lengthwise into ⅛-inch-thick batons

Preheat the oven to 475°F. Trim the broccoli and cut into large florets. Coarsely chop enough of the nice leaves and/or tender stems to equal about 1 cup; set aside. Toss the broccoli florets with 3 tablespoons of the olive oil and the salt and pepper. Arrange on a large rimmed baking sheet and pour ¼ cup water over the florets. Roast until the broccoli is just tender but still has some texture, 12 to 15 minutes. Let cool completely.

In a large skillet, heat 2 tablespoons olive oil over medium-high heat. Add the broccoli leaves and/or stems, sprinkle with a tablespoon or two of water to help them soften in the pan, and cook until tender, about 2 minutes. Season with a pinch each of salt and pepper, remove from the pan, and cool completely.

In a small bowl, toss together the lemon, colatura, chilies, and garlic.

In a large bowl, combine the broccoli leaves and/or stems, the broccoli florets, the onion, and the lemon mixture. Drizzle in the remaining teaspoon of olive oil and adjust the seasoning with pepper. You should not need salt, but if you do, add it sparingly.

Divide the broccoli evenly among four chilled bowls.

Andrew's Note: Colatura can be hard to find, but you can substitute Asian fish sauce—use the best you can get. Colatura tends to be more elegant and refined, while Thai fish sauce can sometimes be a little sweet. Look for a brand of fish sauce with just fish and salt listed on the ingredients label; you don't want to see caramel color, MSG, or other additives.

Marinated Rainbow Chard

Unlike most dense, dark greens, whose stems are too reedy or coarse to eat, Swiss chard has stems that are delicious and warrant cooking. And if you can find gorgeously hued rainbow chard at the market, it would be a tragedy not to make use of all that wonderful color in the stems.

The thing to keep in mind is that the leaves and stems need to be cooked separately, because the stems take much longer to soften. So they should always be added to the pan first. Here they get sautéed in sweet, deeply flavored garlic-scented olive oil until they wilt. Then the greens are added, along with some fresh chopped garlic for pungency. This dish can be made up to 1 day ahead—and the chard is especially compelling after it's had a chance to truly marinate.

SERVES 4

2 bunches Swiss chard (1 pound), **stems trimmed**
½ cup extra-virgin olive oil
6 garlic cloves, 4 smashed and peeled, 2 chopped
Kosher salt

2 tablespoons plus ½ teaspoon moscato vinegar (see Resources, page 357)
½ teaspoon chili flakes
Scant ⅛ teaspoon freshly cracked black pepper

Remove the stems from the chard leaves. Cut the stems in half lengthwise, then into 3-inch lengths. Keep the leaves whole.

Heat a large skillet over medium-high heat. Add ¼ cup of the olive oil and the 4 smashed garlic cloves and cook until the garlic is light golden brown, about 2 minutes. Remove and discard the garlic.

Add the stems to the garlic oil and sprinkle with salt. Cook until the stems are browned in spots, 4 to 5 minutes (if the stems begin to brown too much before they are tender, add a few tablespoons of water). When the stems are almost tender, stir in the 2 tablespoons vinegar. Cook until the stems are shiny and tender, 1 to 2 minutes more. Transfer to a platter.

Return the skillet to medium-high heat, add 2 tablespoons olive oil and the 2 chopped garlic cloves, and cook for 1 minute. Add the chili flakes and cook for 30 seconds. Add the chard leaves, season with salt, and cook until wilted, 1 to 2 minutes. Transfer the greens to a plate and let cool.

Place the greens in a bowl and sprinkle with the remaining 2 tablespoons olive oil and ½ teaspoon vinegar and the pepper. Gently mix in the stems. Let marinate for at least 20 minutes before serving, or for up to 1 day. Store in the refrigerator if marinating for more than 2 hours.

Andrew's Note: You can use regular chard for this recipe if you can't get rainbow chard. Beet greens will also work, though their stems are thinner, so you should cook them a little less.

Cauliflower with Pickles, Anchovies, Capers, and Olives

Served during the Christmas festivities in Naples, this dish is traditionally just boiled cauliflower paired with giardiniera pickles, olives, and anchovies. We roast the cauliflower instead to get a nice toasty flavor. Try to find Romanesco cauliflower and combine it with the common white variety—it's delicious and will add some extra color and variety.

SERVES 4

Two 1-pound heads cauliflower, cored and cut into bite-sized florets
½ cup plus 4 teaspoons extra-virgin olive oil
½ teaspoon kosher salt, plus more to taste
½ teaspoon black pepper, plus more to taste

1 cup drained pickles (recipe follows), **plus about 3 tablespoons of the pickling liquid**
⅓ cup pitted Nocellara or Cerignola olives (about 12), **torn into 2 or 3 pieces each**
2 teaspoons drained capers
8 anchovy fillets

Preheat the oven to 400°F. Toss the cauliflower florets with ½ cup of the olive oil, the salt, and the pepper. Spread on two large rimmed baking sheets. Roast, tossing occasionally, until the cauliflower is tender and golden, 25 to 30 minutes.

Transfer the cauliflower to a bowl and toss with a scant 3 tablespoons pickling liquid and salt and pepper to taste. Spread the cauliflower on a plate. Scatter the pickles over it. Sprinkle the olives and capers next. Arrange the anchovies on top. Sprinkle with more pickling liquid and drizzle with the remaining 4 teaspoons olive oil.

Pickles

MAKES 4 CUPS

2 carrots, peeled and cut into 2-inch lengths
2 celery stalks
½ small fennel bulb
1 small sweet onion, such as Vidalia, quartered
1 small red bell pepper, cored, seeds removed

2 hot red cherry peppers, cored, seeds removed
2 cups white wine vinegar
¼ cup sugar
2 tablespoons plus 2 teaspoons kosher salt

Using a mandoline, slice each carrot piece lengthwise ¼ inch thick; slice the celery crosswise ¼ inch thick; slice the fennel lengthwise ¼ inch thick; and slice the onion ¼ inch thick (you should have about ¾ cup of each vegetable). Using a sharp knife, slice the bell and hot peppers into ¼-inch-wide strips. Combine all the vegetables in a large bowl.

In a small saucepan, combine the vinegar, sugar, and salt and bring to a simmer, stirring until the sugar and salt dissolve. Pour the hot liquid over the vegetables. Let cool to room temperature, then transfer to an airtight container and refrigerate for at least 48 hours. (The pickles will keep for 1 month.)

Marinated Cabbage with Walnuts, Bread Crumbs, and Parmigiano-Reggiano

Cabbage has gotten a bad reputation for being one of those vegetables that is often bland and overcooked. Not here, where it is just soft enough to cut with a fork, but not at all soggy or limp. As a textural contrast, Andrew combines walnuts, bread crumbs, and Parmigiano-Reggiano with oil, almost like a pesto, and uses it to dress the cabbage. I could eat a generous portion of it as a light lunch, but I often have it at the restaurant before a bowl of pasta. While you'd never see a dish like this in Italy, all the building blocks of *cucina povera* are here.

SERVES 4

½ **teaspoon kosher salt, plus more as needed**
8 **ounces large Savoy cabbage leaves** (10 to 12, depending on size)
1 **tablespoon fresh lemon juice**
6 **tablespoons extra-virgin olive oil**

¼ **cup walnuts, finely chopped**
⅓ **cup dried bread crumbs, preferably homemade** (see page 353)
¼ **cup finely grated Parmigiano-Reggiano**
Freshly cracked black pepper

Bring a large pot of salted water to a boil. Fill a large bowl with ice water and salt it generously. Blanch the whole cabbage leaves in the boiling water for 1 minute. Remove from the pot and immediately transfer to the ice water to cool thoroughly. Drain the cabbage and pat completely dry. Transfer to a bowl and refrigerate until chilled.

Toss the cabbage leaves with the lemon juice, ¼ cup of the olive oil, and ¼ teaspoon of the salt. Chill in the refrigerator for up to 1 hour.

Meanwhile, preheat the oven to 325°F, with a rack positioned in the middle. Spread the walnuts on a rimmed baking sheet and toast for 10 to 12 minutes, until golden brown and fragrant. Remove from the oven and allow to cool, then finely chop.

In a small pan, heat the remaining 2 tablespoons olive oil over medium heat. Add the bread crumbs and toast until golden brown, about 5 minutes. Season with the remaining ¼ teaspoon salt and allow to cool.

In a small bowl, mix together the bread crumbs, walnuts, and Parmigiano-Reggiano.

Place a layer of marinated cabbage leaves on a large serving plate and sprinkle with some of the crumb mixture. Repeat the layering until you have used all the ingredients. Serve.

Andrew's Note: This recipe uses only the larger outer cabbage leaves, leaving you with the tender inner leaves to use for soups, slaw, or other dishes.

Roasted Fennel with Lemon and Chilies

Every element of the fennel plant, from seeds to fronds to stems to bulb, goes into this remarkable recipe: the dish is essentially a top-to-bottom love letter to fennel. It's perfect for someone who adores the vegetable, and maybe even more perfect for someone who doesn't—yet. This is more complicated than many of the recipes in this book—it's another dish invented by chef Danny Amend, who trained in French kitchens—but it is well worth the effort.

The fennel stem confit is a great example of what you can do with vegetable trimmings. The trimmings that most of us would usually discard hold all kinds of possibilities. Here, the sliced stems are confited in loads of gorgeous olive oil until very soft. The bulbs themselves are roasted until they condense and their flavors intensify.

Danny also tracked down a very special variety of fennel seed, Lucknow, that he buys from Kalustyan's in New York City. These seeds—smaller, sweeter, and greener than the more common variety—are incredibly aromatic and delicate. If you can't find Lucknow fennel seeds, standard grocery store fennel seeds will also work fine.

SERVES 4

3 fennel bulbs (reserved from the Fennel Conserva, page 351)
2 teaspoons extra-virgin olive oil
½ teaspoon kosher salt
½ teaspoon fennel seeds, preferably Lucknow (see Resources, page 357)
¼ teaspoon chili flakes

¼ teaspoon freshly cracked black pepper
4 shaved rounds red onion
6 tablespoons Fennel Conserva (page 351)
2 teaspoons fresh lemon juice
3 tablespoons chopped fennel fronds (reserved from the Fennel Conserva, page 351)

Preheat the oven to 325°F. Remove the outer layers of the fennel and cleanly slice off the stems where they meet the bulb. Cut each bulb lengthwise in half, then slice each half lengthwise into thirds.

Transfer the fennel pieces to a small casserole dish and toss them with the olive oil, salt, fennel seeds, chili flakes, and black pepper. Cover the dish tightly with aluminum foil and bake until the fennel is very tender, 40 to 50 minutes.

Lower the oven temperature to 325°F. Remove the foil from the dish and continue baking, uncovered, until the fennel has reabsorbed its juices and become firmer, about 30 minutes.

Transfer the fennel to a bowl and toss with the onion, lemon juice, Fennel Conserva, and fennel fronds. Divide among individual plates and serve.

Andrew's Note: The Fennel Conserva will keep for a while in the fridge and would be a great addition to a piece of roasted fish. Or spoon onto grilled bread for a crostini.

Roasted Brussels Sprouts with Almonds and Pecorino

Roasting Brussels sprouts is an easy and spectacular way to cook them. After they are halved and roasted in a superhot oven, their exterior becomes wonderfully dark and crunchy, while the insides stay supple and soft. Once they cool to room temperature, we dress them with lemon juice, roughly chopped toasted almonds, and ragged chunks of tangy Pecorino. Try to find young (aged 4 to 5 months) Pecorino, or feel free to use Manchego, which is widely available.

SERVES 4

5 cups (about 1½ pounds) **trimmed Brussels sprouts, halved through the stem end**
6 tablespoons extra-virgin olive oil, plus more for drizzling
Kosher salt and freshly cracked black pepper

½ cup Pecorino Ginepro or Manchego, cut into ¼-inch jagged pieces (we use a Parmigiano knife)
6 tablespoons roughly chopped toasted skin-on almonds
2 tablespoons fresh lemon juice

Preheat the oven to 500°F. Toss the Brussels sprouts with ¼ cup of the olive oil. Season the sprouts with salt and pepper and spread them out in one layer on a baking sheet. Roast until browned and just tender, 20 to 25 minutes. Let cool.

Put the Brussels sprouts in a medium bowl and add the Pecorino, almonds, lemon juice, and the remaining 2 tablespoons olive oil. Season with salt and pepper and toss to combine.

Divide the Brussels sprouts among four individual plates and finish with a drizzle of olive oil.

Andrew's Note: When people see the word "Pecorino," they think of Pecorino Romano, but there are many different types of Pecorino—which simply means a cheese made from sheep's milk. Romano is generally used in cooked dishes; it's very salty and strong on its own, and it would overwhelm this dish.

VEGETABLES

Pumpkin Agrodolce with Almonds and Spicy Raisins

Sweet and salty, tart and spicy, this autumnal recipe has a lot going for it. Kabocha, also known as Japanese pumpkin, is the best winter squash to use here: it's dense, dry, very sweet, and a little mealy, in a good way. You want a sweet squash to oppose the vinegar—*agrodolce* literally means "sweet sour." We also add a spicy element: raisins plumped in chili-spiked vinegar; they're both fiery and juicy. A finish of toasted almonds or hazelnuts adds a crunchy texture and helps mellow all the intense flavors. This needs to sit overnight, so plan ahead.

SERVES 4

FOR THE SPICY RAISINS
6 tablespoons raisins
⅓ cup moscato vinegar (see Resources, page 357)
⅓ cup white wine vinegar
⅓ cup water
1½ teaspoons chili flakes
½ teaspoon crushed dried Controne chili (see Resources, page 357) **or additional chili flakes**

1 medium kabocha squash (about 3½ pounds), **peeled, halved, seeded, and cut into 8 wedges**
6 tablespoons extra-virgin olive oil, plus more if needed
4 teaspoons kosher salt
Freshly cracked black pepper
¼ cup almonds or hazelnuts
Flaky sea salt, such as Maldon
6 mint leaves, torn

To make the raisins: Place the raisins in a small bowl. In a small saucepan, combine the vinegars and water and bring to a boil. Add the chili flakes and simmer for 10 seconds. Immediately pour the liquid over the raisins and let cool to room temperature.

Preheat the oven to 400°F. Toss the squash with ¼ cup of the olive oil, the salt, and pepper. Arrange the pieces on a rimmed baking sheet (or use two). Roast for 25 minutes. Check the squash; a cake tester should go all the way through the flesh with no resistance; if the squash is not tender, return the pan to the oven and check it every 5 minutes until it is.

Once the squash is tender, flip each piece and continue to roast, checking every 10 minutes, until the squash is relatively dry on the outside and somewhere between cakey and creamy throughout. It should be golden brown with a lightly crisp skin. If it seems to be drying out during this process, drizzle it with additional olive oil.

Transfer the squash to a shallow baking dish or serving platter. Drain the raisins, reserving the liquid, and scatter them evenly over the squash, then pour ⅓ cup of the liquid over all. Drizzle with the remaining 2 tablespoons olive oil. Cover and refrigerate for 24 hours.

The next day, preheat the oven to 350°F, with a rack in the middle of the oven. Spread the nuts on a rimmed baking sheet and toast until golden and fragrant, about 7 minutes. If using hazelnuts, immediately bundle them in a clean dish towel and rub together to remove their papery skins. Let the nuts cool, then coarsely chop them.

To serve, bring the squash to room temperature. Season with flaky sea salt and sprinkle with the nuts and torn mint leaves.

Beets with Pickled Hot Peppers, Walnuts, and Ricotta Salata

This is one of those dishes that transcends the sum of its parts. Sweet roasted beets are topped with salty, creamy cheese; fragrant toasted walnuts; and intensely spicy pickled peppers. Every bite is different—some spicier, some sweeter, some creamier. Harmonious and utterly compelling, this is one of our most popular winter offerings.

SERVES 6

6 medium beets (1¾ pounds)
¾ cup extra-virgin olive oil
**5 teaspoons kosher salt, plus more
  for sprinkling**
¼ cup plus ½ teaspoon red wine vinegar
Freshly cracked black pepper

1½ cups walnuts
1 tablespoon Pickled Hot Peppers
  (page 352)
2 cups shaved ricotta salata
  (8 ounces)

Preheat oven to 375°F. Place the beets in a roasting pan with sides that are higher than the beets. Drizzle with 2 tablespoons of the olive oil, sprinkle with 4 teaspoons of the salt, and toss to combine. Sprinkle 6 tablespoons water and 2 tablespoons of the vinegar over the beets. Cover the pan with aluminum foil and bake until the beets are tender, 1 to 1½ hours. Remove from the oven and let cool; reduce the oven temperature to 325°F.

Peel the beets and slice into ½-inch-thick rounds. Arrange in a single layer on a rimmed baking sheet. Sprinkle with 2 tablespoons olive oil, 2 teaspoons vinegar, ½ teaspoon salt, and pepper to taste. Cover the beets with plastic wrap and refrigerate for at least 2 hours, and up to 3 days. (If marinating for less than 3 hours, you can let them stand at room temperature.)

Meanwhile, spread the walnuts on a rimmed baking sheet. Toast until golden and fragrant, 10 to 12 minutes. Cool, and break into pieces with your hands.

Using tongs or wearing gloves to protect yourself against the spicy peppers, gently toss the beets with 6 tablespoons olive oil, the pickled peppers, and the remaining 1½ tablespoons vinegar and ½ teaspoon salt. Toss in the walnuts.

Spread the beet mixture on a large plate. Top with the ricotta, drizzle with the remaining 2 tablespoons olive oil, and sprinkle with salt.

FISH

I don't think it's going too far to say that Italians worship seafood. Andrew and I thought we knew this from reading about Italian cuisine and eating in Italian restaurants in New York, but we didn't really get it until we saw it for ourselves, on our first trip to Italy together, when we eloped.

We got married in the marble cathedral in Amalfi and then honeymooned on the famous coast, eating seafood in every little trattoria and *osteria* we passed. And it was all incredible. Whether simply grilled, flash-fried, or roasted whole, all kinds of sea creatures in Italy seem to taste like exactly what they are, without a lot of extraneous ingredients or fancy techniques. I remember one pasta dish in particular, *spaghetti ai ricci di mare* (spaghetti with sea urchin), that was jaw-droppingly simple and tasted perfectly briny and sweet, just like the sea itself. Eating in Italy taught us that if you start out with exceptional fish and don't do too much to it, you'll end up with an exceptional dish.

We've taken this approach to heart, and Andrew likes to keep things simple when seasoning seafood. The Italian holy trinity of olive oil, lemon, and garlic features prominently, as do seasonal herbs, which add a fragrant freshness that pairs well with most fish. Beans are another favorite. There is something about their mild, creamy earthiness that works really well with sweet, salty seafood. At Franny's, Andrew combines them with mussels (see page 173), squid (see page 162), and oil-preserved tuna (see page 170).

At home, almost every Saturday night is fish night. Prue and Marco will happily eat shrimp, tuna, and, sometimes, squid. And we hope that by introducing them to a wide variety of seafood, we will make this short list eventually get a little longer.

We are lucky enough to be able to buy our fish at our local greenmarket from Blue Moon Fish, a vendor that sells some of the freshest seafood in all of New York City. The permanently long wait at their stall proves the point. The last thing anyone wants to do on the weekend is stand in a line, but we do it every week, and the kids love to gape at the whole fish, which they find fascinating to look at if not yet to eat. Because all the fish is wild and local, we get to experience the seasonal changes as schools of fish migrate through our waters. In the winter, we delight in blackfish and Boston mackerel; in the summer, we're treated to striped bass, swordfish, and bluefish. With so much farmed fish from all over the world available, it can be easy to forget that local wild seafood is a seasonal thing.

Which brings me to one of the most important points about seafood. For mindful eaters, it can be tricky—we all know our oceans are in trouble and many species are endangered. When buying produce, we look for local first and sustainable second; with seafood, it's the other way around. Of course, the best choices are both sustainable *and* local. But we often pass over the most pristine-looking locally caught fish if we know the species is threatened. For the most part, that means we eat a lot of squid, clams, mackerel, and swordfish, all reeled in nearby off the coast of Long Island, and all fresh and utterly delicious.

But no matter where you live, you should be able to buy sustainable fish once you know what to look for. (There are even phone apps that can tell you.) Our go-to resource is the "Seafood Watch" link on the Monterey Bay Aquarium's website (www.montereybayaquarium .org). On it they list virtually every type of seafood, down to individual species; where the seafood is sourced; and how it is harvested.

And if you check frequently, you can see how things change, often for the worse, but sometimes for the better. For example, take the case of swordfish. A few years ago, swordfish went on the overfished list, and its scarcity was pretty well publicized. Swordfish has always been one of my favorites; there's no other fish with the same mild meatiness and sweet flavor. But I stopped ordering it. And you know what? Thanks to people paying attention and heeding the "overfished" warning, swordfish is back, and for now, at least, is no longer in danger. And we absolutely buy it whenever we can get some nice steaks from a local catch.

Shellfish are also often on the menu both at home and at the restaurant, particularly clams and mussels, which are extremely ocean friendly. We pile clams onto our clam pizza and occasionally toss them with spaghetti or linguine for a pasta dish.

Mussel farming is both easy on the ocean and extremely low-tech. And mussels, by their very nature, are cleaners, filtering the water in which they live. They're immensely popular in Italy, where they're prepared in almost every way imaginable: baked with crispy bread crumbs; steamed and tossed with spaghetti; braised with aromatics and vegetables. During that same first trip to Italy, we had steamed mussels that were spiced with a whopping amount of coarse black pepper, and we've never forgotten them. At Franny's, we've offered mussels in myriad ways, but one of our favorites is Mussels with White Beans and Finocchiona (page 173), a simple mussel and bean stew enriched with fennel-flavored salami.

Another ocean-friendly—and delectable—choice is squid. Most of us are all too familiar with fried calamari, those breaded rubber bands that we grew up dipping in red sauce. I didn't know squid could be prepared in so many better ways—it is a fabulous blank canvas that is highly adaptable. For salads and sautés, Andrew quickly sears squid over high heat to achieve an irresistible crisp tenderness. For pasta dishes, he braises it, and the long-cooked squid takes on a delicate texture and is infused with the aromatics of the sauce.

Then there's the whole *pesce azzurro* ("blue fish") family, which includes anchovies and mackerel. We use anchovies liberally as a seasoning, adding them to salad dressings, crostini, vegetable dishes, and pasta. And mackerel is a staple. The whole fillets can be confited in oil, grilled, roasted, or panfried. The sweet, dense fish doesn't need a lot in terms of seasonings, but a dash of something acidic—vinegar or lemon juice—will bring out its sweeter nature and balance its richness. Plus, mackerel is readily available year-round and surprisingly inexpensive.

As the recipes in this chapter show, sourcing good, fresh, sustainable seafood is definitely the trickiest thing about serving it. Once you've got your hands on the good stuff, the rest is easy.

Sautéed Squid with Lovage Salsa Verde

Salsa verde, a bracing combination of garlic, parsley, vinegar or lemon, capers, and sometimes anchovies, is a rustic Italian sauce that brightens up everything from roasted game to poached chicken to simply grilled fish. Here Andrew uses it to dress tender, quickly sautéed squid, with one major difference: he adds a hefty dose of lovage, a springtime herb with an intense celery flavor that's balanced by an almost candied anise character.

You don't see a lot of lovage in Italy, but it is found in Liguria, one of Italy's most stunning coastal regions. In fact, in a classic linguistic handoff, it's thought that the word "lovage" is a corrupted version of the medieval name for Liguria, where the bushy herb grows freely all over the countryside.

Lovage can be hard to track down (though it's easy to grow yourself). If you can't find it, just substitute more parsley and mint in the salsa verde. It won't have the same flavor, but it will still make for an excellent, zesty dish.

SERVES 4

1½ pounds cleaned squid

FOR THE SALSA VERDE
½ cup finely chopped flat-leaf parsley
¼ cup finely chopped mint
¼ cup finely chopped lovage
4 teaspoons finely chopped drained capers
2 teaspoons finely chopped garlic

½ teaspoon kosher salt
¼ teaspoon freshly cracked black pepper
1 cup extra-virgin olive oil

6 tablespoons extra-virgin olive oil
Kosher salt
Juice of 2 lemons, or to taste

Rinse the squid under cool running water; drain. Cut the bodies into ³⁄₁₆-inch-wide rings; leave the tentacles whole. Transfer to paper towels and pat dry completely, then transfer to a plate.

To make the salsa verde: In a small bowl, combine the parsley, mint, lovage, capers, garlic, salt, and pepper. Stir in the olive oil.

Place a large heavy skillet over high heat and let it get very hot, heating it for a good 5 minutes. Add 3 tablespoons of the olive oil to the skillet and heat until hot but not smoking. Season the squid with salt, then slide half of it into the pan and cook, without moving, for 1 minute. Flip the squid and cook for 30 seconds more. (Do not overcrowd the pan; if your skillet doesn't hold

the squid comfortably, cook it in smaller batches, adding more oil if needed.) Transfer to a bowl. Repeat with the remaining squid and oil.

Toss the squid with 6 tablespoons of the salsa verde and the lemon juice. Spread a thin layer of salsa verde on a platter, top with squid, and serve.

Andrew's Note: Any leftover salsa verde will keep in the fridge for about 24 hours (cover it with a thin layer of oil). You can use it for breakfast the next morning, dabbed on scrambled eggs. Or serve it as a sauce for any kind of seafood or roasted chicken or pork.

Squid Salad with Croutons, Cherry Tomatoes, Olives, and Capers

This vibrant recipe is similar to panzanella, a traditional bread salad served in Italy during the summer. But instead of the usual *cucina povera* mix of stale bread and diced regular tomatoes, Andrew combines toasted croutons and juicy cherry tomatoes with cucumbers and lightly sautéed squid. Big, crisp croutons work really well here—they soak up all the lovely tangy flavors of the oil, vinegar, and tomato (as bread in any panzanella should), but they also retain a nice amount of crunch. To add a more complex note, the salad is tossed with a liberal sprinkling of capers and olives, which echo the brininess of the squid. It is a perfect salad to serve just after that initial summer heat wave, when you want something cooling, light, and crunchy.

SERVES 4 TO 6

FOR THE CROUTONS
1 cup coarsely torn (1-inch chunks)
   country-style bread
2 teaspoons extra-virgin olive oil
Kosher salt and freshly cracked
   black pepper

1½ pounds cleaned squid
About 9 tablespoons extra-virgin olive oil
Kosher salt

1 small Kirby cucumber
2 teaspoons red wine vinegar
½ teaspoon finely chopped garlic
1½ cups cherry tomatoes (about 16), **halved**
½ cup chopped flat-leaf parsley
⅓ cup Taggiasca or other good-quality
   black olives (about 20), **pitted and halved**
¼ cup thinly sliced red onion
4 teaspoons brined capers, drained

To make the croutons: Preheat the oven to 350°F. Toss the bread with the olive oil and season with salt and pepper. Spread on a baking sheet and toast until crisp and very lightly golden, about 10 minutes. Let cool.

Rinse the squid under cool running water; drain. Cut the bodies into ³⁄₁₆-inch-wide rings; leave the tentacles whole. Transfer to paper towels and pat dry completely, then transfer to a plate.

Place a large heavy skillet over high heat and let it get very hot, heating it for a good 5 minutes. Add 3 tablespoons of the olive oil to the skillet. Season the squid with salt, then slide half of it into the pan and cook, without moving, for 1 minute. Flip the squid and cook for 30 seconds more. (Do not overcrowd the pan; if your skillet doesn't hold the squid comfortably, cook it in smaller batches, adding more oil if needed.)

Transfer to a bowl. Repeat with the remaining squid, using about 3 tablespoons oil per batch.

To make the salad, peel the cucumber lengthwise, leaving a strip of skin between each peel to create stripes. Slice the cucumber lengthwise in half and scoop out the seeds. Cut on the diagonal into ¼-inch-thick slices (you should have about ⅓ cup).

In a medium bowl, whisk together the vinegar and garlic. Stir in the squid, tomatoes, croutons, parsley, cucumber, olives, onion, the remaining 3 tablespoons oil, and the capers. Season lightly with salt and pepper.

Andrew's Note: Squid cooks quickly, so have your vegetables prepped and ready to go before you start. Once you do, this dish will come together in minutes.

FISH

Marinated Mackerel with Capers, Croutons, and Herbs

You don't see a lot of mackerel in this country, but it's beloved in Italy, where it's known as a member of the *pesce azzurro* ("blue fish") family, a group that also includes anchovies and sardines. Americans tend to shy away from mackerel because they think it's going to taste strong or fishy. But of all the fish in this family, mackerel is the sweetest and mildest. It's savory, buttery, and rich, and it's good for you, too, loaded with omega-3s.

SERVES 4

FOR THE CROUTONS
⅔ cup coarsely torn (1-inch pieces)
  country-style bread
1 tablespoon extra-virgin olive oil
Kosher salt and freshly cracked
  black pepper

4 skin-on mackerel fillets (about 1¼ pounds)
Kosher salt and freshly cracked
  black pepper
1¼ cups plus 3 tablespoons extra-virgin
  olive oil
8 garlic cloves, thinly sliced

¾ teaspoon red chili flakes
⅔ cup white wine vinegar
⅔ cup moscato vinegar (see Resources, page
  357)
12 large mint sprigs
Zest of 2 lemons, removed in large strips
  with a vegetable peeler
½ cup chopped flat-leaf parsley
8 scallions, thinly sliced on the diagonal
  (about ½ cup)
Juice of ½ lemon, or more to taste
Flaky sea salt, such as Maldon
2 teaspoons brined capers, drained

To make the croutons: Preheat the oven to 350°F. Toss the bread pieces with the olive oil and season with salt and pepper. Spread on a baking sheet and toast until a dark caramel color, 20 to 30 minutes. Let cool.

Season the fish fillets with salt and pepper. Heat a large skillet over high heat, then add 2 tablespoons of olive oil and let it get hot but not smoking. Transfer 2 fillets to the pan, skin side down; if the skin begins to shrink instantly, you know the pan is hot enough. Cook the fish, undisturbed, for 1½ minutes, pressing down on the fillets with a spatula to help brown the skin. Flip the fillets and cook for 10 seconds more. Transfer to a 9-by-13-inch glass baking dish. Repeat with 2 more tablespoons olive oil and the remaining fish fillets.

Reduce the heat to medium and add the garlic and chili flakes to the skillet. Cook, stirring, until fragrant, about 20 seconds. Add the vinegars and mint sprigs, scrape up any browned bits from the bottom of the pan, and pour the mixture over the fish. Add 1 cup olive oil and the lemon zest to the baking dish. Let the fish cool to room temperature, then cover tightly and refrigerate for 4 to 5 hours.

Just before serving the fish, in a bowl, toss together the parsley, scallions, and lemon juice. Stir in the remaining 3 tablespoons olive oil. Taste and add more lemon juice if needed.

To serve, place one mackerel fillet on each plate. Sprinkle with sea salt, and mound the parsley salad on top of the fish. Sprinkle sea salt over each salad. Scatter the croutons and capers over the dish and serve.

Marinated Swordfish with Sweet Peppers, Potatoes, and Olives

August means the start of red pepper season. And as soon as those thick-fleshed, sweet beauties arrive at the farmers' market, we buy a bagful and toss them on the grill until their juices condense and the skin blackens and chars. We drape roasted peppers over crostini and salads, but one night, Andrew decided to do something a little different. He tossed the peppers into the food processor and whirred them up into a smooth red puree that became the base of a complex vinaigrette, heady with fresh oregano and pungent raw garlic.

It's a sweet and tangy sauce that you could pair with any kind of grilled meat or chicken. But we think it works particularly well with chunks of meaty swordfish (the "steak" of the fish world) and soft, fingerling potatoes in this satisfying summer salad.

SERVES 4

Two 6- to 8-ounce swordfish steaks
½ teaspoon kosher salt, plus more to taste
½ teaspoon freshly cracked black pepper, plus more to taste
¼ cup extra-virgin olive oil, plus more to cover the fish
12 ounces fingerling potatoes, peeled
1 large or 2 medium red bell peppers

3 tablespoons finely chopped flat-leaf parsley
2 teaspoons finely chopped oregano
2 teaspoons white wine vinegar, plus more for sprinkling
½ teaspoon finely chopped garlic
12 Nocellara or Cerignola olives, pitted and torn into 2 or 3 pieces each

Season the swordfish with the salt and pepper. Place the fish in a bowl, cover with plastic wrap, and let sit in the refrigerator overnight.

The next day, pat the fish dry. Fill a skillet with enough olive oil to submerge the fish and heat the oil to 160°F. Turn the heat off and drop in the fish. Let the fish cook in the oil until it registers an internal temperature of 125 to 130°F, about 10 minutes. (If the fish does not reach this temperature, return it to low heat until it does.) Transfer the fish to a bowl and let cool; let the oil cool completely, then pour it over the fish.

Bring a pot of highly salted water to a simmer. Add the potatoes and cook until they are tender, about 20 minutes; drain. Once the potatoes are cool, slice them into ¼-inch-thick rounds (you should have about 2 cups).

Heat a wood-fired, charcoal, or gas grill to medium-high heat (see Andrew's Note). Put the peppers on the grill, cover, and cook, turning occasionally, until the skin is black. Let cool.

Peel and seed the peppers. Puree in a food processor until smooth. Scrape the puree into a bowl. Add the ¼ cup olive oil, the parsley, oregano, vinegar, and garlic. Season with salt and pepper.

Remove the fish from the oil and tear it into chunks over a bowl. Add the potatoes and the red pepper dressing and toss gently. Sprinkle the salad with vinegar. Scatter the olives on top. Drizzle the salad with more olive oil and serve.

Andrew's Note: You'll get the best flavor if you roast your peppers on a charcoal grill using wood, or a gas grill using wood chips. The wood smoke adds a ton of flavor to the sweet peppers. You can also use the oven. Line a baking sheet with foil and crank up the broiler. Roast the peppers on the rack nearest the heat source. Let the skin become charred before rotating the peppers to expose another side. The more evenly you char the peppers, the easier they will be to peel.

FISH

Squid Salad with Chickpeas, Olives, and Preserved Meyer Lemon

Meyer lemons are a special winter treat. They are bright and soft at the same time, their juice is sweeter than that of a typical lemon, and their fragrant rinds are absolutely delicious. Little bites of preserved Meyer lemon rind are spectacular in this dish, but you can substitute fresh lemon zest. And the chickpeas seem almost whimsical here—the little rings of squid cup them as if they were made for each other.

SERVES 6

FOR THE CHICKPEAS
1 pound dried chickpeas
2 garlic cloves
10 black peppercorns
1 bay leaf
Grated zest of ½ lemon
1 teaspoon kosher salt

FOR THE SALAD
1 pound cleaned squid
1 garlic clove, finely chopped
Juice of 1 lemon

½ teaspoon kosher salt, plus more to taste
Large pinch of chili flakes
2 Preserved Meyer Lemon quarters (page 349) **or finely grated zest of 2 lemons**
½ cup plus 1 tablespoon extra-virgin olive oil
Freshly cracked black pepper
1 medium fennel bulb, trimmed and outer layer removed
¼ cup chopped pitted black olives, such as Sicilian sal secco
¼ cup chopped flat-leaf parsley

Place the chickpeas in a large bowl and add water to cover by 2 inches. Soak overnight.

Drain the chickpeas and place in a large pot with fresh cold water to cover by 3 inches. Wrap the garlic cloves, peppercorns, bay leaf, and lemon zest in a square of triple-layer cheesecloth and tie with kitchen twine or a knot. Add the sachet and the salt to the pot. Bring to a boil over high heat, reduce the heat to medium, and simmer the chickpeas, uncovered, until tender but firm (they should just be starting to split), 1½ to 2 hours. Allow the chickpeas to cool in the liquid. (You will have extra chickpeas; leftover chickpeas can be stored in the refrigerator for up to 5 days.)

To make the salad: Rinse the squid under cool water; drain. Cut the bodies into ³⁄₁₆-inch-wide rings; leave the tentacles whole. Transfer to paper towels and pat dry, then transfer to a plate.

Mash the garlic to a paste with the side of a knife (or with a mortar and pestle); transfer it to a small bowl. Whisk in the lemon juice, salt, and chili flakes. If using preserved lemon, cut away the

flesh and discard; thinly slice the rind and add it to the bowl. Or add the grated lemon zest. Whisk in ½ cup of the olive oil.

Heat a large skillet over medium-high heat and let it get very hot, heating it for a good 5 minutes. Add 1½ teaspoons of the olive oil and tilt the pan to coat the bottom. Season the squid with salt and pepper. Place half the squid in the pan and cook, without moving, for 1 minute; the squid should be light golden on the bottom. Turn the squid and cook until just opaque and tender, about 1 minute more, and transfer to a large bowl. Repeat with the remaining 1½ teaspoons olive oil and squid.

Using a mandoline or with a very sharp knife, shave the fennel bulb lengthwise into paper-thin slices. Add to the bowl with the squid.

Use a slotted spoon to remove 1½ cups chickpeas (reserve the rest for another use) from the pot and stir into the squid. Add the olives, parsley, and lemon vinaigrette and toss well. Serve.

Pan-Roasted Shrimp with Garlic, Lemon, and Black Pepper

Whole head-on shrimp are truly special. At Franny's, we're always on the lookout for sustainably raised, superlatively delicious shrimp. Over the years, we've used producers from Maine to Maryland, and all the way down to Belize, searching for the best. And when we do find the best, we do very little to them—we throw the seasoned shrimp into a pan and roast them in the wood-burning oven. Then they get tossed with fresh lemon, garlic, a generous amount of cracked black pepper, and really good olive oil (this is the place to use your best stuff). That's all they need.

Sometimes when the plate hits the table, the guests look confused. We serve five to six shrimp per order, and as there's nothing else on the plate (save for a lemon wedge), sometimes folks are a bit disappointed—but that lasts for only a moment; once they take that first bite, the kitchen's rationale becomes clear. High-quality whole shrimp are terrifically rich, nearly as dense and meaty as lobsters. And once we manage to convince our diners that the shrimp are meant to be consumed whole ("Don't peel them, just pop them in your mouth!"), even the initially suspicious guest is won over. Seeking out a source of good head-on shrimp is the most challenging aspect of this dish—the recipe is a cinch once the shrimp are in your kitchen.

SERVES 4

1 large garlic clove, finely chopped
1 tablespoon fresh lemon juice, plus
    more to taste
2 tablespoons plus ½ teaspoon extra-virgin
    olive oil

¼ teaspoon kosher salt, plus more to taste
½ teaspoon freshly cracked black pepper
1½ pounds head-on shrimp, in the shell
2 teaspoons safflower or canola oil
2 lemons, cut into wedges

In a large bowl, whisk together the garlic, lemon juice, 2 tablespoons of the olive oil, the salt, and the pepper. Set aside. Season the shrimp with the remaining ½ teaspoon olive oil and a pinch of salt.

Heat a large skillet over medium-high heat until very hot. Add the canola oil and heat until it almost begins to smoke. Add the shrimp and cook for 45 seconds. Flip the shrimp and continue cooking until just opaque throughout, 15 seconds to 1 minute more. Pour in the dressing and toss to coat.

Divide the shrimp among four bowls, season with more lemon juice and salt to taste, and serve with lemon wedges alongside.

Andrew's Note: When purchasing shrimp, look for sustainably harvested or trap-caught shrimp.

Seared Shrimp with White Beans, Olives, and Herbs

Beans and fish is a classic pairing in Italy; the beans' mild, starchy nature is a great foundation for all kinds of seafood, supporting it without overshadowing its salty ocean flavor. This dish has central and southern Italian sensibilities. White beans are blended into a smooth and earthy puree to use as a bed for the shrimp. The heads definitely make some folks squeamish, but they contain loads of rich, briny juices that seep down into the beans here, imparting an intense salinity to the whole plate.

This dish serves four as an appetizer or as part of a larger meal. If you want to serve it as a main course, it's easy to double the recipe: you'll have enough cooked beans to make double the puree. Then be sure to cook the shrimp in batches so you don't overcrowd the pan.

SERVES 4

FOR THE BEAN PUREE
1 pound dried Controne or cannellini beans
½ cup plus 1 tablespoon extra-virgin
 olive oil
2 tablespoons plus ¼ teaspoon kosher salt
1 small onion (or ½ large), cut in half
3 large garlic cloves, smashed and peeled
1 bay leaf
1 small rosemary sprig
Freshly cracked black pepper

FOR THE SHRIMP
1 pound head-on shrimp, in the shells
Kosher salt and freshly cracked
 black pepper
5 tablespoons extra-virgin olive oil,
 plus more for drizzling
6 tablespoons coarsely chopped pitted
 black Cerignola olives
¼ cup chopped flat-leaf parsley
4 teaspoons chopped fennel fronds
 (optional)
½ teaspoon minced garlic
1 lemon, quartered

Soak the beans in cool water for at least 8 hours, and up to overnight. Drain.

Place the beans in a large pot. Cover with 5 cups water, then add the ½ cup olive oil and 2 tablespoons salt. Wrap the onion, garlic, bay leaf, and rosemary in a piece of cheesecloth and secure with kitchen twine or a knot. Place the sachet in the pot of beans and bring to a boil over medium-high heat. Skim any foamy scum that comes to the surface. Reduce the heat to low to maintain a simmer, cover the pot, and cook the beans until tender, 45 minutes to 1½ hours (depending on the freshness of the beans). Taste regularly to check the tenderness. Remove and discard the sachet and drain the beans, reserving the cooking liquid.

To make the bean puree: Combine 1¼ cups of the beans, ⅓ cup of the reserved cooking liquid, the remaining 1 tablespoon olive oil and ¼ teaspoon salt, and a few turns of black pepper in the work bowl of a food processor and process, scraping the sides down often, until the mixture is smooth. (The puree can be made in advance and stored, covered, in the refrigerator; allow to come to room temperature before serving. You will have extra puree, which can be stored in the refrigerator, covered, for up to 2 days.)

To cook the shrimp: Season the shrimp with salt and pepper. In a large skillet, warm 1 tablespoon of the olive oil over high heat. Add the shrimp and sear on one side until slightly browned,

continued

1 to 2 minutes. Flip the shrimp, remove from the heat, and let stand until cooked through, 2 to 3 minutes.

Meanwhile, using the back of a large spoon, spread the bean puree onto four individual plates.

In a large bowl, toss the cooked shrimp with the remaining ¼ cup olive oil, the olives, parsley, fennel fronds, if using, and garlic. Divide the shrimp among the four plates, mounding them on top of the bean puree. Finish each dish with a squeeze of lemon, a drizzle of olive oil, and a few turns of pepper.

Andrew's Note: After making the bean puree, you will have a good amount of cooked beans left over. They'll keep in the fridge for 5 to 6 days, and they make a great addition to soups and salads. Or, for a delicious spread or dip, mash them up with garlic, extra-virgin olive oil, some chopped parsley, lemon juice, coarse sea salt, and freshly cracked black pepper.

Sautéed Squid with Garlic, Lemon, and Chili

This utterly simple recipe brings the beauty of squid to the forefront. It's the kind of dish you could imagine eating at a little restaurant right on the beach—and its garlicky, saline flavor always reminds us that even on Flatbush Avenue in the heart of Brooklyn, the Atlantic Ocean isn't that far away.

This is a dish that begs for a glass of cold, refreshing white wine or pale rosé to go with it, so you might want to have one at the ready before the squid hit the pan.

SERVES 4

1 large garlic clove, minced
½ teaspoon minced jarred Calabrian chili
  (see Resources, page 357)
1 tablespoon fresh lemon juice
2 tablespoons extra-virgin olive oil

¼ teaspoon kosher salt, plus more to taste
1½ pounds cleaned squid
2 tablespoons safflower or canola oil, plus
  more if needed

| FISH |

In a large bowl, whisk together the garlic, chili, lemon juice, olive oil, and salt.

Rinse the squid under cool running water; drain. Cut the bodies into ³⁄₁₆-inch-wide rings; leave the tentacles whole. Transfer to a paper towel and pat dry completely, then transfer to a plate.

Place a large skillet over high heat and let it get very hot, heating it for a good 5 minutes. Add 1 tablespoon safflower oil to the skillet and heat until hot but not smoking. Season the squid with salt, slide half of it into the pan, and sear, without moving, for 1 minute. Flip the squid and cook for 30 seconds more. (Do not overcrowd the pan; if your skillet doesn't hold the squid comfortably, cook it in smaller batches, using additional oil if needed.) Repeat with the remaining safflower oil and squid. Transfer to the bowl with the garlic mixture and toss to coat. Serve immediately.

Andrew's Note: Achieving a nice sear on the squid is all about getting it thoroughly dry before sliding it into your very hot skillet. Paper towels do a great job of soaking up the moisture, but once the squid is dry, be sure to remove it from the paper towels—they tend to cling after a while and you'll be stuck picking away little bits of towel from the squid.

Tuna Sott'Olio with Shell Beans and Potatoes

Salt-cured overnight and then ever-so-gently confited in extra-virgin olive oil, this tuna takes on a silky richness. This dish was a great way to get our kids started out on seafood.

SERVES 4

FOR THE TUNA CONFIT
1 pound center-cut albacore tuna
1 teaspoon kosher salt
½ teaspoon fennel pollen
3 cups extra-virgin olive oil

FOR THE BEANS
1¼ pounds fresh cranberry beans, shelled
 (about 2 cups)
1 tablespoon kosher salt
1 rosemary sprig
1 garlic clove
1 tablespoon extra-virgin olive oil

FOR THE POTATOES
10 ounces fingerling potatoes, peeled
2 tablespoons kosher salt
1 thyme sprig
1 rosemary sprig
1 head garlic, split horizontally

1 medium red onion, cut in half and
 sliced lengthwise ⅛ inch thick
4 teaspoons fresh lemon juice,
 plus more for drizzling
2 tablespoons extra-virgin olive oil,
 plus more for drizzling
¼ teaspoon kosher salt
¼ teaspoon freshly cracked black pepper
¾ cup flat-leaf parsley leaves
Flaky sea salt, such as Maldon

Cut the tuna into 2 equal pieces. Season with the salt on both sides and sprinkle the fennel pollen on one side. Transfer to a plate, cover, and let sit overnight in the refrigerator.

The next day, preheat the oven to 200°F. Pat the tuna dry and place it in a baking pan that will just barely hold it. Pour the olive oil over the fish and bake until the fish has just cooked through and is opaque (about 115°F), 25 to 35 minutes. Let cool, making sure the oil completely covers the fish (add more oil if needed), then refrigerate. (The tuna can be stored in the refrigerator for up to 2 weeks.)

To make the beans: In a small pot, combine the beans with 1½ cups water and bring to a gentle simmer. Stir in the salt, rosemary, garlic, and olive oil. Cover and cook over low heat until the beans are creamy, 25 to 40 minutes. Remove from the heat and discard the garlic and rosemary. Cool the beans in their cooking liquid. (The beans can be made ahead and refrigerated in an airtight container for up to 5 days.)

To make the potatoes: Place the potatoes in a small pot, add 5 cups water, and heat over medium-high heat until the potatoes just come to a boil. Add the salt, herbs, and garlic, reduce the heat to low, and cook gently until the potatoes offer no resistance when poked with a knife, about 20 minutes. Remove the potatoes from the liquid. Strain the liquid into a bowl and let cool. When the potatoes are cool, cut them into ¼-inch-thick rounds. Add to the cool liquid and set aside. (The potatoes can be prepared up to 1 day ahead and stored in the refrigerator.)

When ready to serve, remove the tuna from the oil and let stand at room temperature for 45 minutes.

Break the tuna into bite-sized pieces. Drain the potatoes and beans and combine in a bowl. Toss with the onion, lemon juice, olive oil, salt, and pepper. Gently fold in the parsley and divide among four plates. Top with the tuna. Sprinkle with a small pinch of sea salt, a crack of pepper, and a few drops of lemon juice, and drizzle with olive oil.

Mussels with White Beans and Finocchiona

As Andrew and I were discussing recipes for this chapter, we came to this dish and I declared, "This is a great one-pot meal!" Though Andrew countered with "Who ever actually uses one pot? Have I ever used only one pot?," I still maintain that this could be prepared, start to finish, in a single big pot—if you've got the beans already cooked.

This serves six as an appetizer, but augmented by a large, leafy green salad and some crusty bread, this hearty, stew-like dish would make a lovely main course for four. Mussels are wonderful to cook with, as their liquor is almost a ready-made sauce. And since fennel, with all its herbaceous sweetness, is a delicious companion for mussels, we take it all the way, using finocchiona (a fennel-flavored salami) along with fennel seeds and a generous pour of Strega or Pernod.

SERVES 4 TO 6

¾ cup extra-virgin olive oil
6 ounces finocchiona (cured fennel sausage), **removed from the casing and cut into 1-by-½-inch-thick batons** (1½ cups)
12 garlic cloves, smashed and peeled
¾ teaspoon fennel seed
¾ teaspoon chili flakes
¼ cup Strega or Pernod

2 cups chopped canned San Marzano tomatoes
1½ cups dry white wine
3½ cups cooked Controne or cannellini beans with their cooking liquid
2 pounds mussels, scrubbed and debearded
1 cup chopped flat-leaf parsley
Toasted crusty bread for serving

In a large Dutch oven, heat 6 tablespoons of the olive oil over medium-high heat. Add the sausage and garlic and let them brown for a minute or two. Stir in the fennel seeds and chili flakes and cook until fragrant. Stir in the Strega and tomatoes and simmer until most of the liquid cooks off. Add the white wine and simmer for 10 minutes.

Stir in the beans, with their cooking liquid, and bring to a boil. Add the mussels, cover, and cook until they have opened, about 5 minutes. Stir in the parsley. Ladle the mussel mixture into individual serving dishes and drizzle each with a tablespoon of olive oil. Serve with toasted bread.

Andrew's Note: Cleaning mussels doesn't have to be a chore, and the smaller Bouchot variety are particularly easy, as their "beards" are pretty insignificant. At Franny's, we speed through pounds and pounds of mussels by simply scrubbing the beards off with a very coarse sponge (I use the thin, green abrasive sponges made by 3M). Be sure to scrub the mussels just before you cook them—they'll die pretty quickly once their beards are removed.

| FISH |

MEAT

Back before there was a Franny's, before we became immersed in pizza, Andrew had another obsession that was part of our lives for years: cured meats.

I don't mean just that he ate a lot of cured meats—which he did. I mean he cured meats at home, using our kitchen as a laboratory and our bathroom as a meat curing room. We had moved to Great Barrington, Massachusetts, to get out of the city for a while, and our shower became Andrew's space of choice for aging all of his experiments. We kept a humidifier running nonstop to create the right moist atmosphere. Every morning when I was brushing my teeth, there'd be something like a cured leg of pork or a string of sausages over my shoulder, reflecting back at me in the mirror.

At the time, there wasn't a lot of information out there on the science of cured meats, especially for Italian *salumi*. Most of the knowledge in Italy was simply handed down from generation to generation. Andrew picked up the basics while we were working at Savoy restaurant with Peter Hoffman, who cured meats in a humidity-and-temperature-controlled wine room. These house-cured meats whetted our appetites for more when we left the restaurant.

After we moved to the Berkshires, Andrew continued his curing education through trial and error. We went through a lot of meat, and a lot of humidifiers. There were some fantastic triumphs, and some sadly inedible failures. In the process, Andrew learned a lot. And eventually I got my bathroom back.

In addition to those dry-aged pork explorations, Andrew came up with recipes for simpler homemade cured meats that don't require temperature-and-humidity-controlled aging. Cured ham, homemade porchetta, and a pork-cheek-and-beef-tongue terrine are staples at Franny's and Bklyn Larder, along with fresh (uncured) homemade sausages and meatballs. All of these are relatively straightforward to make at home—no humidifiers required. These are the recipes you'll find in this chapter.

The advantages of making your own cured meats and fresh sausages include not only being able control the flavors, but also being able to control all the ingredients. There's no doubt that the best-tasting meat comes from heritage breeds raised by small-scale farmers who care deeply about their animals. This kind of meat is worth seeking out. Farmers' markets are good bets, and you can also order it online (see Resources, page 357).

And by making your own fresh sausages, you'll know that they're free of the kinds of additives you find in so many commercial products. Citric acid, nonfat dried milk solids, questionable fillers, and even MSG are all common ingredients. There's really no reason to eat that stuff when making fresh sausage from scratch is not *that* hard to do, and the results are so utterly divine.

In this chapter, you'll find recipes for many types of fresh sausage, including one that doesn't even require a casing—so it's basically as easy as mixing up meatballs. The Pork Sausage (page 185) is quick to pull together, and when it's browned and tossed into Maccheroni with Pork Sausage and Broccoli Rabe (page 206), it's leagues better than even the finest sausages you can buy.

Once you have a sense of how sausages are made, the basic recipes are easy to tweak to your own tastes; you can increase or decrease the salt and chilies, or rejigger the herbs and spices. You can also personalize sausages by how you garnish them. In late summer, you could grill your homemade pork sausages and top them with silky red peppers (see page 180). In the depths of winter, try sautéed greens (see page 180), which cut through the richness of roasted pork fat.

Our Porchetta (page 188) is equally special in a very different way. A rolled log of pork belly and butterflied loin, it's rubbed with fennel pollen, rosemary, lemon, and garlic and roasted until burnished and fragrant. We like to let it cool, then slice it thin and layer it onto sandwiches. But it can also be served hot from the oven and mahogany brown, making for stunning dinner-party fare.

Homemade porchetta—and, for that matter, home-cured ham (see page 186) or Pork Cheek and Beef Tongue Terrine (page 193)—is an intense, multiday project. These are the kind of recipes to attempt when you really want to stretch yourself as a cook. They take time and planning, and some of the ingredients might take some searching out (that half a pig's head in the terrine, for example). But they are worthwhile endeavors—impressive and spectacular to eat—and fun to make if you like nose-to-tail cooking adventures. Of the three, the porchetta is the easiest (you don't need to inject the meat with brine), followed by the ham and then the

terrine. Any true cured-meat devotee will welcome the challenge.

On the simpler end of the spectrum are the Meatballs (page 197). You might not believe that such a straightforward recipe could produce something so outrageously tasty, but try them once, and you'll be devising all sorts of ways to include them in your cooking. They're an integral part of the Tomato, Mozzarella, and Meatball Pizza (page 270), but they're marvelous any time a desire for meatballs hits.

And although you might think otherwise, making your own pancetta (see page 192) is not really any more difficult than making meatballs (it does take time to cure, but there's no work involved in letting it rest for 10 days). It's something any pancetta lover should do at least once, because the payoff is tremendous—a rich and porky piece of meat with deep notes of garlic and rosemary.

All of the recipes in this chapter depend on sourcing high-quality meat. We recommend developing a relationship with a good butcher and asking questions about how the meat is raised. You want to make sure you're starting out with the best ingredients you can get. In the end, your own cured meats, sausages, and meatballs will be so much more flavorful and satisfying than anything you can buy, and you'll happily relish every bite.

Roasted Pork Sausage

Anyone who loves to cook will enjoy the process of making sausage. Once you have the equipment, it isn't hard to do, and it is immensely satisfying. And you can control all the ingredients—everything from the kind of meat to the percentage of fat to the types and amounts of seasonings. We wanted a full-flavored pork sausage that tasted deeply of the heritage pork we use to make it, without spices or other distractions. We add just a touch of Parmigiano-Reggiano to bring out the pork flavor. We suggest that you make this recipe first as written and then, when you get a feel for sausage making, vary it to suit your taste, adding spices such as chili flakes, fennel seed, or black pepper.

There is a learning curve to making sausage, and it does take practice for everything to come out perfectly (for tips, see Sausage Techniques, page 182). The hardest part is filling the casings. You want them full and firm so there aren't air pockets, but not so full that they will explode. However, sausage casings are extremely sturdy, and if you do pop one, just start over with a fresh casing, scraping the meat back into the stuffer so you don't lose any of it.

We grind our own sausage meat, but you can have the butcher grind it for you.

MAKES ABOUT EIGHTEEN 6-INCH LINKS (ABOUT 5½ POUNDS)

FOR THE SAUSAGES
4¼ pounds ground pork shoulder, chilled
10 ounces ground pork belly, chilled
6 ounces Parmigiano-Reggiano,
  finely grated (about 1½ cups)
3 tablespoons kosher salt
5 large garlic cloves, minced
  (about 2 tablespoons)

1 tablespoon freshly cracked black pepper
1½ teaspoons sugar
¼ cup ice water

Natural hog casings (see Resources,
  page 357), **soaked and flushed**
  (see page 182)
Extra-virgin olive oil

To make the sausages: In a large bowl, combine all the ingredients. Using your hands (wear gloves, if you like), fold and mix until all the ingredients are well distributed and the meat and fat bind together. When the mixture becomes noticeably stiff and sticky and starts to leave a greasy film on the sides of the bowl, stop mixing. Undermixing can lead to a dry, crumbly texture and overmixing can lead to tough, rubbery sausages, so you want to make sure the meat is properly mixed.

Slide the entire length of one casing onto the stuffer tube of the sausage maker. Tie a knot in the end of the casing or secure tightly with kitchen twine. (See Sausage Techniques, page 182.) Use a sausage pricker, a pushpin, or a thin needle to poke a few holes in the end of the casing.

With the motor running at medium speed, use one hand to slowly feed the ground meat mixture into the hopper of your sausage maker and the other hand to help guide the meat as it fills the casing. Do not work too quickly, or the casing will overfill and burst. The sausage should feel plump and firm but have a small amount of space to allow for expansion during cooking. When you near the last 3 inches of casing, stop feeding the hopper with meat and remove the sausage from the stuffing tube.

continued

Place the sausage on a large work surface. Tie it tightly with kitchen twine at 6-inch intervals to form individual links. Trim any loose ends of twine. Knot the open end of the casing securely. Using the sausage pricker, pushpin, or needle, prick the sausage casing all over to release air bubbles. Repeat with another casing if necessary.

To cook the sausages: Preheat the oven to 500°F. Bring a large pot of water to a very delicate simmer. Add the sausages (in batches if necessary) and poach just until opaque and firm, about 5 minutes. (At this point, the sausages can be cooled and kept covered in the fridge for up to 5 days.)

Cut the sausages into links and lightly oil them. Arrange on a rimmed baking sheet and roast, turning occasionally, until golden and cooked through, 10 to 12 minutes. (Alternatively, you can sear the sausages in a little oil in a skillet on one side until they turn very brown, about 5 minutes, then flip them and finish them in a 450°F oven until cooked through, about 5 minutes longer. Roasting is easier, but they tend to pick up better color when you sear them first.)

Serving Suggestions

Roasted Green Cabbage: Cut a small green cabbage lengthwise into 8 equal wedges. Pack into a baking pan that holds them in a tight single layer. Sprinkle the cabbage lightly with salt and let it stand for 15 minutes.

Drizzle the cabbage with ½ cup extra-virgin olive oil and sprinkle with ½ teaspoon Controne or other chili flakes. Pour ⅓ cup water over. Cover the pan with foil and bake at 350°F for 45 minutes.

Remove the foil and continue to bake until the water has evaporated and the cabbage is golden, 10 to 20 minutes. Drizzle with 1½ tablespoons red wine vinegar and sprinkle with several turns of cracked black pepper. Serve the hot sausages on top of the cabbage.

Broccoli Rabe: Sauté 3 smashed garlic cloves in ¼ cup extra-virgin olive oil until fragrant and just starting to color. Add ¼ teaspoon chili flakes and 8 cups broccoli rabe. Season with kosher salt and freshly cracked black pepper and sauté until the rabe is wilted and tender, about 5 minutes. Serve alongside the sausages, drizzled with lemon juice and olive oil.

Arugula: Toss 4 cups arugula with 3 tablespoons extra-virgin olive oil, 2 teaspoons fresh lemon juice, and kosher salt and freshly cracked black pepper to taste. Serve with the sausages.

Roasted Peppers: Serve the sausages with the Roasted Peppers on page 30 (don't add the anchovies and capers).

Andrew's Note: The sausage attachment for the KitchenAid (see Resources, page 357) works pretty well for smaller batches of sausage (up to 5 pounds). The only issue is that the equipment tends to heat up from the motor after it's been running for a while, and then when the raw sausage mixture comes in contact with it, the heat will emulsify some of the fat (this hot fat is called "smear"), producing crumbly, unevenly textured sausages. To help avoid smear, chill your attachments as well as your sausage mixture in the fridge for at least an hour before stuffing the casings. And work with purpose so the machine doesn't overheat. This is especially important if your kitchen is very warm.

Fennel Sausage

We developed this assertive sausage as a pizza topping for the Tomato, Mozzarella, and Sausage Pizza (page 269), where it adds a spicy intensity to the cheese and sweet tomato sauce. Made with plenty of garlic, cracked pepper, and red chili, along with the fennel, it's more heavily seasoned than our other sausages. Pan-seared and served hot, it's excellent with soft polenta. Or tuck it into toasted rolls, with some roasted sweet peppers and onions, for a classic sandwich. Wherever you use it, fennel sausage will lend loads of deeply spiced porky flavor.

MAKES ABOUT TEN 6-INCH LINKS (ABOUT 3 POUNDS)

FOR THE SAUSAGES
2 pounds, 10 ounces ground pork shoulder, chilled
6 ounces ground pork belly, chilled
2 tablespoons kosher salt
1 tablespoon finely chopped garlic
2 teaspoons freshly cracked black pepper
1½ teaspoons fennel seeds

½ teaspoon chili flakes
¼ cup ice water

Natural hog casings (see Resources, page 357), **soaked and flushed** (see page 182)
2 tablespoons extra-virgin olive oil

To make the sausages: In a large bowl, combine all the ingredients. Using your hands (wear gloves, if you like), fold and mix together until all the ingredients are well distributed and the meat and fat bind together. When the mixture becomes noticeably stiff and sticky and starts to leave a greasy film on the sides of the bowl, stop mixing. Undermixing can lead to a dry, crumbly texture and overmixing can lead to tough, rubbery sausages, so you want to make sure the meat is properly mixed.

Slide the entire length of one casing onto the stuffer tube of the sausage maker. Tie a knot in the end of the casing or secure tightly with kitchen twine. (See Sausage Techniques, page 182.) Use a sausage pricker, a pushpin, or a thin needle to poke a few holes in the end of the casing.

With the motor running at medium speed, use one hand to slowly feed the ground meat mixture into the hopper of your sausage maker and the other hand to help guide the meat as it fills the casing. Do not work too quickly, or the casing

will overfill and burst. The sausage should feel plump and firm but have a small amount of space to allow for expansion during cooking. When you near the last 3 inches of casing, stop feeding the hopper with meat and remove the sausage from the stuffing tube.

Place the sausage on a large work surface. Tie it tightly with kitchen twine at 6-inch intervals to form individual links. Trim any loose ends of twine. Knot the open end of the casing securely. Using the sausage pricker, pushpin, or needle, prick the sausage casing all over to release air bubbles. (The sausages can be refrigerated, well wrapped, for up to 5 days.)

To cook the sausages: Preheat the oven to 400°F. Cut the sausages into links and lightly oil them. Heat an ovenproof skillet over high heat. Add as many sausages as fit comfortably in the pan and sear until well browned on both sides, about 2 minutes per side. Transfer to the oven and roast until cooked through, about 8 minutes. (If using for pizza, let cool before slicing.)

Sausage Techniques

1. Hog casings are sold dried and salted, and you can find them online (see Resources, page 357). Before making sausages, you need to soak the casings to make them soft and pliable, then flush them with cold water to make sure they are completely rinsed of all residual salt.

2. Unravel the casings and soak them in a large bowl of cool water for 1 hour. Take one casing and fit one end snugly over the faucet in your kitchen sink. Run cool water through the casing for a minute or so to flush it. Transfer the casing to a small bowl of cool water to keep it moist; let one end of the casing hang over the edge of the bowl so that you can easily find it when it's time to stuff. Repeat with the remaining casings.

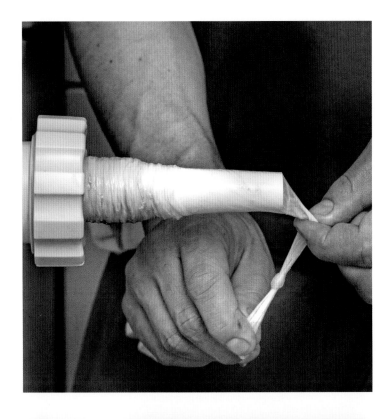

3. If the casings have dried out at all, dip them in water; they need to be well lubricated to easily slide onto the stuffer. Slide the entire length of a casing onto the sausage stuffer, bunching it up and pushing it forward as you go. Then tie a knot at the end.

4. Leave at least 3 inches of unstuffed casing to allow for expansion during tying. Tie the sausage tightly with kitchen twine at 6-inch intervals to form individual links, then tie the open end.

Baked Sausage and Polenta

Essentially a gratin, this dish has a layer of savory ragu rich with homemade sausage (easily made without casings) and dried porcini, another of creamy polenta, and a topping of melted, browned Parmigiano-Reggiano. It's ideal for parties or potlucks, since you can prepare it ahead of time and then bake it when you need it. It also reheats perfectly.

We came up with the recipe to offer at Bklyn Larder, and even though it's fairly wintry fare, it's available all year round. Our customers are devoted to this polenta dish and would holler mightily if we didn't have any in the case—it's become a go-to for folks on their way home from work. Pair it with something lively and fresh such as Citrus Salad with Pistachios, Olives, and Chilies (page 92) or a green salad, and you've got a great weeknight meal.

SERVES 6 TO 8

FOR THE SAUSAGE
1½ pounds ground pork shoulder, chilled
1 tablespoon kosher salt
2¼ tablespoons freshly cracked
  black pepper
2 tablespoons ice water

FOR THE RAGU
¼ ounce (about 2 tablespoons) **dried porcini**
½ cup hot water
½ white onion, finely chopped
2 garlic cloves, finely chopped
¾ teaspoon chopped sage
½ teaspoon finely chopped rosemary
½ cup dry red wine
1 cup chopped canned San Marzano
  tomatoes, drained
2 cups water

FOR THE POLENTA
5½ cups water
1 tablespoon kosher salt
1½ cups polenta
1 cup heavy cream
2 ounces Grana Padano or Parmigiano-
  Reggiano, finely grated
  (about ½ cup)
5 tablespoons unsalted butter, cubed
⅛ teaspoon freshly cracked black pepper

1 ounce Parmigiano-Reggiano, finely grated
(about ¼ cup)

To make the sausage: In a large bowl, combine the pork, salt, pepper, and ice water. Using your hands (wear gloves, if you like), fold and mix together until all the ingredients are well distributed and the meat and fat bind together. When the mixture becomes noticeably stiff and sticky and starts to leave a greasy film on the sides of the bowl, stop mixing. Undermixing can lead to a dry, crumbly texture and overmixing can lead to tough, rubbery sausages, so you want to make sure the meat is properly mixed.

To make the ragu: In a small bowl, stir together the porcini and hot water. Let the mushrooms stand until they are soft and pliable, 20 to 30 minutes. With a slotted spoon, lift out the mushrooms and chop them, then return them to their soaking liquid.

Heat a large skillet over medium-high heat. Brown the sausage in batches, breaking up the meat as it cooks. Remove the cooked sausage with a slotted spoon and transfer it to a paper-towel-lined plate to drain.

When all the sausage is cooked, pour most of the fat from the pan, leaving about 2 tablespoons. Add the onion and garlic and cook until soft, about 10 minutes. Stir in the sage, rosemary, and mushrooms and their liquid. Pour in the wine and cook, scraping up any browned bits in the bottom of the skillet, until the wine has evaporated by about half. Stir in the tomatoes and 2 cups water, bring to a simmer, and simmer gently over medium heat until the sauce is thickened but not dry, about 20 minutes. Keep warm. (The ragu can be cooled, transferred to airtight containers, and refrigerated for up to 5 days. Heat through before using; the sauce is easier to spread when it is warm.)

To make the polenta: In a medium pot, bring the water and salt to a boil. Slowly whisk in the polenta. Simmer over low heat, stirring often,

until tender and thickened, about 20 minutes. Stir in the cream, cheese, and butter and cook for 10 more minutes. Stir in the pepper and remove from the heat.

Lightly oil a 2-quart gratin dish. Spread half the polenta in an even layer in the bottom of the dish. Top with the warm ragu and the sausage, then top with the remaining polenta. Let the casserole stand at room temperature to firm up for at least 2 hours, and up to 6.

Preheat the oven to 450°F. Sprinkle the Parmigiano-Reggiano on top of the casserole and bake until brown and bubbly, 45 minutes to 1 hour. Serve warm. (The casserole can be cooled or refrigerated for up to 5 days; reheat in a 325°F oven until hot and bubbling.)

Pork Sausage

Making this sausage is a breeze—no stuffing involved. We like to sear it up nice and brown and toss it into Maccheroni with Pork Sausage and Broccoli Rabe (page 206), where the little bites of crisp, succulent pork are a great contrast to the bitter greens. But don't stop there—this sausage is so simple and richly flavored, it's ready to be included in all sorts of recipes, especially risottos, ragus, and pasta dishes. Store it in ½-pound packages in the freezer and pull it out when the sausage urge strikes.

MAKES ABOUT 2 POUNDS

1¾ pounds ground pork shoulder, chilled
4 ounces ground pork belly, chilled
¾ teaspoon sugar

4 teaspoons kosher salt
1½ teaspoons cracked black pepper
¼ cup ice water

In a large bowl, combine all the ingredients. Using your hands (wear gloves, if you like), fold and mix together until all the ingredients are well distributed and the meat and fat bind together. When the mixture becomes noticeably stiff and sticky and starts to leave a greasy film on the sides of the bowl, stop mixing. Undermixing can

lead to a dry, crumbly texture and overmixing can lead to tough, rubbery sausages, so you want to make sure the meat is properly mixed. The mixture can be stored, well wrapped, for up to 5 days in the refrigerator or frozen for up to 6 months.

Ham

Traditional *prosciutto cotto* (cooked ham) starts its life as a whole pig leg. At Franny's, we butcher the leg ourselves, but at home, it's easier to buy a 7-pound boned, skinned fresh ham from a butcher and proceed from there. You will need a brining needle (see Resources, page 357), but other than that, it's simply a matter of letting the meat brine for a few days before tying and roasting it. The roasted ham will keep for up to 2 weeks (or longer in the freezer), and you'll be blown away by the results. This is the ham we created for the Prosciutto Cotto, Caciocavallo, and Roasted Pepper Pizza (page 272), but it would make a great addition to an antipasti plate or an earthy vegetable or bean soup, or just slice it for the best ham sandwich you can imagine.

MAKES 5½ TO 6 POUNDS

FOR THE BRINE
8 cups water
393 grams (about 2½ cups) **kosher salt**
237 grams (about 1 cup plus 2 tablespoons)
  sugar
2 onions, halved
8 garlic cloves, smashed and peeled
4 bay leaves
3 dried chiles de árbol
2 teaspoons black peppercorns

36 grams Cure #1 (aka pink curing salt;
  see Andrew's Note, page 192)
6 quarts ice water

**One 7-pound piece boneless, skinless fresh
  ham** (pork leg), **preferably ham sirloin**
  (fat left on)
1 bunch rosemary
1 bunch sage

To make the brine: In a large pot, combine the 8 cups water, salt, sugar, onion, garlic, bay leaves, chiles, and peppercorns. Bring to a simmer and simmer until the sugar and salt are completely dissolved and the onions are soft, about 5 minutes. Remove from the heat and stir in the pink curing salt. Cool completely. (The brine should be very cold when you add the meat.)

Pour the ice water into a receptacle large enough to hold the meat and brine. Add the cooled brine. Add the meat. Cover tightly with plastic wrap or a tight-fitting lid and refrigerate for 24 hours.

Remove the meat from the brine. Fill a brining needle with some of the brine and inject it all over the ham at 1-inch intervals, refilling the needle with more brine for each injection. The meat should feel swollen and firm and filled with brine. Return to the container of brine, cover, and refrigerate for 4 more days.

When ready to cook the ham, remove it from the refrigerator and let stand for 2 to 3 hours so it can come up to room temperature.

Preheat the oven to 300°F. Remove the ham from the brine and pat it dry. Roll the ham into a uniformly shaped bundle (with the fat on the outside) and tie it all around, both crosswise and lengthwise, with butcher twine at 1½-inch intervals, tying the twine as tightly as possible. (The twine should have a net-like appearance when finished.) Stick the rosemary and sage bunches under the twine on the bottom of the ham.

Place the ham on a rack set over a roasting pan. Roast until the meat reaches an internal temperature of 115°F, about 2 hours and 15 minutes.

Increase the oven temperature to 475°F and roast until the meat reaches 135°F, about 30 minutes more; check the temperature every 15 minutes, as the timing may vary. Remove the herbs. Thinly slice to serve.

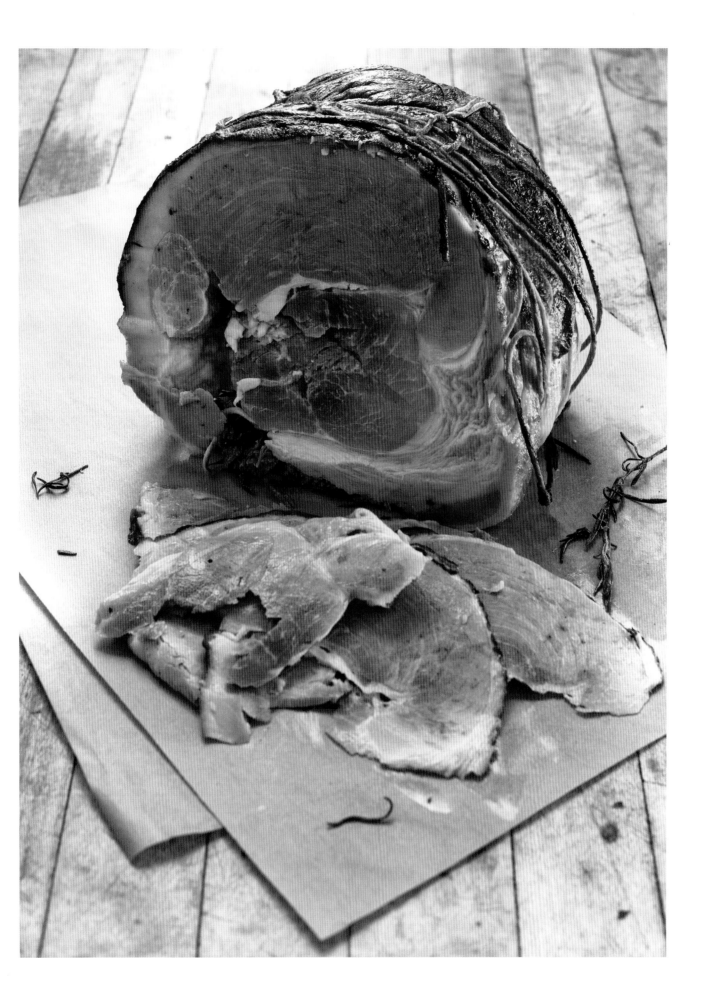

Porchetta

Porchetta is a classic street food in Italy, served from carts and food trucks. Every region has its own version, but most feature fennel and garlic to flavor the pork. In Italy, porchetta is usually made from an entire pig that is deboned, seasoned, rolled up, and slow-roasted until the skin is burnished and crisp. This one is a bit different—we don't use a whole pig, and there's no skin involved. Instead, we roll up the loin (one of the leanest cuts) with the belly (one of the fattiest cuts), spiraling an aromatic paste of rosemary, fennel, lemon, and garlic inside. It's a much more friendly approach for cooking at home, and the result is elegantly rustic fare. We created the recipe to serve thinly sliced as a salumi, but it's also great still hot and glistening brown as a main course, paired with an assertive green salad such as Puntarelle alla Romana (page 94). Then carve up the leftovers the next day and layer them onto crusty bread rubbed with garlic and oil for sandwiches—you'll get at least two superb meals from one gorgeous roast. (If you are planning to primarily serve this hot, and will use it all within 5 days, you can skip the curing in the brine.)

SERVES 10 TO 12

FOR THE BRINE
8 cups water
424 grams (about 2⅔ cups) **kosher salt**
257 grams (about 1¼ cups) **sugar**
2 onions, halved
8 garlic cloves, smashed and peeled
4 bay leaves
3 dried chiles de árbol
2 teaspoons black peppercorns
40 grams Cure #1 (aka pink curing salt; see Andrew's Note, page 192)
6 quarts ice water

One 6¼-pound slab skinless, boneless pork belly
One 3½-pound boneless pork loin roast (butterflied by your butcher; have him leave a ¼-inch fat cap)
2 tablespoons fennel pollen
3 tablespoons finely chopped rosemary
6 garlic cloves, finely chopped
Finely grated zest of 5 lemons
3 tablespoons extra-virgin olive oil

To make the brine: In a large pot, combine the 8 cups water, salt, sugar, onions, garlic, bay leaves, chiles, and peppercorns. Bring to a simmer and simmer, stirring, until the sugar and salt are completely dissolved and the onions are soft. Remove from the heat and stir in the pink curing salt, if using, until dissolved. Cool completely. (The brine should be very cold when you add the meat.)

Pour the ice water into a receptacle large enough to hold the meats and brine. Add the cooled brine.

Place the pork belly fat side down on a large work surface. Using a sharp knife, make long, shallow cuts in the meat (about 1 inch apart) to form a crosshatch pattern. Transfer the pork belly and the loin to the container with the brine. Cover tightly with plastic wrap or a tight-fitting lid and refrigerate for 3 days.

When ready to cook the porchetta, remove the meat from the brine and let stand for 2 to 3 hours so it can come up to room temperature.

continued

188

In a small bowl, stir together the fennel pollen, rosemary, garlic, and lemon zest. Mash in the olive oil until the mixture forms a thick paste.

Preheat the oven to 300°F. Place the belly and loin fat side down on a work surface. Rub the garlic mixture into the surface of the meat, leaving a 1-inch border all around so that the filling doesn't leak out during cooking.

Turn the belly so that its wider end faces you. Arrange the loin on top of the pork at the end closest to you. Roll the belly tightly up around the loin and secure it as tightly as possible in the center with a piece of kitchen twine. (This works best if you have two people doing it, one to hold the meat in place while the other does the tying.) Use two or more pieces of twine to secure the ends of the roll. Then tie the meat at about 1-inch intervals. It should have a tight, almost sausage-like appearance with no bulges.

Transfer the porchetta to a rack set over a roasting pan. Roast until the meat reaches an internal temperature of 115°F, about 1 hour and 45 minutes.

Increase the oven temperature to 500°F and roast until the meat reaches an internal temperature of 135°F, 30 to 45 minutes longer. Let cool completely.

Thinly slice the porchetta to serve. Leftovers will keep in the fridge for up to 5 days if you haven't used the pink salt, and up to 10 days if you have.

Andrew's Note: Talk to your butcher to get the right cuts for this recipe. The actual weights of the two pieces are less important than the measurements, as long as together they weigh exactly 9¾ pounds total (this is important in order for the meat to brine properly with the amount of pink salt given in this recipe). Tell the butcher that you want to be able to roll up the loin in the piece of pork belly so that the belly completely covers the loin. (This is so the fat from the belly can baste the lean loin as the whole thing roasts.) The belly should be as wide as the loin is long so you don't have either the ends of the loin sticking out or too much belly overhanging at the ends.

Porchetta Techniques

1. Arrange the pork belly so that its wider end faces you. Arrange the loin on top of the pork. Roll the belly up over the loin as tightly as possible, tucking the loin into the belly if it starts to creep out.

2. Tie a piece of twine around the center of the roll to secure the meat (as tightly as possible). Use 2 more pieces of twine to secure either end of the roll. Then tie the meat at about 1-inch intervals. It should have a tight, almost sausage-like appearance, with no bulges.

Fresh-Cured Pancetta

Of all the cured pork products you could make, pancetta is the easiest—the gateway meat to the world of salumi. The process is simple and straightforward. After you season the pork belly with rosemary, curing salt, kosher salt, pepper, and garlic, all that's really required is patience: it takes a week to 10 days for the pork to cure and absorb the aromatic flavors. We love to drape thin, crisp slices over herb-butter-topped crostini (page 14). But pancetta is also fantastic in pastas (for example, as a substitute for the hard-to-find guanciale in Mezze Maniche with Guanciale, Chilies, and Ricotta, page 228) and ragus, and it's terrific crisped up and tossed into salads or pasta. Trust us, once you've got homemade pancetta on hand, you'll find plenty of places to use it. And it freezes beautifully for up to 6 months.

MAKES 2 POUNDS

2 pounds boneless, skinless pork belly
2 tablespoons kosher salt
3 grams Cure #1 (aka pink curing salt;
see Andrew's Note)

1½ tablespoons rosemary needles
6 garlic cloves, roughly chopped
1 teaspoon freshly cracked black pepper

Line a small rimmed baking sheet with parchment paper. Place the pork on the pan. In a small cup, combine the kosher and curing salts. Rub half the salt mixture all over the pork—top, sides, and bottom. Let it stand at room temperature until the meat begins to sweat, 5 to 10 minutes. Sprinkle it all over with the remaining salt mixture.

If necessary, turn the pork so it is fat side down, lean side up. Sprinkle the lean side with the rosemary, garlic, and pepper. Cover tightly with plastic wrap and refrigerate overnight.

The next day, the meat will have released a lot of juices. Drain off the liquid and place fresh parchment underneath the meat. Turn the meat fat side up and cover again with plastic wrap. Refrigerate for 7 to 9 days longer (thinner cuts will take less time). To see if it is ready, cut off a small piece and check that it is cured all the way through—it should appear firm, dry to the touch, and more deeply colored than it was originally. Then cook that small piece you just cut off and taste it—the salt will have penetrated all the way to the center if it's fully cured. If not, return the meat to the fridge and check it again in 24 hours.

Andrew's Note: Sodium nitrite, also called Cure #1, Prague powder #1, InstaCure #1, or pink salt, is a preservative. You don't need much, but not only does it extend the shelf life of cured meats, it also gives them a particularly intense flavor and helps keep them from turning brown because of oxidation. You can find it at sausage-making supply stores, and it is easily purchased online (see Resources, page 357). You'll need a scale that can weigh grams for weighing the salt, because a volume measure won't be exact enough. When using curing salt in any of the recipes in the book, it's important to use the exact amounts of meat and salt called for in order for the recipe to work properly; sodium nitrite is a potent chemical, and you need to be careful and precise.

Pork Cheek and Beef Tongue Terrine

Terrines are probably the most elegant members of the salumi family—they are sophisticated, decadent, and refined, and this recipe is no exception. It's based on the Italian *testa* (headcheese), with the addition of chunks of velvety beef tongue. There's no question that this is a big project—you'll need to spread the process out over several days—and it is definitely a major labor of love. And you will need to be able to source half a pig's head to make this, which could take some looking (you will also need a container large enough to hold the pig head, shanks, and 4 gallons of water). But the final product is stunning: rich, silky, and—forgive the pun—heady. If you're someone who likes a challenge and doesn't mind looking dinner in the eye, this recipe is for you.

Once it's made, the terrine will last in the fridge for at least a week, or you can freeze it. This recipe makes two terrines, so you may want to freeze one of them for later. Freezing actually makes it easier to slice. To serve, we like to warm it up slightly so the gelatin in the meat softens, making it luscious and spreadable. People are always excited to see what sort of seasonal accompaniment the Franny's kitchen dreams up for this terrine: in the spring, it's bits of pickled ramps; in the fall, it might be grated fresh horseradish. You could serve it with pickled vegetables or chilies—homemade or something wonderful that you've bought. Caperberries or even cornichons also work well to lend that bright note. A pickle and some toasted good bread is really all you need.

MAKES TWO 8-BY-4-INCH TERRINES; EACH ONE SERVES 12

FOR THE PIG'S HEAD AND SHANKS
½ **pig's head** (about 8 pounds), **cleaned**
5 **pounds skin-on pork shanks**

FOR THE BRINE FOR THE PORK
8 **cups water**
496 **grams** (about 3 cups plus 3 tablespoons)
  kosher salt
374 **grams** (about 1¾ cups) **sugar**
4 **large white onions, halved**
12 **garlic cloves, smashed and peeled**
6 **bay leaves**
6 **dried chiles de árbol**
1½ **tablespoons black peppercorns**
69 **grams Cure #1** (aka pink curing salt)
3½ **gallons** (14 quarts) **ice water**

FOR THE BRINE FOR THE TONGUE
2 **cups water**
116 **grams** (about ⅔ cup) **kosher salt**

50 **grams** (about scant ¼ cup) **sugar**
½ **large white onion**
2 **garlic cloves, smashed and peeled**
1 **bay leaf**
1 **dried chile de árbol**
½ **teaspoon black peppercorns**
10 **grams Cure #1** (aka pink curing salt;
  see Andrew's Note)
6 **cups ice water**

FOR THE BEEF TONGUE
One 2¼-**pound beef tongue**

FOR COOKING THE PORK
2 **large white onions, halved, or more if
  needed**
2 **carrots, peeled and sliced ½ inch thick,
  or more if needed**
2 **celery stalks, sliced ½ inch thick, or more
  if needed**

continued

193

3 bay leaves
3 dried chiles de árbol
1 tablespoon black peppercorns

FOR COOKING THE TONGUE
Two 750-ml bottles dry white wine
¼ cup kosher salt
4 garlic cloves, smashed and peeled
2 bay leaves
2 dried chiles de árbol
1 large white onion, quartered
1 large carrot, diced

1 celery stick, diced
1 teaspoon black peppercorns

FOR SERVING
Flaky sea salt, such as Maldon
Freshly cracked black pepper
Freshly grated horseradish or pickled
  vegetables (such as Pickled Ramps,
  page 353, Pickled Hot Peppers, page 352,
  or Fennel Conserva, page 351)
Toasted country-style bread

Check your pig's head: it should be fairly clean, but if there is a lot of residual hair, use a disposable razor to shave it. The skin adds a nice chewy texture to the terrine, so we try to use as much of it as possible. If the butcher didn't remove the brain, remove and discard it.

To make the brine: In a large pot, combine the 8 cups water, salt, sugar, onion halves, garlic, bay leaves, chiles, and peppercorns. Bring to a simmer and simmer until the sugar and salt are completely dissolved and the onions are soft, about 5 minutes. Remove from the heat and stir in the pink curing salt. Cool completely. (The brine should be very cold before you add the meat.)

Pour the ice water into a receptacle large enough to hold the head, shanks, and brine. Add the cooled brine. Add the head and shanks. Cover tightly with plastic wrap or a tight-fitting lid and refrigerate for 24 hours.

Meanwhile, make the brine for the beef tongue: In a large pot, combine the 2 cups water, salt, sugar, onion, garlic, bay leaf, chile, and peppercorns. Bring to a simmer and simmer until the sugar and salt are completely dissolved and the onions are soft, about 5 minutes. Remove from the heat and stir in the pink curing salt. Cool completely. (The brine should be very cold before you add the meat.)

Pour the ice water into a receptacle large enough to hold the tongue and brine. Add the cooled brine. Add the beef tongue. Cover tightly with plastic wrap or a tight-fitting lid and refrigerate for 24 hours.

The next day, inject the pig's head, shanks, and tongue with brine: Remove the head and shanks from the brine. Fill a brining needle with some of the pork brine and inject it all over the head (especially the cheeks, where there is a lot of meat) and shanks at 1-inch intervals, refilling the needle with more brine for each injection. Return the head and shanks to the brine and refrigerate for 4 more days.

Fill the brining needle with the tongue brine and inject all over the tongue at ½-inch intervals, using the same technique. Return the tongue to the brine and refrigerate for 4 more days.

When ready to cook the pork, remove it from the brine and let stand for 2 to 3 hours so it can come up to room temperature.

Preheat the oven to 500°F. Lay the onions, carrots, and celery in the bottom of a large roasting pan. The bottom of the pan should be completely covered with vegetables so that the pork does not come in contact with the metal surface; add more vegetables if necessary. Scatter the bay leaves, chiles, and peppercorns over the vegetables. Lay the pig's head flat side

continued

down on top of the vegetables, tucking the ears under the head so it doesn't dry out. Add the shanks, skin side down. Pour 3 cups water into the pan. Cover the pan with a double layer of parchment paper and then seal tightly with a double layer of aluminum foil.

Transfer the pan to the oven and cook for 20 minutes. Reduce the temperature to 225°F and roast for 8 hours. The skin should be a burnished mahogany color and the meat should be fork-tender. If it is not, increase the temperature to 300°F and cook until it is tender. Let cool slightly, then transfer the pig's head and shanks to a baking sheet; discard the liquid and vegetables.

While the meat is still warm and pliable, but cool enough to handle, use your hands to pull apart the pork pieces. Have three bowls ready: one for the pieces of meat, which you should break apart into large chunks as you add to the bowl; one for gelatinous material (at Franny's we call this the "goo"), such as fat or soft, sticky skin; and one for waste material, such as glands, veins, grainy bits, gristle, or skin with hair in it. Our rule is that if something doesn't look like you would eat it on the spot, discard it. Slice the pig's ears and add to the bowl of meat. Slice up the tongue and add it to the meat bowl. If not using immediately, cover the bowls of meat and gelatinous material and refrigerate until ready to use.

To cook the beef tongue (you can do this while the pork cooks): Transfer it to a large pot (discard the brine). Add the wine, salt, garlic, bay leaves, chiles, onion, carrot, celery, and peppercorns, then add enough water to cover the tongue by 3 inches and bring to a simmer. Cook, uncovered, at a bare simmer for 4 to 5 hours, until the tongue is very tender; add more hot water if the water level reduces too much (the tongue should stay covered with water). Let the tongue stand in the cooking liquid until cool enough to handle but still warm; the skin will slide off easily while hot but becomes more difficult to remove as it cools.

Starting at the back end of the tongue, peel off the skin. Cut the meat into 1½-inch chunks.

In a food processor, puree the gelatinous pork mixture until smooth. Combine the pig meat and tongue chunks in a large bowl. Add the pureed "goo" and massage it into the meat until the mixture starts to tighten and hold together, about 1 minute.

Line two 8-by-4-inch loaf pans with plastic wrap, leaving an overhang on both sides. Divide the terrine mixture between the pans and press down hard to compress it. Cover with the plastic wrap and bang each pan several times to eliminate air. Weight each terrine down with another pan filled with heavy cans. Refrigerate for at least 8 hours, or overnight. (The terrine will keep for about a week in the fridge. Or, once it is thoroughly chilled, transfer to the freezer and freeze for up to 6 months.)

To serve, unmold the terrines and thinly slice. Place the cold slices on heated plates to help warm them; you don't want the terrine to be hot, just soft, supple, and warm to the touch. You could also put the plates of terrine next to a hot stove to warm them, or heat them in the microwave for about 10 seconds or so per plate. Sprinkle the slices with sea salt and crack black pepper over the tops. Garnish with freshly grated horseradish or pickles and serve with toasted country-style bread.

Andrew's Note: You need 13 pounds of pork here total: if your half pig's head weighs 9 pounds, for example, instead of 8, use 1 pound fewer shanks.

Meatballs

The key component of these light, super-flavorful meatballs is the bread. Instead of using dry bread crumbs (which pull moisture from the meat itself), we soak a cubed country-style loaf in milk to make crumbs that contribute some dairy flavor and a soft texture. With the moisture and binding power of the milk-soaked bread, there's no need to add eggs. The rich pork, sweet veal, and earthy beef all get their due, and they are brightened by fresh lemon zest and sharp cheese; these are spectacular meatballs. They are also relatively easy to make, because instead of frying them, you simply pop a baking sheet of meatballs into a very hot oven and roast them until they're crisp and brown all over. They're great on our pizza, but they'd be excellent just about anywhere—in sliders and sandwiches, with pasta, or on a mound of soft polenta. But you may find yourself devouring them straight from the pan.

MAKES 4 TO 4½ DOZEN MEATBALLS

6 ounces day-old country-style bread, crust removed
¾ cup whole milk
1 pound ground beef, chilled
1 pound ground veal, chilled
1 pound ground pork, chilled
1 cup finely chopped onion

2 ounces Parmigiano-Reggiano, finely grated (about ½ cup)
½ cup chopped flat-leaf parsley
3 garlic cloves, minced
2 tablespoons kosher salt
2¼ teaspoons freshly cracked black pepper
Finely grated zest of 1 lemon
Extra-virgin olive oil

Preheat the oven to 500°F. Cut the bread into ½-inch cubes and place in a bowl. You should have about 4 cups. Pour the milk over and let stand until the bread has absorbed most of the liquid.

In a large bowl, gently fold together the beef, veal, pork, onion, bread, cheese, parsley, garlic, salt, pepper, and lemon zest. Mix only until just combined—keep the mixture as loose as possible.

Roll the meat into Ping Pong–sized balls and place at least an inch apart on two large rimmed baking sheets. It's easiest to shape very cold meat, so if the mixture warms up, chill it again until cold. Brush the meatballs generously with olive oil.

Roast the meatballs, turning several times, until golden and cooked through, about 10 minutes.

Andrew's Note: As you're mixing your meats, bread, and seasonings together, be thorough but gentle. If you're too aggressive and you overmix, your meatballs could end up a little tough. Mix just enough to evenly distribute the ingredients, no more.

PASTA

Everyone thinks that pasta is the easiest thing in the world to cook—you just boil up a big pot of spaghetti, drain, and top with a premade sauce and a handful of grated cheese. It's the last-minute dinner to end all last-minute dinners— quick, easy, satisfying. But the very best pasta dishes are so much more than that: truly al dente noodles that taste of wheat, imbued with the aromatics in the sauce—be it a few cloves of lightly browned garlic and a fat pinch of chili flakes, some ripe tomatoes quickly warmed and glossed with olive oil, or slowly simmered squid spiked with salty capers. In a great pasta dish, all of the elements are integrated and perfectly calibrated—the shape of the noodles and the consistency of the sauce, the type and amount of cheese (if any), the chili heat or lack thereof. They all work together to create a blissful harmony of flavors and textures in the bowl.

Although Andrew and I had been eating pasta our whole lives, it wasn't until he started making it at home in earnest, studying recipes from his favorite Italian cookbooks (by Giuliano Bugialli, Marcella Hazan, and Fred Plotkin), that we started to fully appreciate the differences between a perfectly good pasta dish and a phenomenal one. Ingredients are key, of course. But so is technique. And one of the most important pasta lessons that Andrew ever learned was a classic Italian method for cooking pasta that, for some reason, is not embraced in the United States.

It might be because it's slightly more complicated than the American standard of boil-drain-pour-on-the-marinara. In the States, the first time the pasta meets the sauce is when you twirl it all together with a fork. There is no real unity of flavors—and the noodles are usually overcooked and limp. This is definitely not the case in Italy, where one of the hallmarks of a properly cooked pasta dish is al dente noodles that are seasoned fully with the flavors of the sauce.

Achieving this pasta perfection is a two-step process (see Pasta Techniques, page 214, for more details). Step 1 is to undercook the pasta by about 2 minutes. This ensures that the pasta maintains an essential spine of chewiness. Step 2 is to finish cooking the noodles in the sauce, which, ideally, you've just simmered together in a skillet on another burner. Finishing the pasta in the sauce gives the noodles a chance to meld with and absorb all the good flavors in the pan. It makes for a deeper-tasting dish in which all the ingredients are wedded into a well-balanced whole. It takes practice to get the timing down (you'll need to get to know different shapes and brands of pasta), but once you do, the pasta will emerge supple, intensely flavored, and with a toothsome bite.

Andrew started cooking pasta like this at home way before we opened Franny's,

but we quickly discovered that it was one thing to be able to make, say, a great *cacio e pepe* in our home kitchen, and another thing entirely to do it consistently in a very busy restaurant. After a few months of struggling, we decided to take pasta off the menu until we could remodel the kitchen and put in a proper pasta tank, which we did in a few years. But in your kitchen, the Italian two-step method should work well, and we highly recommend giving it a try, adapting your own favorite pasta recipes, as well as the ones in this chapter.

Most of the recipes you'll find here are based on Italian classics that we've altered to some degree. Andrew always strives to keep the core elements of the original dish intact. His tweaks are subtle, like adding a touch of shrimp stock to bring out the sweet sea flavor in his Spaghettini with Shrimp (page 211) or using aromatic Meyer lemons in his *alla limone* (see page 237). He makes a version of *puttanesca* (see page 216) that omits the tomato but ramps up the flavor of the other ingredients (anchovies, capers, garlic) by browning them thoroughly. For the most part, he leaves well enough alone. Cooks in Italy know what they are doing.

This is also true when it comes to ingredients. In Italy, it's pretty easy to find high-quality pasta made by small artisanal producers in every little supermarket. Luckily, these pastas are becoming more and more available here too. Pasta from artisan producers might cost more, but supporting a true craftsman is well worth the higher price tag, especially since you end up with an excellent product. Frequently the business has been family-run for generations; perhaps the wheat is grown near the same village where the pasta is produced. That pricey bag of artisanal Italian pasta may reflect the livelihood and pride of an entire community. With all that heritage, tradition, and expertise going for it, how could it not be superior?

For dry pasta, we like to buy from the Campagna region, where many of the best Italian pasta producers are located. A town called Gragnano, near Naples, has seven or eight amazing artisanal pasta makers alone.

Italian artisanal dry pasta is made with *grano duro* (hard-grain) durum wheat. It has a golden yellow color and is extruded through rugged bronze dies that in many cases have been in use for decades or longer. It's slowly air-dried for a minimum of 24 hours (and up to 72 hours), helping to make it dense and resilient. Sauce adheres perfectly to its porous, textured surface, and thanks to its density, the pasta holds its shape and toothsome character after cooking.

Industrially made dry pasta, on the other hand, is shoved through Teflon-coated dies, a process that greatly speeds up extrusion and production but results in a reedy, slick (nonstick) noodle. Commercial pasta is also made from a more yielding, cheaper strain of wheat, and it is rapidly dried with heaters, essentially parcooking the noodles. Large-scale industrially made pasta is inferior to artisanal pasta in all respects: it breaks down in water, becoming flabby and mushy, and sauce slides away from its slippery surface.

If you take the time to track down the best pasta and other ingredients and then use the two-step pasta cooking method, you're pretty much guaranteed a fantastic meal. But there are a few final touches that can make it even better, such as finishing a skillet full of well-sauced pasta with an emulsifying spoonful of butter, a fragrant splash of olive oil, a sprinkle of creamy cheese, or a combination of all three. Then, once the pasta is plated, a drizzle of olive oil and maybe a little very coarsely grated cheese will make all the flavors pop. At the end, when you're finished with your meal, you should have no more than a few teaspoons of pasta sauce at the bottom—just enough for a single swipe of your bread to finish everything off.

Bucatini with Ramps

There's always a bit of a frenzy when ramps start showing up at the greenmarkets in spring. After a long, cold winter, it's a treat to bite into something fresh, sharp, and green-tasting, and ramps are some of the first alliums to sprout after the thaw. These leafy wild members of the lily family are a cause for celebration, heralding the real end of winter.

Make this dish with the first ramps of the season—slim, pencil-thin ones. The younger the ramp, the sweeter it is. And when you have tender young ramps, you can separate the tops from the bottoms and use the bulbs whole and unsliced. (As ramps mature and grow, they get bigger, thicker, and tougher, making slicing a necessity; see Andrew's Note on page 18.) Plus, the long, lean shape of a young ramp echoes that of the bucatini, making for a really beautiful presentation full of silky textures.

SERVES 4

6 ounces young ramps, ⅛ to ¼ inch thick, ends trimmed
6 tablespoons unsalted butter
Kosher salt
½ teaspoon chili flakes

1 pound bucatini
¼ cup finely grated Parmigiano-Reggiano
About 3 tablespoons finely grated Pecorino Romano, plus more if desired

Rinse the ramps under cold running water to remove any grit and dry them well on paper towels. Separate the leaves from the bulbs. Cut the dark green leaves into 3-inch pieces and leave the bulbs whole.

In a very large skillet (or a Dutch oven; see page 215 for tips), melt the butter over high heat. Add the ramp bulbs and cook until golden, 2 to 3 minutes. Season with a large pinch of salt and the chili flakes. Add the ramp greens and toss until wilted, about 1 minute. Add 2 tablespoons water to the pan. Remove from the heat.

In a large pot of well-salted boiling water, cook the pasta according to the package instructions until 2 minutes shy of al dente; drain.

Toss the bucatini into the skillet with the ramps, along with the Parmigiano-Reggiano. Cook over medium heat until the pasta is al dente, 1 to 2 minutes, adding more water if the sauce seems dry.

Divide the pasta among four individual serving plates or bowls and finish each with 2 teaspoons or more of Pecorino Romano.

Mezze Maniche with Asparagus and Ricotta

This dish is all about the ricotta: it melts easily on the warm noodles, completely coating the mezze maniche—a short, substantial, tube-shaped pasta—to create an upscale mac-and-cheese. The result is a beautiful milky pasta sauce that's velvety and luscious and sets off the grassy sweet flavor of the asparagus. Don't skimp on the black pepper; a generous amount of kick cuts through the richness of the ricotta.

SERVES 4

2 pounds asparagus, trimmed
¼ cup extra-virgin olive oil, plus more
  for drizzling
½ teaspoon kosher salt, or more to taste
2½ tablespoons unsalted butter

1 pound mezze maniche (or penne or rigatoni)
½ teaspoon freshly cracked black pepper,
  or more to taste
½ cup fresh ricotta

Slice the asparagus lengthwise in half. Cut crosswise into 1½-inch pieces (you should have about 7 cups).

In a very large skillet (or a Dutch oven; see page 215 for tips), warm the olive oil over medium-high heat. Add the asparagus and salt and cook until the asparagus begins to turn golden, about 2 minutes. Add 1 tablespoon of the butter. Continue cooking until the asparagus is golden all over, about 2 minutes more. Add 2 tablespoons water to the pan. Remove from the heat.

In a large pot of well-salted boiling water, cook the pasta according to the package instructions until 2 minutes shy of al dente; drain.

Toss the mezze maniche into the skillet with the asparagus, the remaining 1½ tablespoons butter, and the pepper. Cook over medium heat until the pasta is al dente, 1 to 2 minutes, adding more water if the sauce seems dry. Taste and adjust the seasonings if necessary.

Divide the pasta among four individual serving plates or bowls and finish each with ricotta and a drizzle of olive oil.

Andrew's Note: You have to use freshly ground pepper here if you want the dish to have a spicy-hot flavor. Pre-ground pepper doesn't really taste like much. When a recipe calls for a lot of black pepper for seasoning, taste as you go. Depending on the quality of the pepper and where it was grown, you might need to use more or less.

Spaghetti with Artichokes

The flavors in this recipe are very Roman: a combination of artichokes and Pecorino Romano, along with chili, garlic, and parsley, is something you'd see in a trattoria in the Eternal City. We like the addition of the softer Parmigiano-Reggiano, which imparts a milky creaminess to balance out the Pecorino's piquant saltiness.

SERVES 4

8 small or 4 large artichokes, trimmed
  (see page 124)
**¾ cup extra-virgin olive oil, plus more for
  drizzling**
8 garlic cloves, smashed and peeled
2 teaspoons kosher salt
½ teaspoon chili flakes
½ cup water

1 pound spaghetti
½ cup chopped flat-leaf parsley
**3 tablespoons finely grated Parmigiano-
  Reggiano**
1 tablespoon unsalted butter
¼ teaspoon freshly cracked black pepper
**4 teaspoons finely grated Pecorino
  Romano, plus more if desired**

Halve the artichokes lengthwise, then slice lengthwise into ¼-inch-thick slices.

In a very large skillet (or a Dutch oven; see page 215 for tips), warm the olive oil over medium-high heat. Add the artichokes, garlic, and salt and cook until the artichokes are nicely browned and a little soft and the garlic is golden around the edges, 6 to 7 minutes. Add the chili flakes and cook for 1 minute. Add the water (just enough to not quite cover the artichokes) and let simmer until the artichokes are very soft, about 2 minutes. There should still be some liquid remaining in the pan. Remove from the heat.

Meanwhile, in a large pot of well-salted boiling water, cook the pasta according to the package instructions until 2 minutes shy of al dente; drain.

Toss the spaghetti into the skillet with the artichokes, along with the parsley, Parmigiano-Reggiano, butter, and pepper, and cook until the pasta is just al dente, 1 to 2 minutes, adding 2 tablespoons water if the sauce seems dry.

Divide the pasta among four individual serving plates or bowls and finish each with a drizzle of olive oil and a teaspoon or more of Pecorino Romano.

Maccheroni with Pork Sausage and Broccoli Rabe

Broccoli rabe and sausage is a classic Italian combination you've probably seen hundreds of times—with good reason: the bitter, spicy greens make a pitch-perfect companion to rich, fatty sausage. Here the chewy, toothsome pasta adds a nice neutral element, breaking up the intensity of the sausage and greens.

SERVES 4

¼ cup extra-virgin olive oil
10 ounces **Pork Sausage** (page 185), formed into 4 equal patties
4 garlic cloves, smashed and peeled
½ teaspoon chili flakes
1 bunch broccoli rabe, trimmed and cut into bite-sized pieces (4 cups)

1 pound maccheroni
1 tablespoon unsalted butter
3 tablespoons finely grated Parmigiano-Reggiano, plus more for serving
½ teaspoon freshly cracked black pepper
Kosher salt

In a very large skillet (or a Dutch oven; see page 215 for tips), warm the olive oil over medium-high heat. Add the sausage patties and brown on both sides, 4 to 6 minutes total. Break up the meat with a spoon (the inside will still be pink and undercooked). Add the garlic and cook until golden, about 2 minutes. Add the chili flakes and cook until fragrant, about 30 seconds. Toss in the broccoli rabe and cook until wilted and tender, about 5 minutes. Add 2 tablespoons water to the pan. Remove from the heat.

In a large pot of well-salted boiling water, cook the pasta according to the package instructions until 2 minutes shy of al dente; drain.

Toss the maccheroni into the skillet with the sausage and broccoli rabe mixture. Cook over medium heat for 1 minute, then add the butter and cook until the pasta is al dente, 1 to 2 minutes, adding more water if the sauce seems dry. Stir in the Parmigiano-Reggiano and pepper and cook for another 30 seconds. Season to taste with salt.

Divide the pasta among four individual serving plates or bowls and finish each with a generous sprinkle of cheese.

Penne with Zucchini and Mint

With its dense, firm texture that can withstand high cooking temperatures, Romanesco zucchini works really well in this early summer pasta dish. Unlike the usual zucchini, it can actually pick up some caramelized brown color in the pan without falling apart. Zucchini tends to be a mild-tasting vegetable, so browning it deeply is important for the flavor here.

To add some body to this otherwise delicate dish, Andrew uses a combination of butter and olive oil—the butter adds richness and helps to emulsify the sauce, and the oil contributes a floral note and a slight bite. Mint and zucchini are a classic Italian combination, and this delicious pasta will show you why.

SERVES 4

1¾ pounds zucchini, preferably Romanesco, trimmed
¼ cup extra-virgin olive oil, plus more for drizzling
Kosher salt
1 pound penne
4 tablespoons unsalted butter

8 garlic cloves, smashed and peeled
¼ cup plus a scant 3 tablespoons finely grated Parmigiano-Reggiano, plus more if desired
3 tablespoons chopped mint
¼ teaspoon freshly cracked black pepper

Slice each zucchini into 2-inch-by-¼-inch batons (you will have about 5 cups).

In a very large skillet (or a Dutch oven; see page 215 for tips), warm 2 tablespoons of the olive oil over high heat. Add half the zucchini, season with salt, and cook, without moving it, until dark golden and almost tender, 2 to 3 minutes. With a slotted spoon, transfer the zucchini to a paper-towel-lined plate. Add another 2 tablespoons olive oil to the skillet and repeat with the remaining zucchini. Add 2 tablespoons water to the pan. Remove from the heat.

In a large pot of well-salted boiling water, cook the pasta according to the package instructions until 2 minutes shy of al dente; drain.

In the same skillet, melt 3 tablespoons of the butter over medium heat. Add the garlic and cook for 2 to 3 minutes. Toss in the penne and zucchini, and cook until the pasta is al dente, 1 to 2 minutes, adding more water if the sauce seems dry. Toss in the ¼ cup Parmigiano-Reggiano and the remaining tablespoon of butter. Add the mint and season to taste with salt and the pepper.

Divide the pasta among four individual serving plates or bowls and finish each with a drizzle of olive oil and 2 teaspoons or more cheese.

Spaghetti with Herbs and Ricotta

When fresh herbs finally arrive at the farmers' market in the early summer, we rush home with fragrant bundles to make this creamy, light spaghetti. The ricotta acts as a vehicle for all the lovely herbs, allowing them to cling to the pasta without making the dish heavy. This recipe calls for leafy, soft herbs—parsley, mint, and basil; woody, intensely flavored herbs such as rosemary or thyme would overpower the delicacy and sweetness of the cheese. If you're lucky enough to have some earth or a window box in which to plant an annual herb garden, this is a brilliant way to make use of that sudden surplus that seems to happen all at once.

SERVES 4

½ cup extra-virgin olive oil, plus more
 for drizzling
4 garlic cloves, smashed and peeled
½ teaspoon chili flakes
1 pound spaghetti
½ cup fresh ricotta
¼ teaspoon freshly cracked black pepper,
 plus more to taste

Kosher salt
1 tablespoon unsalted butter
½ cup coarsely chopped flat-leaf parsley
¼ cup coarsely chopped basil
¼ cup coarsely chopped mint
¼ cup coarsely grated Parmigiano-
 Reggiano, plus more if desired

In a very large skillet (or a Dutch oven; see page 215 for tips), warm the olive oil over medium-high heat. Add the garlic and cook until fragrant and light golden, about 3 minutes. Add the chili flakes and cook for 30 seconds more. Add 2 tablespoons water to the pan. Remove from the heat.

In a large pot of well-salted boiling water, cook the pasta according to the package instructions until 2 minutes shy of al dente; drain and reserve a cup or two of the pasta water.

Season the ricotta with salt and pepper.

Toss the spaghetti into the skillet with the garlic, along with the butter and pepper. Cook over medium heat until the pasta is just al dente, 1 to 2 minutes. Then add the ricotta, herbs, and Parmigiano-Reggiano to the pasta and toss with tongs until the ricotta loosely coats the spaghetti, adding more pasta water as needed to smooth out the texture.

Divide the pasta among four individual serving plates or bowls. Finish each with a drizzle of olive oil and more Parmigiano-Reggiano, if desired.

PASTA

210

Spaghettini with Shrimp

This is a very nontraditional way to make pasta, borrowing on the French technique of using stock as a foundation for sauce. In Italy, you don't normally see pasta prepared with stock, but here it works to intensify the delicate flavor of sweet, fresh shrimp. This recipe takes longer to make than most others in this chapter, but the process is fairly straight-forward. For the stock, whole shrimp are peeled, separating the shells from the meat, and the shells and heads are toasted to bring out their flavor and add a layer of caramelization to the sauce. Then the pan is deglazed with a dash of white vermouth, which imparts a lovely herbal quality and complexity.

Once you have the stock, the rest of the dish is utterly simple: reduce the stock with a little garlic and pinch of chili, then brown the shrimp. Delicate spaghettini tangles around the golden-edged shrimp, and a finish of scallions and lemon adds a sunny brilliance.

SERVES 4

¼ cup extra-virgin olive oil, plus more
  for drizzling
1½ pounds large shrimp, peeled and
  deveined
Kosher salt
3 tablespoons unsalted butter
4 garlic cloves, smashed and peeled

½ teaspoon chili flakes
4 cups Shrimp Stock (page 350)
1 pound spaghettini
½ cup thinly sliced scallions
Juice of 1 lemon, or to taste
½ teaspoon freshly cracked black pepper

In a very large skillet (or a Dutch oven; see page 215 for tips), warm ¼ cup of the olive oil over medium-high heat. Season the shrimp with salt. Once the oil is hot and shimmering, add the shrimp (cook in batches if necessary) and sear, without moving it, until the undersides are brown. Transfer the shrimp to a bowl. (If you cook the shrimp on both sides, it will overcook when added to the pasta.)

Return the skillet to the heat and add 1 tablespoon of the butter, the garlic, and the chili flakes and cook until the garlic is fragrant and golden, about 2 minutes. Pour in the shrimp stock, bring to a simmer, and simmer until reduced by half, 10 to 15 minutes.

While the sauce reduces, bring a large pot of well-salted water to a boil. Cook the pasta according to the package instructions until 2 minutes shy of al dente; drain.

Toss the spaghettini into the skillet with the reduced stock, along with the scallions. Cook over medium heat until the pasta is al dente, 1 to 2 minutes. Toss in the shrimp, the remaining 2 tablespoons butter, the lemon juice, and the pepper, and stir to combine and heat through.

Divide the pasta among four individual serving plates or bowls and finish each with a drizzle of olive oil.

Andrew's Note: While you could use purchased shrimp stock for this recipe, it might not have the same depth of flavor as the homemade. And this is such a bare-bones dish, it pays to take the time to make your own stock. (Plus, prepared shrimp stock can be hard to find.)

Bucatini Fra Diavolo

A gutsy, punchy "red sauce" pasta is just right for the beginning of summer—here the Pecorino Romano lends a salty bite, and the spicy chili flakes add a sharp kick that is especially welcome when the weather starts to warm. We make this dish just before fresh tomatoes start showing up at the market but while bunches of herbs are available in abundance.

Don't imagine this as the *fra diavolo* (Italian for "brother devil," because of the fiery seasoning) you might remember from Italian restaurant menus in the '80s. This recipe was inspired by one in Fred Plotkin's *The Authentic Pasta Book*. Aside from the aroma of the fresh herbs, the secret to this sauce is a copious hit of olive oil. It adds a fruity richness that plays beautifully off the chili and tomatoes.

SERVES 4

¾ cup extra-virgin olive oil, plus more for drizzling
8 garlic cloves, smashed and peeled
1 teaspoon chili flakes
2 cups San Marzano tomato puree
Kosher salt
1 pound bucatini
¼ cup finely chopped basil

¼ cup finely chopped mint
¼ cup finely chopped flat-leaf parsley
1 tablespoon unsalted butter
3 tablespoons finely grated Parmigiano-Reggiano
¼ teaspoon freshly cracked black pepper
Scant 3 tablespoons finely grated Pecorino Romano, plus more if desired

In a very large skillet (or a Dutch oven; see page 215 for tips), warm the olive oil over medium-high heat. Add the garlic and cook until fragrant and golden, about 3 minutes. Add the chili flakes and cook for 30 seconds more. Add the tomato puree, season with salt to taste, and cook until the oil separates, the tomato solids start to fry, and the sauce has thickened, 10 to 12 minutes. Add 2 tablespoons water to the pan. Remove from the heat.

In a large pot of well-salted boiling water, cook the pasta according to the package instructions until 2 minutes shy of al dente; drain.

Toss the bucatini into the skillet with the tomato sauce, herbs, and butter. Cook over medium heat until the pasta is just al dente, 1 to 2 minutes. Stir in the Parmigiano-Reggiano and pepper, adding more water if the sauce seems dry.

Divide the pasta among four individual serving plates or bowls and finish each with 2 teaspoons or more Pecorino Romano and a drizzle of olive oil.

Pasta Techniques

1. There's an art and a science to matching pasta shape to sauce. Sauces that are fairly fluid and smooth, such as the one in Linguine with Meyer Lemon (page 237), are lovely paired with long pastas like linguine, spaghetti, or bucatini; the sauce will drape and wrap the noodles.

2. When there's a lot of stuff or bits in the sauce (see Maccheroni with Pork Sausage and Broccoli Rabe, page 206), short pastas have the necessary nooks and crannies to give all the elements of a chunkier sauce a place to congregate. Large tubular pastas, such as rigatoni and paccheri, have wide holes that can capture the big chunks of a meat ragu, whole beans, or bite-sized pieces of seafood. So, when picking your pasta size and shape, think about the texture of your sauce and pair them accordingly.

3. Always make sure your pasta cooking water is adequately salted. Most Americans add a pinch of salt to the pot, but pasta needs a generous amount of salt in the water to bring out its wheaty flavor. The water should taste markedly salty, like the ocean—use about ⅓ cup kosher salt per large pot of water (and don't worry, most of the salt ends up going down the drain with the pasta water). As the pasta cooks, it absorbs salt and becomes seasoned through and through.

4. The best pan for simmering pasta and sauce together is a wide deep skillet or sauté pan. A 14-inch pan may seem enormous, but it's actually ideal for sauce and pasta to feed 4 to 6 people (about a pound of noodles). The recipes in this chapter are written for this amount. However, if you halve everything to feed 2 or 3, a 10- or 12-inch skillet will work fine.

5. Another option is to use a Dutch oven. Dutch ovens have higher sides than skillets, making it harder to evaporate liquid. They also retain heat beautifully—which is good for braises but not for pasta, as too much residual heat in the pot can wilt the noodles. If using a Dutch oven, make sure the sauce is cooked down until it's thick before you add the pasta, then go light when adding water to the pan. As soon as the pasta is ready, serve it or transfer it to a warmed serving platter. You don't want it to sit in the hot pot and continue to cook.

6. After the pasta is added to the pan with the sauce, let it cook until the pasta absorbs the flavor of the sauce, 1 to 3 minutes. If the pan looks dry, you can add a little plain water. Don't use the pasta cooking water here; it could make the sauce too salty.

Bucatini alla Puttanesca

If you love to make Italian food at home, you probably have all these ingredients in your pantry or refrigerator at this very moment. While this dish is bursting with savory flavors, the translation of *puttanesca* is rather unsavory. Let's just say that this classic Italian preparation is named after the ladies of the night who, when arriving home in the wee hours, could whip up a satisfying meal using ingredients they had on hand. If you can find canned Italian cherry tomatoes, use them. The sweetness of cherry tomatoes is most welcome against the salty, briny flavors of the capers, olives, and anchovies (though you could substitute canned diced tomatoes). When you're craving a bowl of pasta swimming in big, bold flavors, this puttanesca more than fits the bill.

SERVES 4

¼ cup extra virgin olive oil, plus more for drizzling
4 large cloves garlic, smashed and peeled
4 tablespoons unsalted butter
9 anchovy fillets
½ teaspoon chili flakes
1 teaspoon dried oregano
2 cups canned Italian cherry tomatoes or canned diced tomatoes, drained

3 tablespoons salt-packed capers, soaked, rinsed, and drained (see Andrew's Note, page 30)
1 pound bucatini
½ cup Nocellara or Cerignola olives, pitted and chopped
½ cup chopped flat-leaf parsley
Kosher salt and freshly cracked black pepper

In a very large skillet (or a Dutch oven; see page 215 for tips), warm the olive oil over medium-high heat. Add the garlic and cook until golden brown, about 1 minute. Add the butter, anchovies, chili flakes, and oregano and cook for 2 minutes, breaking up the anchovy fillets with the back of a large spoon until they dissolve. Add the tomatoes and capers and cook, breaking up the tomatoes, until much of the liquid has evaporated and the oil has separated out and puddled on the sauce's surface, about 10 minutes. Remove from the heat.

In a large pot of well-salted boiling water, cook the pasta according to the package instructions until 2 minutes shy of al dente; drain.

Toss the bucatini into the skillet with the tomato mixture along with the olives and parsley. Cook over medium heat until the pasta is al dente, 1 to 2 minutes, adding a few tablespoons of water if the sauce seems dry. Season to taste with salt and pepper.

Divide the pasta among four individual serving plates or bowls and finish each with a drizzle of olive oil.

Linguine with Tomatoes, Basil, and Parmigiano-Reggiano

Here's a fantastic dish to make at the height of tomato season. We especially love to use Ramapo tomatoes (from Maxwell's Farm in New Jersey), which while technically not heirloom tomatoes have the flavor of them. The hybrid was originally developed at Rutgers University in 1968, and we think it is one of the finest beefsteak tomatoes in existence. Ramapo tomatoes are intensely red and have an intoxicating perfume. When genuinely ripe, they are very soft, very juicy, and deeply sweet. Their skin is more delicate than that of conventional tomatoes, making them a great choice for this dish—you don't get any tough, unappealing curls of skin accumulating in your sauce. After you bring the tomatoes home from the market, let them sit on your counter for 2 to 4 days   you'll be rewarded with absurdly ripe, concentrated tomato flavor. The sweetness will remind you that a tomato is botanically a fruit. Unfortunately, many farms stopped growing those tomatoes because they are fragile and don't travel well. If you can't get them, use the best, ripest tomatoes you can get.

Once you've got ripe tomatoes, this sauce comes together quickly. There's no need to develop any flavors, since the tomatoes are full of flavor already. You want the fresh, vibrant essence of tomato to shine. Add a few torn basil leaves, and it's perfect—though an extra sprinkle of Parmigiano-Reggiano doesn't hurt.

SERVES 4

½ cup extra-virgin olive oil, plus more
  for drizzling
4 garlic cloves, coarsely chopped
1¾ pounds ripe tomatoes, cored and
  chopped (about 5 cups)
1 pound linguine

1 tablespoon unsalted butter
12 basil leaves, torn
¼ cup finely grated Parmigiano-Reggiano,
  plus more for serving
Kosher salt

In a very large skillet (or a Dutch oven; see page 215 for tips), warm the olive oil over medium-high heat. Add the garlic and cook until fragrant, about 2 minutes. Add the tomatoes and cook for 5 minutes, until they start to break down and most of the liquid evaporates. Add 2 tablespoons water to the pan. Remove from the heat.

In a large pot of well-salted boiling water, cook the pasta according to the package instructions until 2 minutes shy of al dente; drain.

Toss the linguine into the skillet with the tomatoes, butter, and basil. Cook over medium heat until the pasta is just al dente, 1 to 2 minutes. Toss in the Parmigiano-Reggiano

and season to taste with salt, adding more water if the sauce seems dry.

Divide the pasta among four individual serving plates or bowls and finish each with a drizzle of oil and a sprinkle of cheese.

Andrew's Note: I'm not a fan of basil chiffonade—that is, finely slivered basil. The long strips seem overwrought, and all that contact with the knife basically just bruises the tender leaves. Instead, pull off the leaves from the basil branches and tear them into small pieces before adding them to the pasta; torn basil just tastes better!

Paccheri with Swordfish, Olives, Capers, and Mint

People often think of swordfish as a strong-flavored fish, but I think that's more about its texture, which is meaty and dense. The flesh is actually sweet and mild. And for this dish, swordfish's density is an advantage, allowing for lovely, resilient chunks that can stand up to the al dente pasta. Their size and texture goes well with the pasta called *paccheri* (in Italian it means "a slap in the mouth")—the bits of fish nestle nicely inside the wide openings of the pasta—but you can also use rigatoni or any other large tubular shape. The pungency of chili flakes, mint, and fennel seeds make a nice contrast to the gentle saline flavor of the fish.

SERVES 4 TO 6

1½ pounds skinless swordfish steaks, cut into 1-inch-by-1-inch-by-½-inch chunks
Kosher salt and freshly cracked black pepper
½ cup extra-virgin olive oil, plus more for drizzling
3 tablespoons salt-packed capers, soaked, rinsed, and drained (see Andrew's Note, page 30), **or drained brined capers**
¼ cup Nocellara or Cerignola olives, pitted and roughly chopped
4 teaspoons chopped garlic
1 teaspoon fennel seeds, preferably Sicilian (see Andrew's Note)
1 teaspoon chili flakes
1 pound paccheri (see the headnote)
¼ cup chopped flat-leaf parsley
3 tablespoons chopped mint
Fresh lemon juice

Season the fish with salt and pepper. In a very large skillet (or a Dutch oven; see page 215 for tips), warm ¼ cup of the olive oil over high heat. Add the fish and cook, without moving, until browned on one side, about 2 minutes. (Cook in batches if necessary to avoid overcrowding the pan.) Transfer the fish to a platter and set aside.

In the same skillet, warm the remaining ¼ cup olive oil over medium-high heat. Add the capers and fry until they start to brown, 1 to 2 minutes. Add the olives, garlic, fennel seeds, and chili flakes and cook until everything is toasty and fragrant, about 2 minutes. Add 2 tablespoons of water to the pan. Remove from the heat.

In a large pot of well-salted boiling water, cook the pasta according to the package instructions until 2 minutes shy of al dente; drain.

Toss the paccheri into the skillet with the caper mixture, along with the swordfish. Cook over medium heat until the pasta is al dente, 1 to 2 minutes, adding more water if the sauce seems dry. Stir in the parsley and mint and season with salt, pepper, and lemon juice.

Divide the pasta among four individual serving plates or bowls and finish each with drizzle of olive oil.

Andrew's Note: Here we use fennel seeds from Sicily—they are shorter, fatter, and more fragrant than the typical fennel seeds. You can get them at Manicaretti (see Resources, page 357).

Paccheri with Squid, Cherry Tomatoes, Peppers, and Capers

To do this dish justice, you need to cook the squid low and slow. During the braising process, a deeply flavored, sea-sweet broth develops, providing an ideal base for the sauce. If tomatoes and peppers aren't in season, experiment with other seasonal vegetables—fresh peas in the spring, or shell beans in early autumn.

SERVES 4 TO 6

1¼ **pounds cleaned squid, tentacles and heads separated**
½ **cup plus 1 tablespoon extra-virgin olive oil, plus more for drizzling**
Kosher salt
¼ **cup salt-packed capers, soaked, rinsed, and drained** (see Andrew's Note, page 30)
2 **cups** (about 28) **cherry tomatoes**

¾ **cup diced red bell pepper**
2½ **tablespoons chopped garlic**
6 **tablespoons finely chopped flat-leaf parsley**
1 **teaspoon chili flakes**
1 **cup dry white wine**
1 **pound paccheri or other pasta** (see Andrew's Note)

Rinse the squid under cool running water; drain. Pat dry with paper towels, then transfer to a plate.

Heat a very large skillet (or a Dutch oven; see page 215 for tips) over high heat until very hot, about 5 minutes. Add 2 tablespoons of the olive oil. Season the squid with salt, then add about half the squid to the pan and cook, without moving it, until browned on one side. Transfer to a plate. (Do not overcrowd the pan; if it doesn't hold half the squid comfortably, cook it in 3 instead of 2 batches, using 2 tablespoons oil for each batch.) Repeat with the remaining squid.

Add 3 tablespoons olive oil to the pan and reduce the heat to medium-high. Add the capers and sauté until they begin to brown, 2 to 3 minutes. Transfer the capers to the plate with the squid. Add the remaining 2 tablespoons olive oil to the pan, stir in the tomatoes and bell pepper, and cook for 2 minutes. At this point the bottom of the pan should have a nice brown *fond* (the bits sticking to the bottom of the pan). Add the garlic, 2 tablespoons of the parsley, and the chili flakes and cook until the garlic is fragrant, about 2 minutes.

Return the squid and capers to the pan, pour in the white wine, and cook until the wine is reduced by half. Add ½ cup water, cover the pan, and simmer over low heat until the squid is tender, about 20 minutes.

While the squid simmers, in a large pot of well-salted boiling water, cook the pasta according to the package instructions until 2 minutes shy of al dente; drain.

When the squid is just tender, add the pasta to the pan and cook over medium heat, tossing well, until the pasta is al dente, 1 to 2 minutes. Add the remaining ¼ cup parsley and toss to combine. If the sauce seems dry, add a little water.

Divide the pasta among four individual serving plates or bowls and finish each with a drizzle of olive oil.

Andrew's Note: If you can't find paccheri, look for calamarata, which is basically half a paccheri noodle, and works perfectly, since it's almost the same size as the length of the squid pieces. If you can't find either one, substitute spaghetti, bucatini, or even linguine.

Spaghetti with Chickpeas

It's not often that you see a starchy ingredient like chickpeas tossed in with pasta, but it's done beautifully in Italy, and this is actually a relatively light and nutritious dish. Because there's no cheese, the flavors maintain a discernible brightness. Browning and crisping the chickpeas in olive oil intensifies their nutty flavor. Once they go into the pan, resist the urge to move them around—let them sit and sizzle, soaking up the olive oil and turning golden and crunchy. The flavor of the chickpeas is heightened by the pungent notes of garlic and chili, and anchovy lends its classic savory saltiness.

SERVES 4

¾ cup extra-virgin olive oil, plus more
  for drizzling
2 cups drained cooked chickpeas
  (see page 34)
8 garlic cloves, smashed and peeled
4 anchovy fillets
½ teaspoon chili flakes

1 pound spaghetti
½ cup finely chopped flat-leaf parsley
¼ cup finely chopped mint
¼ teaspoon freshly cracked black pepper
Juice of ½ lemon
Kosher salt

In a very large skillet (or a Dutch oven; see page 215 for tips), warm ½ cup of the olive oil over high heat until shimmering. Add the chickpeas and fry, without stirring, until they are darkly colored on one side, 3 to 5 minutes. Add another ¼ cup olive oil and the garlic cloves and cook until the garlic is fragrant and light golden, about 2 minutes. Add the anchovies and cook, stirring and mashing, until they dissolve. Add the chili flakes and cook for 30 seconds. Add 2 tablespoons water to the pan. Remove from the heat.

In a large pot of well-salted boiling water, cook the pasta according to the package instructions until 2 minutes shy of al dente; drain.

Toss the spaghetti into the skillet with the chickpeas, herbs, and pepper. Cook, tossing, until the pasta is al dente, about 1 to 2 minutes, adding more water if the sauce seems dry. Add the lemon juice and season with salt to taste.

Divide the pasta among four individual serving plates or bowls and finish each with a drizzle of olive oil.

Andrew's Note: People don't often think of adding lemon juice to pasta, but it's a great complement to pastas that are on the richer, starchier side. It can really transform a dish, contributing brightness and complexity.

Penne with Broccoli

We usually make this dish in the late summer and early fall, when the best local broccoli is available at our farmers' market. Supermarket broccoli stems can be bland and woody, but at the farmers' market, the entire stalk (florets, leaves, stems) is flavorful and tender. With good seasonal broccoli, there's no need to limit yourself to florets—cook it all; it's delicious.

Since broccoli is a pretty powerful-tasting vegetable, it can stand up to a good amount of garlic and chili: two sweet, pungent cloves of garlic per person isn't overdoing it here. And be diligent when it comes to browning the broccoli. In this recipe, the browning is almost an ingredient in itself, providing a solid flavor foundation for all the other elements of the dish.

SERVES 4

(or a Dutch oven; see page 215 for tips)

7 tablespoons extra-virgin olive oil, plus more for drizzling
8 cups 1-inch broccoli florets and peeled tender stems (see Andrew's Notes) (from about 2 pounds broccoli)
1 teaspoon kosher salt
8 garlic cloves, crushed and peeled
½ teaspoon chili flakes

1 pound penne
1 tablespoon unsalted butter
¼ teaspoon freshly cracked black pepper
3 tablespoons finely grated Parmigiano-Reggiano
4 teaspoons finely grated Pecorino Romano, plus more if desired

In a very large skillet (or a Dutch oven; see page 215 for tips), warm 3 tablespoons of the olive oil over medium-high heat. Add the broccoli and ½ teaspoon of the salt. Once the broccoli has absorbed the olive oil, add the remaining ¼ cup oil, increase the heat to high, and let the broccoli get very brown and tender, about 7 minutes. Add the garlic and chili flakes and cook until fragrant, about 30 seconds. Add 2 tablespoons water to the pan. Remove from the heat.

In a large pot of well-salted boiling water, cook the pasta according to the package instructions until 2 minutes shy of al dente; drain.

Toss the penne into the skillet with the broccoli, butter, and pepper. Cook over medium heat until the pasta is al dente, 1 to 2 minutes, adding more water if the sauce seems dry. Stir in the Parmigiano-Reggiano and season with the remaining ½ teaspoon salt.

Divide the pasta among four individual serving plates or bowls and finish each with 1 teaspoon Pecorino Romano. Drizzle with olive oil and sprinkle with additional Pecorino, if desired.

Andrew's Notes: Depending on how you cut your broccoli, you could also use mezze maniche, rigatoni, or maccheroni here. Just make sure to cut the broccoli to approximate the pasta's size and shape to make this dish work best.

If you want to use whole broccoli stalks here instead of just the florets, peel the stems and cut them into pieces the same size as the florets (and the pasta), and cook them along with the florets. You can toss in the leaves too—they have great flavor.

Fusilli with Black Kale Pesto

This pesto dish calls for kale in place of handfuls of perfumed basil leaves, making for an altogether quieter, softer, and warmer pasta. With the toothy, satisfying chunks of walnuts and the Parmigiano-Reggiano, fusilli works well for this dish—all those curves and crevices are a great vehicle for the sauce. Kale is one of those hardy greens you can find all winter long, and this is an out-of-the-ordinary way to use it. In the dead of winter, treat yourself to this bright-tasting dish, bursting with green freshness and fragrant lemon zest.

SERVES 4

½ cup plus 2 tablespoons walnuts
½ cup plus ¾ teaspoon kosher salt, or more to taste
12 ounces (about 1 bunch) Tuscan kale, center ribs removed
¾ cup extra-virgin olive oil, plus more for drizzling

8 garlic cloves, thinly sliced
Finely grated zest of 1 lemon
1 pound fusilli
¼ cup finely grated Parmigiano-Reggiano, plus more if desired

Preheat the oven to 350°F. Spread the walnuts on a rimmed baking sheet. Toast until golden and fragrant, 7 to 10 minutes. Set aside.

In a large pot, bring 4 quarts water and the ½ cup of salt to a boil. Prepare a bowl of ice water. Add the kale leaves to the pot and cook until tender, 2 to 3 minutes. Using tongs, immediately transfer the kale to the ice water to cool. Drain, squeeze the excess water from the greens, and transfer to a plate (it's okay if they retain a bit of water, as long as they aren't dripping).

In a very large skillet (or a Dutch oven; see page 215 for tips), warm ¼ cup of the olive oil over medium-low heat. Add the garlic and cook until tender but not browned, about 2 minutes. Add 2 tablespoons water to the pan. Remove from the heat.

In a food processor, combine the walnuts, kale, garlic-oil mixture, the remaining ½ cup oil, the remaining ¾ teaspoon salt, and the lemon zest. Pulse until the mixture forms a coarse paste, then transfer the pesto to the large skillet.

In a large pot of well-salted boiling water, cook the pasta according to the package instructions until 2 minutes shy of al dente; drain.

Toss the fusilli into the skillet with the pesto. Cook over medium heat until the pasta is al dente, 1 to 2 minutes, adding more water if the sauce seems dry. Taste and add more salt if needed.

Divide the pasta among four individual serving plates or bowls and finish each with a tablespoon or more of Parmigiano-Reggiano and a drizzle of olive oil.

Penne with Spicy Cauliflower

The secret to deeply flavored cauliflower is cooking it until it's good and caramelized all over; the darker it gets, the richer it will taste.

One thing to keep in mind: cauliflower releases more water than broccoli, meaning it takes longer to brown, so make sure to get the pan piping hot before adding it. Cooked cauliflower has a pleasant soft texture, and here the garnish of crisp bread crumbs provides a lovely contrast. The bread crumbs for this dish are bigger than usual, like a cross between a crumb and a crouton, with loads of texture and crunch. Don't try to substitute store-bought bread crumbs; they won't have the same effect.

SERVES 4

⅓ cup 1-inch pieces country-style bread
⅔ cup plus 2 teaspoons extra-virgin olive oil, plus more for drizzling
1 large head cauliflower, trimmed and cored
8 garlic cloves, coarsely chopped
Kosher salt
1 pound penne

2½ tablespoons unsalted butter
2 teaspoons chili flakes
¼ cup finely grated Parmigiano-Reggiano
Freshly cracked black pepper
3 tablespoons finely grated Pecorino Romano, plus more if desired

Preheat the oven to 300°F. In a large bowl, toss the bread pieces with the 2 teaspoons olive oil. Spread them out on a baking sheet and toast until they are dry, about 10 minutes. Increase the heat to 400°F and toast until the bread is dark golden brown, about 10 minutes more.

Crumble the croutons into small pieces or pulse very coarsely in a food processor; you want them to still have some texture.

Cut the cauliflower into pieces about twice the size of a penne noodle.

In a very large skillet (or a Dutch oven; see page 215 for tips), warm ⅓ cup of the olive oil over medium-high heat. Add half the cauliflower and cook until the cauliflower is well browned, about 5 minutes. Add half the garlic and cook for 30 seconds. Season with salt and transfer to a bowl. Repeat with the remaining ⅓ cup olive oil, cauliflower, and garlic. Season with salt and add to the bowl. Set the pan aside.

In a large pot of well-salted boiling water, cook the pasta according to the package instructions until 2 minutes shy of al dente; drain.

Return all of the cauliflower to the skillet, add 1 tablespoon of the butter and the chili flakes, and cook over medium heat for 30 seconds. Add 2 tablespoons water and a large pinch of salt and simmer until the cauliflower is tender, 2 to 3 minutes.

Add the penne to the skillet, along with the remaining 1½ tablespoons butter and the Parmigiano-Reggiano. Toss until a nice emulsified sauce forms and the pasta is al dente, 1 to 2 minutes, adding more water if the sauce seems dry. Season generously with pepper, then remove from the heat and toss in the bread crumbs and Pecorino Romano; toss again.

Divide the pasta among four individual serving plates or bowls and finish each with a drizzle of olive oil and more Pecorino, if desired.

Andrew's Note: If you get cauliflower from the farmers' market, be sure to use the chopped leaves—they are sweet and mild and will add a great deal of flavor and texture to the dish.

Penne with Cabbage and Provolone Piccante

This hearty pasta was inspired by a Northern Italian dish from Val d'Aosta made with cabbage and Fontina. We use provolone instead of Fontina. It's still soft and moist enough to create a creamy sauce that coats the noodles and cabbage, but its slightly sharp finish adds some complexity to the mix. This is a great dish to turn to in the winter when you want something warm and indulgent.

SERVES 4

½ cup extra virgin olive oil, plus more
  for drizzling
One 2-pound green cabbage, cored and cut
  into 1-inch squares (about 9 cups)
4 large garlic cloves, crushed and peeled
Kosher salt

4 tablespoons unsalted butter
½ teaspoon chili flakes
1 pound penne
½ cup plus 2 tablespoons grated provolone
  piccante, plus more if desired
Freshly cracked black pepper

In a very large skillet (or a Dutch oven; see page 215 for tips), warm the olive oil over medium-high heat. Add the cabbage and cook, stirring often, until it turns golden, 7 to 8 minutes. Add the garlic, a pinch of salt, 2 tablespoons of the butter, and the chili flakes. Cook until the garlic is light golden and fragrant, 2 to 3 minutes. Add 2 tablespoons water to the pan. Remove from the heat.

In a large pot of well-salted boiling water, cook the pasta according to the package instructions until 2 minutes shy of al dente; drain.

Toss the penne into the skillet with the cabbage, and the remaining 2 tablespoons butter. Cook over medium heat until the pasta is al dente, 1 to 2 minutes, adding a little more water if the sauce seems dry. Add ½ cup of the provolone and black pepper to taste.

Divide the pasta among four individual serving plates or bowls and finish each with ½ tablespoon or more cheese and a drizzle of olive oil.

Andrew's Note: This is a recipe made for regular green cabbage. Red cabbage is too sweet, and the color isn't right for the dish. Savoy cabbage could work as well.

Mezze Maniche with Guanciale, Chilies, and Ricotta

This is our version of *alla gricia* (a classic Roman dish) made with guanciale—rich, cured hog jowl. The star of the show here is the guanciale. There is some well-made commercially available guanciale, but it can be hard to find, so feel free to substitute pancetta (or even bacon). Pancetta has less fat and is less gamey than guanciale, but it will still be delicious in its own, milder way. A sprinkle of chili is toasted in the rendered guanciale fat, yielding a nice prickle of heat. Tossing ricotta in at the end creates a lush and creamy sauce, with a mildness that softens some of the more rustic aspects of the guanciale. This has all the best elements of a classic *alla gricia*, but the sharp corners have been rounded off for a more elegant dish.

SERVES 4

**12 ounces guanciale, pancetta,
 or bacon, diced** (generous 2 cups)
¼ teaspoon chili flakes
1 pound mezze maniche
 (or penne or rigatoni)

2 tablespoons unsalted butter
**1 tablespoon plus 4 teaspoons finely grated
 Pecorino Romano, plus more if desired**
½ cup fresh ricotta
Extra-virgin olive oil

Heat a very large skillet (or a Dutch oven; see page 215 for tips) over medium-high heat. Add the guanciale and cook, stirring, until it is golden and much of the fat has rendered, about 5 minutes. Pour off all but 3 tablespoons of the fat. Add the chili flakes and cook over medium heat for 30 seconds. Add 2 tablespoons water to the pan. Remove from the heat.

In a large pot of well-salted boiling water, cook the pasta according to the package instructions until 2 minutes shy of al dente; drain.

Toss the mezze maniche into the skillet with the guanciale, butter, and 1 tablespoon of the Pecorino Romano. Cook, stirring occasionally, for 30 seconds. Add the ricotta and cook until the pasta is al dente and a loose, creamy sauce has formed, 1 to 2 minutes. Add more water if necessary.

Divide the pasta among four individual serving plates or bowls and finish each with 1 teaspoon or more of Pecorino and a drizzle of olive oil.

Spaghetti with White Puttanesca

This dish was a happy accident. Andrew was testing a standard—i.e., tomato-based—puttanesca recipe for this book in which he added all the other elements (save the parsley) before the tomato. It looked and smelled gorgeous in the pan, so we tasted it and found it to be fantastic on its own, without the tomatoes.

To bring out the most flavor from these few ingredients, make sure to get your pan extremely hot before attempting to fry the capers and anchovies until they are brown and sizzling. Once the anchovies have dissolved and the capers are nicely crisp, add the garlic and chili flakes, letting them toast and the flavors develop. Really good olives add both some funkiness and some fruitiness, and parsley lends a nice herbal quality to the heady aromas.

SERVES 4

½ cup extra-virgin olive oil, plus more
  for drizzling
8 anchovy fillets
¼ cup salt-packed capers, soaked, drained,
  and rinsed (see Andrew's note, page 30)
1 cup pitted and sliced Nocellara or
  Cerignola olives

8 fat garlic cloves, smashed and peeled
½ teaspoon chili flakes
1 pound spaghetti
¾ cup chopped flat-leaf parsley
Kosher salt

In a very large skillet (or a Dutch oven; see page 215 for tips), warm ¼ cup of the olive oil over medium-high heat until very hot. Add the anchovies and capers and cook, stirring occasionally, until nicely browned, about 3 minutes. Add the remaining ¼ cup olive oil, the olives, garlic, and chili flakes and cook until the garlic is golden, about 3 minutes. Add 2 tablespoons water to the pan. Remove from the heat.

In a large pot of well-salted boiling water, cook the pasta according to the package instructions until 2 minutes shy of al dente; drain.

Toss the spaghetti into the skillet with the caper-anchovy mixture. Cook over medium heat until the pasta is al dente, 1 to 2 minutes, adding additional water if the sauce seems dry. Toss in the parsley and season with salt to taste.

Divide the pasta among four individual serving plates or bowls and finish each with a drizzle of olive oil.

Andrew's Note: While we say that good-quality ingredients are important all the time, in this recipe, they are critical. Mushy, bland supermarket Kalamata olives will just not cut it, and this is certainly a dish calling for top-shelf anchovies, and salt-packed capers. If you pull out all the stops, this simple pasta will surprise you.

Rigatoni with Spicy Salami and Tomato

An alternative to a traditional pasta amatriciana (spicy tomato sauce made with cured pork guanciale), this soul-satisfying dish was born thanks to a test batch of salami that we made for Bklyn Larder. Somehow we'd gotten the chili proportions off and while it wasn't spicy enough to sell as sopressata, it was too spicy to sell as regular salami. So Andrew sliced the salami up, crisped it in a pan, and added our house tomato sauce and plenty of olive oil and cheese. It's a simple dish with lusty, soul-satisfying flavors, bolstered with lots of chili.

SERVES 4

8 ounces spicy sopressata, casings removed
2 tablespoons extra-virgin olive oil, plus more for drizzling
½ teaspoon chili flakes

2 cups Basic Tomato Sauce (page 349)
1 pound rigatoni
¼ cup finely grated Pecorino Romano, plus more for serving

Cut the sopressata into batons about 2 inches long and ¼ inch thick.

In a very large skillet (or a Dutch oven; see page 215 for tips), warm the olive oil over medium-high heat. Add the sopressata and cook, stirring occasionally, until it has crisped and rendered some of its fat. Add the chili flakes and cook for 30 seconds, then add the tomato sauce and cook over high heat until most of the liquid has evaporated, about 8 minutes. Remove from the heat.

In a large pot of well-salted boiling water, cook the pasta according to the package instructions until 2 minutes shy of al dente; drain.

Toss the rigatoni into the skillet with the sopressata and tomato mixture and cook over medium heat, stirring occasionally, until the pasta is al dente and the sauce has reduced and clings to the pasta, 2 to 3 minutes. Add the Pecorino Romano, then add a few tablespoons of water if the sauce seems dry.

Divide the pasta among four individual serving plates or bowls and finish each with a sprinkling of Pecorino and a drizzle of olive oil.

PASTA

Fusilli with Pork Sausage Ragu

This is one of the most popular dishes at Franny's. Instead of taking big cuts of meat and braising them until they fall apart, we grind the meat and aggressively season it, thereby making a kind of ad hoc sausage meat. The flavor notes here are very much those of Southern Italy, with a touch of rich tomato paste and a dash of chili. Pancetta, with its porky richness, adds another dimension. Fusilli, offering up all those nooks and crannies in which the sausage can hide, makes the perfect companion to this ragu.

SERVES 4 TO 6

2 tablespoons unsalted butter
2 tablespoons extra-virgin olive oil
2½ pounds coarsely ground pork
⅔ cup ¼-inch-diced pancetta (3½ ounces)
½ teaspoon chili flakes
3 large garlic cloves, minced
1 medium onion, minced
⅔ cup finely diced carrots
⅔ cup finely diced celery
⅔ cup chopped flat-leaf parsley
3½ tablespoons tomato paste

⅔ cup dry red wine
One 14-ounce can Italian cherry tomatoes, drained and smashed, or canned diced tomatoes
2 cups water
2 teaspoons kosher salt, plus more to taste
Freshly cracked black pepper
1 pound fusilli
Finely grated Parmigiano-Reggiano and fresh ricotta for finishing

In a heavy stockpot or a Dutch oven, melt the butter with the olive oil over medium-high heat. Add the ground pork (cook in batches if necessary) and cook just until golden; be careful not to overbrown. Using a slotted spoon, remove the meat from the pot and set aside.

Add the pancetta to the pot and cook gently over medium heat until the fat is rendered and the meat begins to crisp. Stir in the chili flakes and garlic and cook until fragrant, about 1 minute. Add the onion, carrots, celery, and parsley and cook until the onion is translucent, 10 to 15 minutes. Stir in the tomato paste and cook for 2 minutes, then add the red wine and bring to a simmer.

Add the pork to the pot, along with the tomatoes, water, and salt. Bring the mixture to a simmer, cover the pot with a tight-fitting lid, and simmer for 40 minutes.

Remove the lid and continue to simmer until the ragu has thickened nicely, 15 to 20 minutes longer. Season to taste with salt and pepper.

Let the ragu cool to room temperature, then refrigerate until thoroughly chilled.

Remove and discard about two-thirds of the fat that has settled on the surface of the ragu, leaving the remaining third to be incorporated back into the sauce.

In a large pot of well-salted boiling water, cook the pasta according to the package instructions until 2 minutes shy of al dente; drain.

While the pasta is cooking, in a very large skillet (or a Dutch oven; see page 215 for tips), warm the ragu over medium heat.

Toss the fusilli into the skillet with the ragu and cook until al dente, 1 to 2 minutes. If the sauce seems dry, add a few tablespoons of water.

Divide the pasta among four individual serving plates or bowls. Finish each with a sprinkle of Parmigiano-Reggiano and a dollop of ricotta.

Linguine with Bottarga di Muggine

Bottarga, the pressed dried roe of certain fish, is a fabulous Italian pantry item that is underappreciated in the United States. It keeps forever and adds a unique richness and brininess to whatever you use it with. We like to use mullet bottarga, as it's milder and more delicate than tuna bottarga. The mullet roe has a delicate salinity, a hint of bitterness, and a touch of sweetness that pairs really well with buttery noodles.

Bottarga is easy to use; just shave some on the top of your pasta, and it will meld into the sauce, imparting a sea-salty taste. The heat and steam of the noodles blooms the flavors of bottarga. Use a fine Microplane zester here, which will get the bottarga almost powdery: the more surface area you expose, the more aromatics you'll gain.

SERVES 4

1 pound linguine
⅓ cup water
2 tablespoons unsalted butter
½ teaspoon freshly cracked black pepper

Juice of 1½ lemons, or more to taste
⅔ cup finely grated bottarga di muggine
 (see Resources, page 357)
About 4 teaspoons extra-virgin olive oil

In a large pot of well-salted boiling water, cook the pasta according to the package instructions until 2 minutes shy of al dente; drain.

Meanwhile, in a very large skillet (or a Dutch oven; see page 215 for tips), combine 2 tablespoons water, the butter, and the pepper and stir over medium-high heat until the butter has melted. Add the pasta, toss to coat, and cook until the pasta is al dente, 1 to 2 minutes, adding additional water if the pasta seems dry. Stir in the lemon juice.

Divide the pasta among four individual serving plates or bowls and finish each with about 2½ tablespoons of the grated bottarga and about 1 teaspoon olive oil; sprinkle on more lemon juice if needed.

Linguine with Meyer Lemon

Pairing lemon with pasta is just brilliant, as it lightens up what could be a very heavy dish. While the Northern Italian rendition uses a mix of cream and lemon juice, this has a silky butter sauce made with lemon zest as well as juice—it's a bright, clean-flavored, lemony pasta. Serve this in winter, when sweet, thin-skinned Meyer lemons are available and you start craving a comforting yet sunny-tasting dish like this. But don't sweat it if you don't have Meyer lemons; regular lemon sweetened with a squeeze of tangerine works beautifully in their place (see the variation).

We add a drizzle of olive oil—ideally a light, aromatic Ligurian oil—just before serving so that the fragrance of the warmed oil melds with the sauce. Our kids beg for this: when she was only two years old, Prue used to shout, "More lemon!"

SERVES 4

1 pound linguine
6 tablespoons unsalted butter
½ teaspoon freshly cracked black pepper
Finely grated zest of 2 Meyer lemons
¼ cup finely grated Parmigiano-Reggiano, plus more if desired

Juice of 1 Meyer lemon
½ teaspoon kosher salt, or more to taste
Extra-virgin olive oil

In a large pot of well-salted boiling water, cook the pasta according to the package instructions until 2 minutes shy of al dente; drain.

In a very large skillet (or a Dutch oven; see page 215 for tips) set over medium-low heat, combine the linguine and ¼ cup water. Stir in the butter, pepper, and lemon zest. Increase the heat to medium and use a pair of tongs to toss the pasta. If the pasta seems dry, add a little additional water. Stir in the cheese, lemon juice, and salt; toss again and cook until the sauce has thickened slightly and only a little liquid remains in the pan and the pasta is al dente (increase the heat to high if necessary).

Divide the pasta among four individual serving plates or bowls and finish each with a drizzle of olive oil and more cheese, if desired.

Variation

Linguine with Lemon and Tangerine:
Substitute the zest of 1 regular lemon and 1 tangerine for the Meyer lemon zest and the juice of ½ lemon and ½ tangerine for the Meyer lemon juice.

Farro Spaghetti with Anchovies, Chilies, and Garlic

Pasta made from whole-grain farro (an heirloom grain that is a close cousin to wheat) is richer, nuttier, and earthier than that made from regular wheat flour. This is a perfect winter dish; farro's heft and body will feel comforting and fortifying. Originally we based this dish on a pasta with anchovies and walnuts we'd eaten in Naples. But because the farro itself was nutty, we ended up nixing the walnuts, though we kept the anchovies and brightened everything with a squeeze of lemon and some spicy chili. If you can't find farro pasta, you can use whole wheat pasta in its place.

SERVES 4

½ cup extra-virgin olive oil, plus more
  for drizzling
8 garlic cloves, smashed and peeled
10 anchovy fillets
½ teaspoon chili flakes
1 pound farro spaghetti (or use whole wheat)

⅓ cup chopped flat-leaf parsley
¼ teaspoon freshly cracked black pepper
Juice of ½ lemon
2 to 3 tablespoons finely grated Pecorino
  Romano

In a very large skillet (or a Dutch oven; see page 215 for tips), heat the olive oil over medium-high heat. Stir in the garlic and anchovies and cook until the anchovies are dissolved and the garlic is beginning to color, 2 to 3 minutes. Add the chili flakes and cook for about 30 seconds. Add 2 tablespoons water to the pan. Remove from the heat.

In a large pot of well-salted boiling water, cook the pasta according to the package instructions until 2 minutes shy of al dente; drain.

Toss the spaghetti into the skillet with the garlic-anchovy mixture, parsley, and pepper. Cook over medium heat until the pasta is al dente, 1 to 2 minutes. Stir in the lemon juice and a little more water if the pasta seems dry.

Divide the pasta among four individual serving plates or bowls and finish each with a sprinkle of Pecorino Romano and a drizzle of olive oil.

PIZZA

Pizza just might be the perfect food, a magical substance that pleases most people, of most ages, most of the time. People never seem to tire of pizza. We've been eating at Franny's, as a couple and then as a family, many times a week for the eight years we've been open. And I can honestly say that I have never gotten sick of pizza. Neither have our regulars. Whether it's a quick solo bite at the bar on the way home from work, a date-night feast, or a weekend lunch with out-of-town guests, a meal at Franny's always (or nearly always) seems to include at least one pizza.

That was part of the plan when we opened. We wanted to create a place where our friends could come every night—where people would crave the food and want to come back again and again. So far, so good. And once we came up with the idea of opening a pizza restaurant, it seemed obvious.

The concept was a given—but getting the pizza itself right was another matter. Other than a love of pizza and our trips to Italy, we didn't have a lot to go on. When we opened Franny's, we were at the forefront of a pizza renaissance. While there are now artisanal, wood-fired, brick-oven pizza restaurants in San Francisco, Los Angeles, Seattle, Chicago, . . . virtually everywhere, when we opened, there were only a handful. We love that we caught this new-style pizza wave right at the beginning.

Before we opened in our original space, we hired a third-generation brick-oven builder from Naples to build our hulking brick oven, and then we got to work. When Andrew looks back on the early days of Franny's, he is genuinely appalled: we opened a restaurant based on a food that we didn't really know how to cook. (Chalk it up to youthful naïveté and optimism.) For the first few weeks after we opened, Andrew rolled out the pizza dough with a rolling pin, and the result was all wrong; the rolled-out crusts were crackery and dry. And he cooked the tomato sauce on the stove, as you would for pasta, which stripped it of all its complexity and vibrancy.

But one of the many things I love about Andrew is that he is always researching, reading books, tweaking, experimenting, and not resting until a dish is right. He and the other folks in the kitchen taught each other how to cook pizza, handing knowledge back and forth. The recipes and techniques in this chapter, all of which are based on the traditional Neapolitan-style pizza, represent years of experience.

The pizza made in Naples is taken so seriously in Italy that some pizzas have been designated with governmental protection. To be called a *pizza Margherita* in Italy, a pizza has to meet strict guidelines that govern everything from the type of flour used in the dough to the temperature at which it is baked. True Neapolitan-style pizza is soft throughout (the dough is tender and chewy), and there's a restrained amount of cheese and sauce (both of very high quality). Overall, pizza in Naples is a subtler affair than pizza in America. While Andrew and I respect and admire authentic Neapolitan pizza, and have learned so much from it, we've ultimately gone our own way. Our pizza is a little bit different from anything you'd find in Naples, or anywhere else in this country, for that matter.

Of course, the foundation of any pizza is the dough. Ours is yeasty and deeply flavorful, with just the right balance of crispness and chewiness. Stretching the pizza out by

hand means it puffs spectacularly in the hot oven and forms a few large bubbles around the edges, which take on a crackling black char. The key to the flavor and texture is using a small amount of yeast and letting the dough rise slowly in the fridge, where it has a chance to develop complexity and nuance. We strongly advise against using instant yeast to hurry things along. Patience, we've learned, is part and parcel of making great pizza.

Then there's the sauce. It turns out that the easiest sauce is in fact the best. Taking our cue from Naples, we puree high-quality canned San Marzano tomatoes, then season them aggressively. That's all you need for a bright, lush sauce, and it couldn't be simpler to do.

When it comes to the toppings, there's plenty of room for creativity. But whatever you choose to put on your pizza, use a light hand. You want balance: balance between the sauce and the dough, between the cheese and the anchovy, and so on. Some of our pizza toppings are as traditional as can be (see our version of a Margherita, page 264), while others are purely of our own invention (Tomato, Provolone Piccante, and Roasted Onion Pizza, page 266). Some, of course, are decidedly seasonal (like our Flowering Broccoli Pizza, page 252), in keeping with our overall philosophy.

Whatever the ingredients we put on our pizzas, we make sure they are superb.

We buy the best cheeses we can find, and they're worth every penny. For most of our pizzas, that means buffalo mozzarella, which adds a distinct creamy complexity and depth of flavor. For more elaborate pizzas with other meats, you can use either buffalo mozzarella or a good-quality fresh cow's-milk mozzarella. We've done it both ways, and while we've ultimately come to prefer the more pronounced taste of the buffalo, the buttery milkiness of the cow's-milk cheese next to the pungency of sausage or meatballs is also marvelous. As long as the cheese you buy is fresh and well made, whichever mozzarella you choose will be delicious.

Pizza is a great blank canvas for whatever you love, so feel free to change things up to suit your taste. Skip the capers if you're not a fan, or pile them on if you are. Or swap out roasted eggplant for roasted peppers or add olives or anchovies to the Tomato, Garlic, Oregano, and Extra-Virgin Olive Oil Pizza (page 276). Start out with a simple pizza and build from there—if you like onions and sausage together, by all means put them both on your pizza. If you like things spicy, add a generous amount of chili flakes. That said, all of the recipes in this chapter are perfectly calibrated, so we do recommend making them as written at least once— especially the Clam, Chili, and Parsley Pizza (page 263). Follow the recipe to the letter, and you'll be bowled over by its gorgeous, briny perfection.

For baking pizza at home, we came up with a method using a conventional oven that results in a close approximation of the puffed, charred pizzas you get from a wood-fired brick oven (though without the wood-smoke flavor). You do need a pizza stone. If you don't have one, buy the thickest, sturdiest one you can find. Preheat the stone in a 500°F oven for an hour. When you slide in your pizza, the fierce heat from the stone will immediately start baking the bottom crust. Then, after 3 minutes, turn off the oven and turn on the broiler, which will blister the top of the pizza, so your pizza is basically cooked from both top and bottom.

If your oven has a separate broiler, you can still use this technique, but it will require an extra step. After cooking the pizza on the stone in the oven, preheat the broiler. Use tongs to move the half-baked pizza onto a baking sheet and run it under the broiler until the top of the pizza browns, about a minute or two. The results will be just as good.

All of the recipes in this chapter make four individual pizzas. At the restaurant, it's rare for a table of four to order, say, four sausage pizzas or four white pizzas. People order an array of choices, since pizza is ideal for sharing (another part of what makes it so appealing). At home, you could do the same thing and improvise four different pizzas. Don't feel hemmed in. Make the dough and then top each round individually and separately.

For example, you could start out with an EVOO pizza (see page 250) and the Escarole with Meyer Lemon, Parmigiano-Reggiano, and Black Pepper (page 88), then move on to a Flowering Broccoli Pizza (page 252). Wrap things up with a hearty Tomato, Mozzarella, and Sausage Pizza (page 269) and a creamy Buffalo Mozzarella, Ricotta, Garlic, Oregano, and Hot Pepper Pizza (page 258) as the "cheese course." Get the kids involved in the process, letting them help top the pizza. It's just the kind of cooking that kids love to be a part of. And there's no need to fret about timing. Share each pizza as you make it, and no one will go hungry waiting. (If you're lucky enough to have a dual-oven setup in your home kitchen, buy two pizza stones and make two pizzas at once!)

Although making pizza does take some advance preparation, with a little planning and practice, your dinner can take shape pretty quickly. Freeze a bunch of individually portioned sauces and dough balls, then put them in the fridge to defrost before you start your day. You'll have fresh homemade pizza fixings at the ready when you get home. Pizza at home can satisfy an urgent craving, or it can be the centerpiece of a convivial dinner with good friends.

Franny's Pizza Dough

We opened a pizza place with a lot to learn about making pizza. Our first pizzas were wildly inconsistent; we were honestly amazed that anyone who ate one ever came back. We knew what we were looking for: a chewy, flavorful thin crust, burnished all over from the oven and crisp on the bottom, with a few of those delicious bubbles that rise and brown here and there on a great pizza.

Andrew read everything he could about the science of yeast doughs, and he experimented with the amount of yeast, the amount and protein content of the flour, the amount of salt, the amount of kneading, and the rising time. The winning formula (which took years to find; we only just stopped playing around with it recently) is actually very easy. We use the bare minimum of yeast. We let the dough proof (aka rise) slowly, at least overnight, in the fridge, so it becomes way more flavorful than it would rising faster at a warmer temperature, and the gluten develops perfectly—the secret to a chewy, gorgeous crust. Then, after the dough is brought back to room temperature, it's ready to be stretched out (do not roll it!). This method means you'll want to start making your pizza at least 24 hours, and preferably 48 hours, ahead.

While it's not something we do at Franny's, we discovered that this dough freezes really well. If you want to freeze it, after shaping the dough into balls, tightly wrap each ball individually in plastic wrap, place in a resealable freezer bag, and freeze (for up to 3 months). Defrost overnight, or for at least 12 hours, in the refrigerator, or for 2 to 4 hours at room temperature, before using. Feel free to double this recipe if you are feeding a crowd.

MAKES 2 POUNDS, ENOUGH FOR FOUR 12-INCH PIZZAS

2 packed teaspoons fresh yeast (10 grams) **or 1½ teaspoons dry active yeast**
1¾ cups cold water

4½ cups all-purpose flour
2 teaspoons kosher salt

If using fresh yeast, mix the water and yeast together in the bowl of a stand mixer until the yeast is dissolved. If using active dry yeast, mix the water and yeast in the bowl and let sit until the yeast is foamy, about 5 minutes.

Using the dough hook, beat in the flour and salt and mix until a smooth, slightly elastic dough forms, 2 to 3 minutes; do not knead. Place the dough in an oiled bowl, turn the dough to coat, cover loosely with plastic, and refrigerate for at least 24 hours, and up to 48 hours, to proof. (At Franny's we let it proof for 48 hours, at which

point we feel the dough has the optimal texture and flavor, but you've got some leeway at home.)

When you are ready to make the pizza, divide the dough into 4 equal pieces. Shape each piece by using the palm of your hand to rotate the dough clockwise until a tight, compact ball has formed. Turn the dough over. Working from the outside in, pinch and twist the edges of the dough into the center to make a very tight ball. Put the dough on a baking sheet and return to the refrigerator to rest for at least 4 hours, and up to 12 hours.

continued

When you are ready to make the pizzas, remove the dough from the refrigerator and let it sit at room temperature for at least 30 minutes (take the dough out of the fridge while you preheat the pizza stone). You can let it sit out longer, as long as it doesn't get too soft and floppy, which would make it difficult to shape; soft dough is also more likely to stick to the baking sheet or pizza peel, making it harder to slide onto the stone. If the dough gets too soft, stick it back in the fridge for 10 minutes or so to give it a chance to firm up. Shape and top as directed in the individual pizza recipes.

Franny's Pizza Sauce

This pizza sauce is so simple it's almost shocking: all you do is blend uncooked canned tomatoes with a good dose of salt and pepper. Then you spoon it onto the unbaked crust, and the high heat of the oven cooks the sauce just enough to accentuate the tomato flavor and thicken it—no need to simmer it on the stove. And keeping the ingredients to a bare minimum means you'll be able to taste the crust and other toppings without the sauce dominating the pizza.

As far as the texture goes, it's really up to you, but we like to leave some small chunks in there (about the size of a pea)—the sauce shouldn't be completely chunky, but we also don't want it entirely smooth. If you've got plenty of room in your freezer, make two or even three batches. Freeze in plastic bags, in individual pizza-sized portions (about 3 tablespoons per pizza), and it will defrost in a flash and be ready for you when you need it.

MAKES ABOUT 2½ CUPS

One 28-ounce can whole San Marzano tomatoes, drained
½ teaspoon kosher salt, or more to taste
¼ teaspoon freshly cracked black pepper

Using a food mill fitted with the large-holed disk, or a food processor, puree the tomatoes until slightly coarse and loose, not completely smooth. Season with the salt and pepper.

Andrew's Note: Most Italian cooking experts agree that San Marzanos are the best sauce tomatoes in the world. Their flesh is dense, there are fewer seeds, and their strong, sweet flavor is balanced with acidity. San Marzano tomatoes have been designated as the only tomatoes that can be used for true Neapolitan pizza—only tomatoes grown in the San Marzano region from seeds dating back to the original cultivar, and according to strict standards, can receive the Denominazione d'Origine Protetta (DOP) label. If you do not see the prominently displayed DOP label, you are not getting certified San Marzanos. At the restaurant, we usually use the Strianese brand, but there are many others widely available, such as Cento, La Valle, and Caluccio—just look for the DOP label and you'll know you're getting an authentic product. If you can't find DOP San Marzanos, make sure you substitute another tomato with a good balance of sweetness and acidity.

Pizza Techniques

1. Lightly flour an upside-down baking sheet or a pizza peel. You'll use this to transfer the dough onto your pizza stone.

2. Place a dough ball on a lightly floured work surface. Dust the top of the dough with additional flour, and use your fingertips to flatten the dough into a round. Forming the dough into nice even rounds takes practice, but don't worry—even if your dough comes out lopsided and a little funny-looking, the pizza will still taste great.

3. Holding the dough in front of you as you would hold a steering wheel (with hands positioned at ten o'clock and two o'clock), rotate the dough several times, stretching it as you do so. Let the weight of the dough help stretch it. Then move your fists about 6 inches apart and place the dough over your knuckles. Toss the dough in a circle over your knuckles, using your fists to stretch the dough. Try to maintain as even a thickness as possible, with the edges of the dough slightly thicker. Continue until you have a 12-inch round.

4. Carefully set the dough on the floured baking sheet or a pizza peel. Patch any tears or holes in the dough.

5. Use a light touch when topping the dough. You need fewer ingredients and less of them than you might think. You want to be able to taste the charred pizza crust itself, not just the toppings.

6. Before sliding the pizza onto the pizza stone, give the baking sheet (or peel) a shake to make sure the pizza isn't sticking anywhere. If it is, lift up the stuck part and sprinkle more flour underneath it. The pizza needs to easily slide from baking sheet to stone.

7. If you don't have a pizza peel, use tongs to remove the pizza from the oven and transfer to a platter or a cutting board.

8. As a finishing touch to the pizza, a sprinkling of sea salt, a drizzle of olive oil, and often a handful of grated Parmigiano-Reggiano or Grana Padano after the pizza is baked adds yet another layer of flavor and texture.

Extra-Virgin Olive Oil and Sea Salt Pizza

On one of our early trips to Italy, we went into a Roman restaurant and ordered a *pizza bianca*, anticipating one of the cheesy white pizzas we always got in New York. When it arrived, we were confused—it looked like focaccia, without any cheese at all, just a smattering of herbs and a sheen of olive oil. But, as so often happens in Italy, the first bite took away all our doubts. The pizza was perfect in its simplicity, and we came straight home to replicate it.

Very early in the restaurant's tenure, we made this pizza with fresh rosemary and thin slivers of garlic baked on top. That's still the way my mother, Barbara, orders it. While that version is totally delicious, we stripped it down even further and finish the pizza with just a sprinkle of big, crunchy flakes of sea salt.

Of all the pizzas at Franny's, this is the one that lets you taste the bare elements of our pizza the most. There's no missing the satisfying char that develops, or the slight tang of the yeast. And it's a great showcase for super-high-quality olive oil. At the restaurant, this pizza is a true test for any new cook—getting one out of a 900°F wood-fired oven at the right time can be tricky. Fortunately for you, this pizza is actually much easier to make at home. And it's a great way to start off your meal.

MAKES FOUR 12-INCH PIZZAS, SERVING 4 TO 6

Franny's Pizza Dough (page 245)
All-purpose flour

¼ cup extra-virgin olive oil, plus more for drizzling
Sea salt

Preheat the oven to 500°F, with a pizza stone on a rack in the top third of the oven. Let heat for 1 hour. Remove the pizza dough from the refrigerator at least 30 minutes before baking.

Turn a large baking sheet upside down, or use a pizza peel. Dust the surface with flour. Form one piece of the dough into a 12-inch round (see page 248) and set it on the baking sheet or peel.

Working quickly, drizzle the dough with 1 tablespoon of the olive oil.

Jiggle the pizza gently on the pan (or peel) to make sure it is not sticking (if it is, loosen it and sprinkle a little more flour under the area where it stuck). Slide the pizza onto the hot stone, making sure to start at the stone's back end so that the entire pizza will fit on it.

Cook the pizza for 3 minutes. Turn on the broiler. Broil the pizza until golden, crisp, and a bit blistery and charred in places, 2 to 4 minutes (watch it carefully to see that it does not burn). If you don't have a peel, use tongs to slide the pizza onto a large platter. Finish with a drizzle of olive oil and a generous sprinkling of sea salt.

Repeat with the remaining dough and toppings.

Andrew's Note: Because this pizza's only topping is the olive oil, you need to keep a closer eye on it than you do with the other pizzas. Without the weight and moisture of sauce and/or cheese, bubbles tend to form, so the dough can rise and then char fairly quickly. If you see big bubbles rising, just give them a few bangs with the handle of a wooden spoon or puncture them with a paring knife.

Flowering Broccoli Pizza

One of our favorite vendors at Brooklyn's Grand Army Plaza Greenmarket is Kira Kinney's Evolutionary Organics. And from her stall one very early spring, this pizza was born. Kira grows overwintered greens that blossom into sweet little sprouts by about April. Flowering kale, flowering broccoli, even flowering bok choy—topped with yellow and white buds, these plants are almost like an edible bouquet of wildflowers, a welcome sight after a long winter.

Chef John Adler came up with this simple, vibrant pizza as a great way to get some greens on the menu at a time when they are in short supply. There's no tomato sauce, because the pizza doesn't need it—the focus is all on the interplay among the broccoli leaves, stems, and flowers. Some of the leaves will char a touch (delicious), and the stems roast just enough to take on a complex sweetness. Finished with some sharp Pecorino Romano and a squeeze of lemon, this has swayed many a pizza traditionalist at the restaurant. Regular broccoli rabe would work fine here too. Just pull the florets apart into small pieces and slice the stems into ¼-inch-thick slivers.

MAKES FOUR 12-INCH PIZZAS, SERVING 4 TO 6

Franny's Pizza Dough (page 245)
8 ounces flowering greens, such as broccoli rabe
All-purpose flour
4 small garlic cloves, shaved into paper-thin slices with a knife or a mandoline
Chili flakes

4 ounces Parmigiano-Reggiano or Grana Padano, finely grated (about 1 cup)
¼ cup extra-virgin olive oil, plus more for drizzling
2 ounces Pecorino Romano, finely grated (about ½ cup)
2 lemons, halved

Preheat the oven to 500°F, with a pizza stone on a rack in the top third of the oven. Let heat for 1 hour. Remove the pizza dough from the refrigerator at least 30 minutes before baking.

Coarsely chop the tops of the flowering greens. Trim away any woody stem ends and cut the remaining stems into halves or quarters (¼ inch thick is good; you should have about 4 cups greens and stems total).

Turn a large baking sheet upside down, or use a pizza peel. Dust the surface with flour. Form one piece of the dough into a 12-inch round (see page 248) and set it on the baking sheet or peel.

Working quickly, scatter the dough with one-fourth of the garlic and a pinch of chili flakes followed by one-fourth of the greens. Sprinkle

with one-fourth of the Parmagiano-Reggiano and drizzle with 1 tablespoon of the olive oil.

Jiggle the pizza gently on the pan (or peel) to make sure it is not sticking (if it is, loosen it and sprinkle a little more flour under the area where it stuck). Slide the pizza onto the hot stone, making sure to start at the stone's back end so that the entire pizza will fit on it.

Cook the pizza for 3 minutes. Turn on the broiler. Broil the pizza until golden, crisp, and a bit blistery and charred in places, 2 to 4 minutes (watch it carefully to see that it does not burn). If you don't have a peel, use tongs to slide the pizza onto a large platter. Drizzle with more olive oil, sprinkle with one-fourth of the Pecorino Romano, and squeeze the juice of ½ lemon over the top.

Repeat with the remaining dough and toppings.

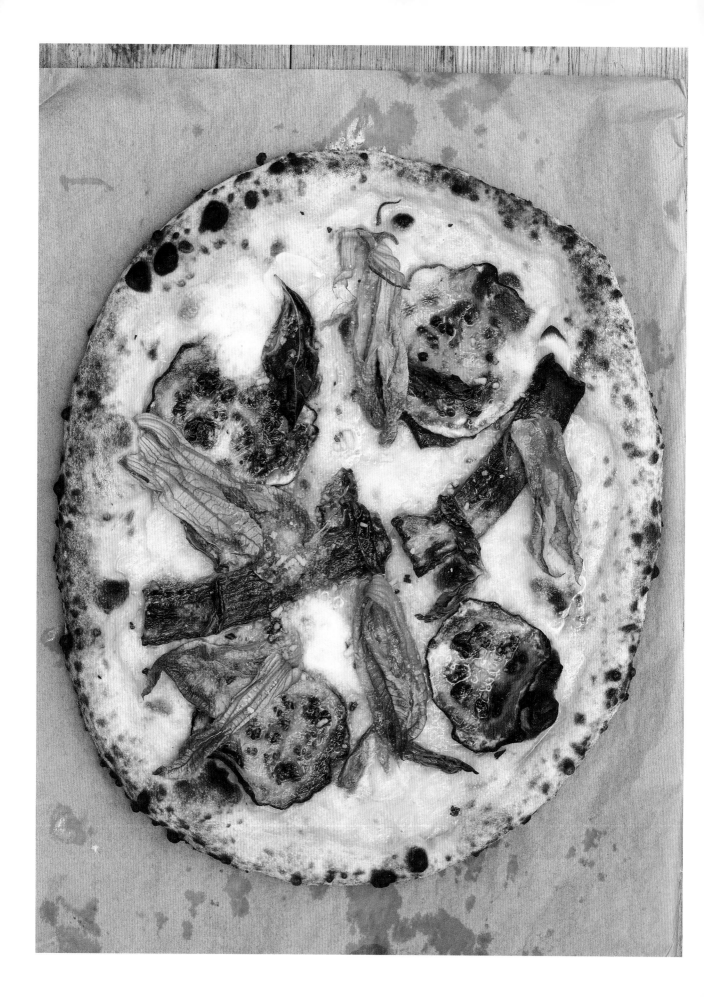

Zucchini, Buffalo Mozzarella, and Basil Pizza

On a trip to Rome, Andrew stopped to grab some lunch at Volpetti. It's his favorite food shop in Rome, with a self-service restaurant next door. It was summer, prime zucchini season, so Andrew ordered pizza topped with mozzarella, zucchini, and zucchini blossoms. Coming up with a version that worked for Franny's, though, was a struggle. Originally the zucchini slices went on raw, and when the pizza emerged from the oven, the zucchini was bland and almost watery. It was Chef Danny Amend's clever idea to roast the slices first, condensing them and developing their flavor, and then the pizza came out perfectly. When we have access to them, we add zucchini blossoms to this pizza as well—they make for a stunning presentation.

MAKES FOUR 12-INCH PIZZAS, SERVING 4 TO 6

FOR THE ZUCCHINI
4 medium zucchini, trimmed
2 tablespoons extra-virgin olive oil
¾ teaspoon kosher salt

FOR THE PIZZA
Franny's Pizza Dough (page 245)
All-purpose flour
4 small garlic cloves, shaved into paper-thin slices with a knife or a mandoline

½ teaspoon chili flakes
12 ounces fresh mozzarella, preferably buffalo, pulled into bite-sized pieces (about 2 cups)
1 bunch basil
Scant 3 tablespoons extra-virgin olive oil, plus more for drizzling
2 ounces Parmigiano-Reggiano or Grana Padano, finely grated (about ½ cup)
Sea salt

To make the zucchini: Preheat the oven to 450°F. Slice each zucchini lengthwise into ¼-inch-thick slabs. Spread them in a single layer on a rimmed baking sheet. Drizzle with the olive oil and sprinkle with the salt. Roast until just tender but not limp, 7 to 10 minutes. Cool. (You can roast the zucchini 8 hours ahead; store at room temperature.)

Increase the oven temperature to 500°F, arrange a rack in the top third of the oven, and place a pizza stone on the rack. Let heat for 1 hour. Remove the pizza dough from the refrigerator at least 30 minutes before baking.

Turn a large baking sheet upside down, or use a pizza peel. Dust the surface with flour. Form one piece of the dough into a 12-inch round (see page 248) and set it on the baking sheet or peel.

Working quickly, scatter the dough with one-fourth of the garlic and a generous pinch of chili flakes. Arrange one-fourth of the zucchini slices

on top of the pizza. Scatter one-fourth of the mozzarella and 5 to 7 basil leaves, depending on their size, over the zucchini. Drizzle with 2 teaspoons of the oil.

Jiggle the pizza gently on the pan (or peel) to make sure it is not sticking (if it is, loosen it and sprinkle a little more flour under the area where it stuck). Slide the pizza onto the hot stone, making sure to start at the stone's back end so that the entire pizza will fit on it.

Cook the pizza for 3 minutes. Turn on the broiler. Broil the pizza until golden, crisp, and a bit blistery and charred in places, 2 to 4 minutes (watch it carefully to see that it does not burn). If you don't have a peel, use tongs to slide the pizza onto a large platter. Sprinkle with one-fourth of the Parmigiano-Reggiano and a pinch of sea salt, and drizzle with more olive oil.

Repeat with the remaining dough and toppings.

Ricotta, Buffalo Mozzarella, Oregano, and Cherry Tomato Pizza

The classic Neapolitan *pizza filetti* studded with fresh cherry tomatoes was the inspiration for this pizza. But instead of scattering raw cherry tomatoes over the dough, we slow-roast the tomatoes first. They're almost identical to those we use on our roasted cherry tomato and ricotta crostini (see page 26). If you want to make a big batch, they will hold, submerged in olive oil and stored in the fridge, for at least a couple of weeks. They're delicious on everything: salad, pasta, even scrambled eggs. And on this pizza the little bursts of tart-sweet concentrated tomato flavor are just terrific paired with the creamy ricotta and buffalo mozzarella.

MAKES FOUR 12-INCH PIZZAS, SERVING 4 TO 6

FOR THE TOMATOES
2 cups cherry tomatoes, halved
2 teaspoons extra-virgin olive oil,
  plus more to taste
¼ teaspoon kosher salt
Pinch of freshly cracked black pepper

FOR THE PIZZA
Franny's Pizza Dough (page 245)
All-purpose flour

5 ounces (½ cup) **fresh ricotta**
12 ounces fresh mozzarella, preferably
  buffalo, pulled into bite-sized pieces
  (about 2 cups)
1 large bunch basil
2 tablespoons extra-virgin olive oil,
  plus more for drizzling
2 ounces Parmigiano-Reggiano or Grana
  Padano, finely grated (about ½ cup)
Sea salt

To roast the tomatoes: Preheat the oven to 225°F. Arrange the tomatoes cut side up on a rimmed baking sheet. Drizzle with the olive oil and season with the salt and pepper. Roast until the tomatoes have lost 50 percent of their volume, 1½ to 2 hours. Cool.

Transfer the tomatoes to a container and cover with olive oil. (They will keep in the fridge for 2 weeks.)

When you are ready to bake the pizzas, preheat the oven to 500°F, with a pizza stone on a rack in the top third of the oven. Let heat for 1 hour. Remove the pizza dough from the refrigerator at least 30 minutes before baking.

Turn a large baking sheet upside down, or use a pizza peel. Dust the surface with flour. Form one piece of the dough into a 12-inch round (see page 248) and set it on the baking sheet or peel.

Working quickly, dot the dough with one-fourth of the ricotta, followed by one-fourth of the mozzarella. Scatter 5 to 7 basil leaves

(depending on their size) over the pizza and drizzle with 1½ teaspoons of the olive oil.

Jiggle the pizza gently on the pan (or peel) to make sure it is not sticking (if it is, loosen it and sprinkle a little more flour under the area where it stuck). Slide the pizza onto the hot stone, making sure to start at the stone's back end so that the entire pizza will fit on it.

Cook the pizza for 3 minutes. Turn on the broiler. Broil the pizza until golden, crisp, and a bit blistery and charred in places, 2 to 4 minutes (watch it carefully to see that it does not burn). If you don't have a peel, use tongs to slide the pizza onto a large platter.

Top the pizza with one-fourth of the tomatoes (about 12) and 1 tablespoon of the tomato oil. Sprinkle with one-fourth of the Parmigiano-Reggiano and a pinch of sea salt and drizzle with additional olive oil.

Repeat with the remaining dough and toppings.

PIZZA

Buffalo Mozzarella, Ricotta, Garlic, Oregano, and Hot Pepper Pizza

A pizza for cheese lovers, this is everything a white pizza should be. Of course, it's mostly about the cheese—with ultrafresh, high-quality ricotta and buffalo mozzarella and a salty sprinkling of Parmigiano-Reggiano, it's dairy in all its glory. Throw in grassy oregano, pungent garlic, and spicy house-pickled peppers, and you've got something really special. This pizza had gone through many makeovers, but it hasn't changed since we landed on this version. (Though in the summer, we do swap out the oregano for fresh basil leaves.)

There's nothing wrong with leaving the hot peppers off, but their sweet bite paired with a touch of spicy heat makes this pizza what it is. The first year that we pickled peppers, we bought about two hundred pounds of summer-ripe Hungarian hots. We ran out of them by the following January. Come August, our chefs, Danny Amend and John Adler, were determined to make enough to last year-round. Five hundred pounds turned out to be enough. If you're someone who enjoys things spicy, pickle more peppers than you think you'll need. They're that good.

MAKES FOUR 12-INCH PIZZAS, SERVING 4 TO 6

Franny's Pizza Dough (page 245)
All-purpose flour
4 small garlic cloves, shaved into paper-thin slices
12 ounces fresh mozzarella, preferably buffalo, pulled into bite-sized pieces (about 2 cups)
5 ounces (about ½ cup) **fresh ricotta**

4 to 6 teaspoons minced Pickled Hot Peppers (page 352), **to taste**
4 pinches dried oregano or 1 bunch basil
¼ cup extra-virgin olive oil, plus more for drizzling
Sea salt
2 ounces Parmigiano-Reggiano finely grated (about ½ cup)

Preheat the oven to 500°F, with a pizza stone on a rack in the top third of the oven. Let heat for 1 hour. Remove the pizza dough from the refrigerator at least 30 minutes before baking.

Turn a large baking sheet upside down, or use a pizza peel. Dust the surface with flour. Form one piece of the dough into a 12-inch round (see page 248) and set it on the baking sheet or peel.

Working quickly, scatter the dough with one-fourth of the garlic, followed by one-fourth of the mozzarella. Dot one-fourth of the ricotta over the top, followed by one-fourth of the hot peppers. Sprinkle with a pinch of oregano (or 7 to 10 basil leaves). Drizzle with 1 tablespoon of the olive oil and sprinkle with a pinch of salt.

Jiggle the pizza gently on the pan (or peel) to make sure it is not sticking (if it is, loosen it and

sprinkle a little more flour under the area where it stuck). Slide the pizza onto the hot stone, making sure to start at the stone's back end so that the entire pizza will fit on it.

Cook the pizza for 3 minutes. Turn on the broiler. Broil the pizza until golden, crisp, and a bit blistery and charred in places, 2 to 4 minutes (watch it carefully to see that it does not burn). If you don't have a peel, use tongs to slide the pizza onto a large platter. Sprinkle with one-fourth of the Parmigiano-Reggiano, drizzle with additional oil, and sprinkle with salt.

Repeat with the remaining dough and toppings.

Andrew's Note: Our house-pickled hot peppers are fantastic with this pizza, but you can also use store-bought pickled hot peppers, chopped.

Anchovy, Garlic, Chili, Caper, and Pecorino Pizza

Chef John Adler created this pizza, and it's one of my favorites because I lean toward pizzas without tomato sauce. They feel lighter and are more focused, flavorwise, and they almost always wind up a bit crunchier.

The key here is to chop the capers and anchovies, which makes it easier to disperse them evenly over the pizza. This ensures a great balance—you get a little bit of briny-salty goodness in each bite. Surprisingly, though this pizza is essentially smothered with anchovies, some of the most staunch anchovy haters find they enjoy them when they try this pizza. Hard lines can be drawn when it comes to anchovies, and I think that has a lot to do with people having experienced nothing but the crummy fillets on the take-out pizzas of their childhood. Bad anchovies are terrible, but good ones, such as those packed in olive oil and imported from Italy or Spain—Agostina Recca (see Resources, page 357) are fantastic—are nuanced, saline, and not at all "fishy." They are absolutely worth spending a little extra money on, and if you do, even your anchovy-averse teenager may be swayed by this delicious pizza.

MAKES FOUR 12-INCH PIZZAS, SERVING 4 TO 6

Franny's Pizza Dough (page 245)
All-purpose flour
16 to 24 anchovy fillets, depending on size,
coarsely chopped
4 teaspoons drained capers, chopped
8 small garlic cloves, shaved into
paper-thin slices
Dried oregano (see Andrew's Note)

Chili flakes
4 ounces Parmigiano-Reggiano,
finely grated (about 1 cup)
2 ounces Pecorino Romano, finely grated
(about ½ cup)
2 lemons, halved
Extra-virgin olive oil for drizzling

Preheat the oven to 500°F, with a pizza stone on a rack in the top third of the oven. Let heat for 1 hour. Remove the pizza dough from the refrigerator at least 30 minutes before baking.

Turn a large baking sheet upside down, or use a pizza peel. Dust the surface with flour. Form one piece of the dough into a 12-inch round (see page 248) and set it on the baking sheet or peel.

Working quickly, scatter the dough with one-fourth of the anchovies, capers, and garlic. Sprinkle with a pinch each of oregano and chili flakes. Scatter one-fourth of the Parmigiano-Reggiano over the pizza.

Jiggle the pizza gently on the pan (or peel) to make sure it is not sticking (if it is, loosen it and sprinkle a little more flour under the area where it

stuck). Slide the pizza onto the hot stone, making sure to start at the stone's back end so that the entire pizza will fit on it.

Cook the pizza for 3 minutes. Turn on the broiler. Broil the pizza until golden, crisp, and a bit blistery and charred in places, 2 to 4 minutes (watch it carefully to see that it does not burn). If you don't have a peel, use tongs to slide the pizza onto a large platter. Scatter one-fourth of the Pecorino Romano and squeeze the juice of ½ lemon over the pizza. Finish with a drizzling of olive oil.

Repeat with the remaining dough and toppings.

Andrew's Note: If you can find dried oregano imported from Sicily that's still on the stem, use it here. It has a unique, pungent flavor.

PIZZA

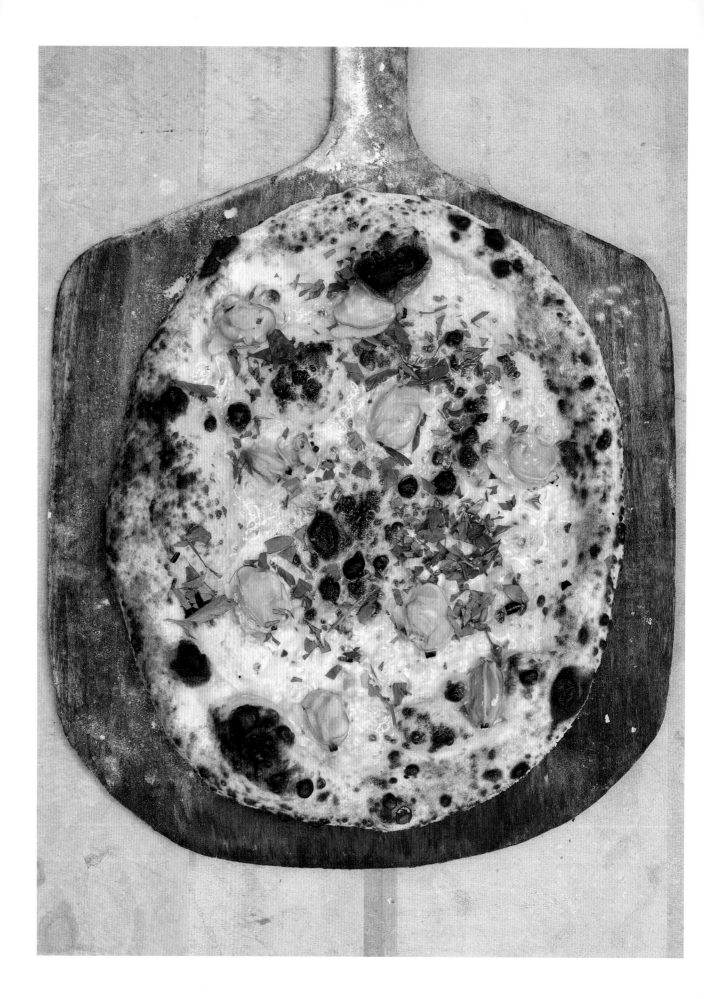

Clam, Chili, and Parsley Pizza

There's not much on Franny's menu that reflects Andrew's training in classic French cuisine, with the prominent exception of our clam pizza. You wouldn't necessarily think so, as clam pizza is an Italian-American staple, especially in New Haven. But ours is significantly different. Andrew steams sweet littleneck clams with onions, garlic, and wine, then simmers the clam broth with a little heavy cream. This intense shellfish glaze gets painted on the dough, adding a depth of clam flavor that you don't get in the usual clam pizza. Plus, the cream sauce bubbles and caramelizes in the oven, adding even more complexity and a richness that we cut with a touch of chili and a generous handful of fresh parsley.

It's a magical combination that developed a following as soon as we put it on the menu. Former *New York Times* restaurant critic Frank Bruni waxed poetic about this pizza, and it was so popular back in the early days of the restaurant that if we had a busy night, we'd sometimes run out. And when that happened, a few folks would be truly heartbroken.

You'll notice that the clam pizza is a bit more labor-intensive than the other pizzas, but none of the steps is hard. And the results are so worth it.

MAKES FOUR 12-INCH PIZZAS, SERVING 4 TO 6

Franny's Pizza Dough (page 245)
¼ **cup extra-virgin olive oil, plus more for drizzling**
½ **Spanish onion, cut into chunks**
4 **garlic cloves, smashed and peeled**
1¼ **cups dry white wine**

4½ **dozen littleneck clams** (about 6 pounds), **scrubbed well**
1½ **cups heavy cream**
All-purpose flour
Chili flakes
½ **cup chopped parsley**

Preheat the oven to 500°F, with a pizza stone on a rack in the top third of the oven. Let heat for 1 hour. Remove the pizza dough from the refrigerator at least 30 minutes before baking.

While the oven heats, place ¼ cup olive oil in a large pot over medium heat. Add the onion and sauté until it is limp, about 5 minutes. Add the garlic, reduce the heat to low, and cook for 7 minutes, until the edges are golden. Add the wine and bring to a simmer. Add the clams, cover the pot, and cook until the clams start to open, about 10 minutes. As they open, transfer them to a large bowl. When all the clams are cooked, simmer the liquid in the pot until it reduces to a thick glaze, about 10 minutes. Add the cream, bring to a simmer, and reduce by a quarter, 10 to 15 minutes longer. Strain through a fine-

mesh sieve into a bowl and set aside. It thickens as it cools.

Meanwhile, when the clams are cool, pluck out the meat and discard the shells.

Turn a large baking sheet upside down, or use a pizza peel. Dust the surface with flour. Form one piece of the dough into a 12-inch round (see page 248) and set it on the baking sheet or peel.

Working quickly, paint the entire surface of the pizza with one-fourth of the glaze. Scatter the clams over the pizza and sprinkle with chili flakes.

Jiggle the pizza gently on the pan (or peel) to make sure it is not sticking (if it is, loosen it and sprinkle a little more flour under the area where it stuck). Slide the pizza onto the hot stone, making

continued

sure to start at the stone's back end so that the entire pizza will fit on it.

Cook the pizza for 3 minutes. Turn on the broiler. Broil the pizza until golden, crisp, and a bit blistery and charred in places, 2 to 4 minutes (watch it carefully to see that it does not burn). If you don't have a peel, use tongs to slide the

pizza onto a large platter. Drizzle with oil and scatter with one-fourth of the parsley.

Repeat with the remaining dough and toppings.

Andrew's Note: Finish this pizza with a squeeze of lemon juice. It adds a bright note of acidity that helps cut the richness of the cream.

Tomato, Buffalo Mozzarella, and Basil Pizza

Without a doubt, this is the most classic, the most revered, and the most truly Neapolitan pizza on our menu. It is also Andrew's year-round favorite, even though the basil comes and goes with the change of the seasons. For most Americans, this is what they think of when they think of artisanal pizza—a perfect balance of bright-flavored tomato sauce; creamy, tangy mozzarella (we use buffalo mozzarella); and fragrant basil leaves, all on a charred and puffed crust. We like to add a finish of grated Parmigiano-Reggiano and very good olive oil, which isn't something you really see done in Naples. But it's a delicious crowning touch, and we stand by the unorthodoxy.

MAKES FOUR 12-INCH PIZZAS, SERVING 4 TO 6

Franny's Pizza Dough (page 245)
All-purpose flour
¾ cup Franny's Pizza Sauce (page 246)
12 ounces buffalo mozzarella, pulled into bite-sized pieces (about 2 cups)

1 bunch basil
2 ounces Parmigiano-Reggiano or Grana Padano, finely grated (about ½ cup)
Sea salt
Extra-virgin olive oil for drizzling

Preheat the oven to 500°F, with a pizza stone on a rack in the top third of the oven. Let heat for 1 hour. Remove the pizza dough from the refrigerator at least 30 minutes before baking.

Turn a large baking sheet upside down, or use a pizza peel. Dust the surface with flour. Form one piece of the dough into a 12-inch round (see page 248) and set it on the baking sheet or peel.

Working quickly, spread one-fourth of the tomato sauce over the dough, then scatter one-fourth of the mozzarella over the pizza. Top with 5 to 7 basil leaves, depending on their size.

Jiggle the pizza gently on the pan (or peel) to make sure it is not sticking (if it is, loosen it and sprinkle a little more flour under the area where it

stuck). Slide the pizza onto the hot stone, making sure to start at the stone's back end so that the entire pizza will fit on it.

Cook the pizza for 3 minutes. Turn on the broiler. Broil the pizza until golden, crisp, and a bit blistery and charred in places, 2 to 4 minutes (watch it carefully to see that it does not burn). If you don't have a peel, use tongs to slide the pizza onto a large platter. Sprinkle with one-fourth of the Parmigiano-Reggiano and a pinch of sea salt and drizzle with one-fourth of the olive oil.

Repeat with the remaining dough and toppings.

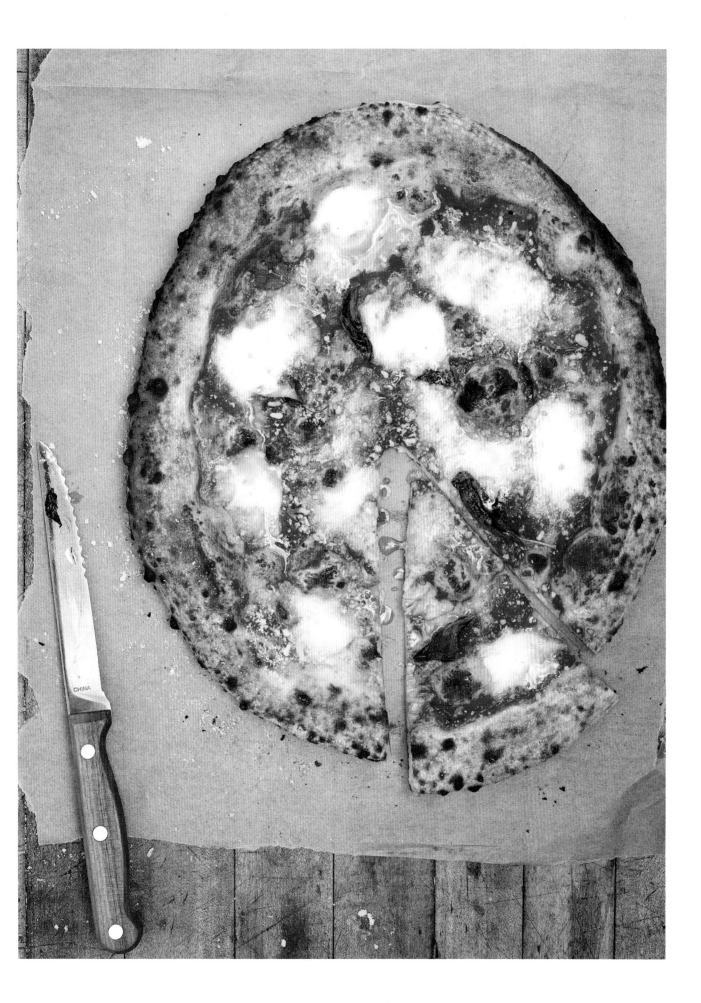

Tomato, Provolone Piccante, and Roasted Onion Pizza

There is nothing traditional about this pizza. We came up with it as a way to use provolone piccante—a wonderfully funky aged cow's-milk cheese that melts beautifully—on one of our pizzas. Provolone piccante is perfect with roasted onions—big, juicy rings that provide a honeyed contrast to the piquant aged cheese. When this pizza emerges from our oven, people's heads whip around, wondering where the incredible smell is coming from. And it's a great option for vegetarians who are craving something hearty.

MAKES FOUR 12-INCH PIZZAS, SERVING 4 TO 6

FOR THE ROASTED ONIONS
1 medium onion
2 tablespoons extra-virgin olive oil
¼ teaspoon kosher salt
Pinch of freshly cracked black pepper

FOR THE PIZZA
Franny's Pizza Dough (page 245)
All-purpose flour
¾ cup Franny's Pizza Sauce (page 246)

Dried oregano, preferably Sicilian
(see Andrew's Note, page 260)
4 ounces Calabrese olives, pitted and torn in half (about 1 cup)
5½ ounces Provolone Piccante cheese, coarsely ground (about 1 cup; see Andrew's Note)
2 ounces Parmigiano-Reggiano, finely grated (about ½ cup)
Extra-virgin olive oil for drizzling

To roast the onions: Preheat the oven to 475°F. Cut the onion into ¾-inch-thick slices. Transfer the slices to a baking sheet, keeping them as intact as possible. Drizzle with the oil and season with the salt and pepper.

Roast the onions until brown and singed on the edges, 20 to 30 minutes. Cool completely, then separate into rings. You can use the onions as soon as they are cool or store in the refrigerator for up to 5 days.

When you are ready to bake the pizza, preheat the oven to 500°F, with a pizza stone on a rack in the top third of the oven. Let heat for 1 hour. Remove the pizza dough from the refrigerator at least 30 minutes before baking.

Turn a large baking sheet upside down, or use a pizza peel. Dust the surface with flour. Form one piece of the dough into a 12-inch round (see page 248) and set it on the baking sheet or peel.

Working quickly, spread one-fourth of the tomato sauce over the dough. Sprinkle with oregano. Scatter one-fourth of the onion rings over the

sauce, and then one-fourth of the olives. Scatter one-fourth of the provolone over the pizza.

Jiggle the pizza gently on the pan (or peel) to make sure it is not sticking (if it is, loosen it and sprinkle a little more flour under the area where it stuck). Slide the pizza onto the hot stone, making sure to start at the stone's back end so that the entire pizza will fit on it.

Cook the pizza for 3 minutes. Turn on the broiler. Broil the pizza until golden, crisp, and a bit charred in places, 2 to 4 minutes (watch it carefully to see that it does not burn). If you don't have a peel, use tongs to slide the pizza onto a large platter. Sprinkle with one-fourth of the Parmigiano-Reggiano and a pinch of sea salt and drizzle with olive oil.

Repeat with the remaining dough and toppings.

Andrew's Notes: To get the proper grind for this cheese, cut it into 1-inch pieces and grind in a food processor until it resembles bread crumbs.

If you can't get provolone piccante, substitute caciocavallo.

Tomato, Mozzarella, and Sausage Pizza

Many people (mostly parents or their young children) come into Franny's asking for a pizza with pepperoni. We've never gone the pepperoni route, but our homemade sausage, sliced into thin rounds that sizzle in the oven, satisfies most folks' need for a spicy pork product gilding their pizza. This pizza is a big hit with kids, including ours. When Prue was little, we'd have the kitchen roast up a plate of the sausage and watch her demolish it. Now when a sausage pizza hits our table, Marco goes right to work, picking the slices off one by one.

MAKES FOUR 12-INCH PIZZAS, SERVING 4 TO 6

Franny's Pizza Dough (page 245)
All-purpose flour
¾ **cup Franny's Pizza Sauce** (page 246)
5 ounces fresh mozzarella, preferably buffalo, pulled into bite-sized pieces (about ¾ cup)

10 ounces Fennel Sausage (page 181), **cut into ¼-inch-thick rounds**
2 ounces Parmigiano-Reggiano or Grana Padano, finely grated (about ½ cup)
Sea salt
2 tablespoons extra-virgin olive oil

Preheat the oven to 500°F, with a pizza stone on a rack in the top third of the oven. Let heat for 1 hour. Remove the pizza dough from the refrigerator at least 30 minutes before baking.

Turn a large baking sheet upside down, or use a pizza peel. Dust the surface with flour. Form one piece of the dough into a 12-inch round (see page 248) and set it on the baking sheet or peel.

Working quickly, spread one-fourth of the tomato sauce over the dough. Scatter one-fourth of the mozzarella and one-fourth of the sausage over the sauce.

Jiggle the pizza gently on the pan (or peel) to make sure it is not sticking (if it is, loosen it and sprinkle a little more flour under the area where it stuck). Slide the pizza onto the hot stone, making sure to start at the stone's back end so that the entire pizza will fit on it.

Cook the pizza for 3 minutes. Turn on the broiler. Broil the pizza until golden, crisp, and a bit blistery and charred in places, 2 to 4 minutes (watch it carefully to see that it does not burn). If you don't have a peel, use tongs to slide the pizza onto a large platter. Sprinkle with one-fourth of the Parmigiano-Reggiano and a pinch of sea salt and drizzle with olive oil.

Repeat with the remaining dough and toppings.

Andrew's Note: You can substitute store-bought sausage for the homemade; just be sure to seek out a good, sweet Italian variety. Cook it first before slicing and adding to the pizza.

Tomato, Mozzarella, and Meatball Pizza

We had a meatball pizza on the menu when we first opened. This was back in the days when Andrew was making everything himself, and after a few months of rolling meatball after meatball, he got sick to death of them. And he was tired of watching the meatballs roll off the pizzas and into the wood fire, which is actually pretty funny if you're not standing in front of a pizza oven for ten hours at a time. So the pizza came off the menu (other items met that same fate; when Andrew got tired of making something, it got nixed, which left me with the unenviable task of explaining this to customers).

Once we had more experience and a well-oiled kitchen staff in place, we brought the meatball pizza back. This time around, the kitchen had the great idea of making the meatballs much larger, roasting them, and then slicing them into wedges, thus solving two problems—the kitchen crew doesn't have to make as many meatballs, and the wedges don't roll off into the fire.

These meatballs are outrageously delicious, and while they're great on the pizza, they'd be tasty elsewhere too—in sliders or on top of spaghetti.

MAKES FOUR 12-INCH PIZZAS, SERVING 4 TO 6

Franny's Pizza Dough (page 245)
All-purpose flour
¾ cup Franny's Pizza Sauce (page 246)
5 ounces fresh mozzarella, preferably buffalo, pulled into bite-sized pieces (about 1¼ cups)

12 Meatballs (page 197), **cut into quarters**
2 ounces Parmigiano-Reggiano, finely grated (about ½ cup)
2 tablespoons extra-virgin olive oil
Sea salt

Preheat the oven to 500°F, with a pizza stone on a rack in the top third of the oven. Let heat for 1 hour. Remove the pizza dough from the refrigerator at least 30 minutes before baking.

Turn a large baking sheet upside down, or use a pizza peel. Dust the surface with flour. Form one piece of the dough into a 12-inch round (see page 248) and set it on the baking sheet or peel.

Working quickly, spread one-fourth of the tomato sauce over the dough. Scatter one-fourth of the mozzarella and one-fourth of the meatballs over the sauce.

Jiggle the pizza gently on the pan (or peel) to make sure it is not sticking (if it is, loosen it and

sprinkle a little more flour under the area where it stuck). Slide the pizza onto the hot stone, making sure to start at the stone's back end so that the entire pizza will fit on it.

Cook the pizza for 3 minutes. Turn on the broiler. Broil the pizza until golden, crisp, and a bit blistery and charred in places, 2 to 4 minutes (watch it carefully to see that it does not burn). If you don't have a peel, use tongs to slide the pizza onto a large platter. Sprinkle with one-fourth of the Parmigiano-Reggiano and a pinch of sea salt and drizzle with 1½ teaspoons of the olive oil.

Repeat with the remaining dough and toppings.

Prosciutto Cotto, Caciocavallo, and Roasted Pepper Pizza

I think our chefs, Danny Amend and John Adler, created this pizza because they wanted an excuse to make their own ham at the restaurant. If that's something you also want to try at home, by all means, make our prosciutto cotto. But if not, a good store-bought ham will work just fine. Some of our guests call it the "ham and cheese pizza," and while I wouldn't want to call it that on our menu, it's a fairly accurate description—though with the addition of silky roasted peppers, it's a pretty elegant ham and cheese. Some of the pieces of ham curl up around the edges, getting all crispy and irresistible. And the caciocavallo lends a delicious creamy tanginess next to the soft, sweet peppers.

MAKES FOUR 12-INCH PIZZAS, SERVING 4 TO 6

1 large red bell pepper
Franny's Pizza Dough (page 245)
All-purpose flour
6 ounces caciocavallo, finely grated
(about 1½ cups)
12 ounces prosciutto cotto, homemade (see
page 186), **or other good-quality sliced
baked ham, torn into bite-sized pieces**

Sea salt
2 ounces Parmigiano-Reggiano,
finely grated (about ½ cup)
¼ cup extra-virgin olive oil

Preheat the oven to 500°F, with a pizza stone on a rack in the top third of the oven. Let heat for 1 hour. Remove the pizza dough from the refrigerator at least 30 minutes before baking.

Meanwhile, place the pepper over a high flame on the stovetop and char the pepper, turning it occasionally, until it is blackened all over but not falling apart. (If you have a gas stove, broil the peppers instead.) Place the pepper in a deep bowl, cover with aluminum foil, and let stand for 10 minutes. Using your fingers or a paring knife, scrape off the blackened pepper skin. Remove and discard the seeds and cut the pepper into ¼-inch-wide strips.

Turn a large baking sheet upside down, or use a pizza peel. Dust the surface with flour. Form one piece of the dough into a 12-inch round (see page 248) and set it on the baking sheet or peel.

Working quickly, scatter the dough with one-fourth of the caciocavallo, followed by one-fourth of the ham and a pinch of sea salt.

Jiggle the pizza gently on the pan (or peel) to make sure it is not sticking (if it is, loosen it and sprinkle a little more flour under the area where it stuck). Slide the pizza onto the hot stone, making sure to start at the stone's back end so that the entire pizza will fit on it.

Cook the pizza for 3 minutes. Turn on the broiler. Broil the pizza until golden, crisp, and a bit blistery and charred in places, 2 to 4 minutes (watch it carefully to see that it does not burn). If you don't have a peel, use tongs to slide the pizza onto a large platter. Distribute one-fourth of the roasted peppers over the pizza. Sprinkle with one-fourth of the Parmigiano-Reggiano and the sea salt, and drizzle with 1 tablespoon of olive oil.

Repeat with the remaining dough and toppings.

Andrew's Note: Don't use regular prosciutto here—it will just dry out in the oven. A good, moist, light pink, freshly baked or boiled prosciutto cotto is what you want. Avoid deli ham, which is filled with preservatives.

Mushroom Pizza

While mushrooms certainly have seasons, there are so many good producers growing lovely cultivated mushrooms year-round, there's no reason not to turn to this pizza whenever you're in the mood for the savory satisfaction that can only come from mushrooms. Any variety will do—the more the merrier to yield 2¼ pounds total. The kitchen roasts them through, letting the mushrooms release their liquid, condense, and take on a golden color. Then they get tossed with a bit of raw garlic, fresh rosemary and sage, and a splash of white wine vinegar. The touch of acid is a surprising addition here, but it contributes some nice complexity to an otherwise fairly straightforward pizza. Though straightforward isn't a bad thing when it comes to mushrooms—their earthy richness is all this pizza really needs.

MAKES FOUR 12-INCH PIZZAS, SERVING 4 TO 6

Franny's Pizza Dough (page 245)

FOR THE MUSHROOMS
6 ounces cremini mushrooms
6 ounces button mushrooms
6 ounces shiitake mushrooms
6 ounces trumpet mushrooms
6 ounces hen-of-the-woods mushrooms
6 ounces oyster mushrooms
½ cup extra-virgin olive oil
1 teaspoon kosher salt
½ teaspoon freshly cracked black pepper

1 teaspoon finely chopped rosemary
1 teaspoon finely chopped sage
1 teaspoon finely chopped garlic
1 tablespoon white wine vinegar
8 ounces mozzarella, preferably buffalo, pulled into bite-sized pieces
(about 1 ⅓ cups)
1 ounce Parmigiano-Reggiano, finely grated
(about ¼ cup)
Sea salt
Extra-virgin olive oil for drizzling

Preheat the oven to 500°F, with a pizza stone on a rack in the top third of the oven. Let heat for 1 hour. Remove the pizza dough from the refrigerator at least 30 minutes before baking.

Meanwhile, clean the mushrooms with a damp paper towel. Cut into bite-sized pieces. Divide the olive oil between two large skillets and heat over high heat until the oil begins to ripple but is not smoking. Add the cremini, button, and shiitake mushrooms to one pan; add the trumpet, hen-of-the-woods, and oyster mushrooms to the other. Cook the mushrooms for 1 minute, tossing them constantly, then reduce the heat to medium. Add half the salt and pepper to each pan and cook until the mushrooms are well caramelized, 3 to 5 minutes more. Remove from the heat and transfer the mushrooms to a large bowl. Add the

herbs and toss for 30 seconds, then stir in the garlic and vinegar. Let cool.

Turn a large baking sheet upside down, or use a pizza peel. Dust the surface with flour. Form one piece of the dough into a 12-inch round (see page 248) and set it on the baking sheet or peel.

Working quickly, scatter the dough with one-fourth of the mushroom mixture and then one-fourth of the mozzarella.

Jiggle the pizza gently on the pan to make sure it is not sticking (if it is, loosen it and sprinkle a little more flour under the area where it stuck). Slide the pizza onto the hot stone, making sure to start at the stone's back end so that the entire pizza will fit on it.

Cook the pizza for 3 minutes. Turn on the broiler. Broil the pizza until golden, crisp, and a bit blistery and charred in places, 2 to 4 minutes (watch it carefully to see that it does not burn). If you don't have a peel, use tongs to slide the pizza onto a large platter. Sprinkle with one-fourth of the Parmigiano-Reggiano and the sea salt. Finish with a drizzling of olive oil.

Repeat with the remaining dough and toppings.

Andrew's Note: I make this pizza using a combination of whatever mushrooms are looking good at the moment. I group the mushrooms with similar cooking times and cook them in the same pan. You don't want to mix a short-cooking mushroom with one that needs longer to cook. Then mix all the mushrooms together with the aromatics before topping the pizzas.

Tomato, Garlic, Oregano, and Extra-Virgin Olive Oil Pizza

This is a pizza that some folks initially just didn't get. It's a cheeseless tomato-sauced pizza—but it's entirely traditional, a true Neapolitan pizza. Called *pizza marinara*, it consists of a red slick of tomato sauce, plenty of garlic and oregano, and lots of olive oil. It doesn't need any cheese—Naples knows what it's doing. And having this pizza on the menu means we've been able to offer something to vegans that they very rarely get to eat: good pizza. At home, this would make a lovely addition to a meal that perhaps featured protein elsewhere. This is definitely one of those times to pull out your very best olive oil—be liberal applying it.

MAKES FOUR 12-INCH PIZZAS, SERVING 4 TO 6

Franny's Pizza Dough (page 245)
All-purpose flour
1 cup Franny's Pizza Sauce (page 246)
12 or 13 Calabrese olives, pitted
**4 small garlic cloves, shaved into
  paper-thin slices**

Dried oregano, preferably Sicilian
  (see Andrew's Note, page 260)
Sea salt
6 tablespoons extra-virgin olive oil

Preheat the oven to 500°F, with a pizza stone on a rack in the top third of the oven. Let heat for 1 hour. Remove the pizza dough from the refrigerator at least 30 minutes before baking.

Turn a large baking sheet upside down, or use a pizza peel. Dust the surface with flour. Form one piece of the dough into a 12-inch round (see page 248) and set it on the baking sheet or peel.

Working quickly, spread one-fourth of the tomato sauce over the crust. Scatter one-fourth of the olives and garlic over the sauce. Sprinkle the pizza with dried oregano and a pinch of sea salt.

Jiggle the pizza gently on the pan to make sure it is not sticking (if it is, loosen it and sprinkle a little more flour under the area where it stuck). Slide the pizza onto the hot stone, making sure to start at the stone's back end so that the entire pizza will fit on it.

Cook the pizza for 3 minutes. Turn on the broiler. Broil the pizza until golden, crisp, and a bit blistery and charred in places, 2 to 4 minutes (watch it carefully to see that it does not burn). If you don't have a peel, use tongs to slide the pizza onto a large platter. Sprinkle with sea salt and drizzle with 1½ tablespoons of the olive oil.

Repeat with the remaining dough and toppings.

Pizza Rustica

Though the Neapolitan name for this traditional recipe uses the word "pizza," it's actually a creamy tart. It wouldn't make sense on the menu at Franny's, but it's perfect for our provisions shop, Bklyn Larder. It's quite sturdy and therefore is good picnic fare—lovely to eat at the park or the beach. And it's a great way to use up leftover salami scraps if you have any—though the tart is so good, it's totally worth buying salami just for it. The buttery short-crust pastry, made with white wine and lemon, has a touch of sweetness, and with the savory richness of the cured meat and the milky ricotta, the result is divine. Next to a cool, crunchy salad, this would make an elegant lunch, or even brunch.

SERVES 8 TO 10

FOR THE CRUST
2¾ **cups all-purpose flour**
4 **teaspoons sugar**
1½ **teaspoons kosher salt**
Grated zest of 1 lemon
12 **tablespoons** (1½ sticks) **unsalted butter, cubed and chilled**
1 **large egg, plus 1 egg beaten with 1 tablespoon water for an egg wash for the top**
1 **large egg white**
2 **tablespoons dry white wine**

FOR THE FILLING
2 **cups** (1¼ pounds) **ricotta**
3 **ounces Pecorino Romano cheese, finely grated** (about ¾ cup)
2 **large eggs**
1 **large egg yolk**
¼ **teaspoon kosher salt**
8 **ounces fresh mozzarella, cut into ¼-inch cubes**
One 2-ounce piece salami, cut into ¼-inch cubes
One 2-ounce piece prosciutto cotto or other mild baked ham, cut into ¼-inch cubes
½ **teaspoon freshly cracked black pepper**
¼ **teaspoon chili flakes**
2 **tablespoons chopped flat-leaf parsley**

To make the crust: In a large bowl, combine the flour, sugar, salt, and lemon zest. Toss in the butter. Cover the bowl with plastic wrap and freeze for 10 minutes.

Transfer the mixture to a food processor and pulse until it resembles coarse crumbs. Add the egg and egg white and pulse until combined. With the food processor running, add the wine and process until the dough just comes together.

Turn the dough out into a bowl and briefly knead it. Divide the dough into 2 pieces, one about 16 ounces, the other about 8 ounces. Shape each piece into a round, wrap it in plastic wrap, and refrigerate for at least 2 hours before rolling.

Preheat the oven to 325°F. On a lightly floured surface, roll the larger round of dough into a 12-inch circle. Transfer it to a 9-inch springform pan (the dough won't come all the way up the sides). Line the crust with parchment paper and fill it with dried beans or pie weights.

Bake the crust for 20 minutes. Remove the parchment and beans or weights and bake for 5 to 10 minutes longer, until the shell is golden brown. Let cool completely. Increase the oven temperature to 350°F.

To make the filling: In a food processor, combine the ricotta, Pecorino Romano, eggs, and yolk and process until smooth. Scrape the mixture into a bowl and fold in the rest of the filling ingredients. Pour the filling into the cooled tart shell.

On a lightly floured surface, roll out the smaller dough round to a 10-inch circle. Cut it into 1-inch-wide strips. Lay half the strips over the filling, spacing them about ¼ inch apart. Weave the remaining strips over and under the first strips, forming a lattice. Press the ends of the strips into the bottom crust.

Brush with the egg wash, and bake until the filling is just set, about 40 minutes. Serve warm or at room temperature.

DESSERTS

Italians are known for their sumptuous pastries and cakes. But after a meal made up of some combination of cured meats, crostini, salads, pasta, and pizza, it can seem like too much. To us, a few perfect sweet bites after a satisfying meal are the ideal way to close the evening.

In Italy, a few bites of something sweet is most likely to consist of gelato. Cold and creamy, intensely flavored, and luscious, it has to be the most popular dessert in Italy. There's a *gelateria* on practically every corner and they are always packed, especially on warm nights, when people spill out the doors, waiting for their frozen treats. Italians eat gelato for dessert after dinner, as a midafternoon snack, and even for breakfast in parts of Sicily, stuffed into a brioche.

So, from the beginning, gelato has featured prominently on our menu. And just as with our pizza dough, Andrew has been tinkering with our gelato recipes since day one. He's perpetually trying to make them better, tweaking the ratio of milk to cream, the amount of sugar, and the flavorings. When we first started, our ice-cream gear consisted of a rather old-fashioned salt-and-wooden-bucket contraption. It was at least an electric, not a hand-crank, model, but it made loads of noise and it took forever to churn. Even after we upgraded to a small home model that had its own compressor, Andrew spent hours every day churning our gelati and sorbetti. When we opened Bklyn Larder and decided to sell pints of our gelati and sorbetti there, we invested in a large-capacity machine that churns out batches in under fifteen minutes. But all of the recipes in this chapter will work in a small home-kitchen machine, just like the one we used to rely on.

Although the definition of gelato varies depending on whom you ask, we say that what gives gelato its character is its density: most ice creams are churned full of air to make them light; gelati are not. With a bowl of gelato, you're getting more of everything—more cream, more flavor, more satisfaction, which is why gelato is usually more expensive than ice cream.

You'll sometimes see egg yolks in gelato recipes, but we leave them out. Egg yolks work well as a stabilizer for homemade frozen desserts, keeping the texture pliant and ice-crystal-free, but they also mask the purity of flavor that we want and add a heaviness we'd rather avoid. Instead, we use a professional gelato stabilizer. At home, you can substitute xanthan gum, which is easy to find in health food stores and large supermarkets and helps achieve the right dreamy texture (see Andrew's Note, page 284).

Because a silky texture is what you are striving for, you don't want to overchurn these gelati; when your base has reached the texture of soft-serve, you're done. And while you can make gelati and sorbetti ahead and store them in the freezer for up to a week, serving them right out of the ice-cream machine is a spectacular treat. It might take a bit of planning to get the timing right (you have to know how long your machine takes to churn a batch, since machines are different in this regard), but the active work once the base is in the machine is nil. And because there are no eggs in our gelati bases, you can refrigerate them for up to 10 days, then churn when needed. So, while you're tidying things up or enjoying that last glass of wine at the table, your gelato can be spinning away. And believe me, your guests will be blown away by a scoop or two of homemade rich, subtle Mascarpone

Honey Gelato (page 288) straight from your ice-cream machine, soft and velvety.

Another wonderfully pure, creamy dessert to serve after a pizza or pasta meal is panna cotta. Our panna cotta (see page 310) is divine and, unlike gelato, doesn't require any special equipment. It's uncommonly luscious, filling and coating your mouth with silky, sweet dairy. And that's the real secret: high-quality dairy. Make panna cotta with the absolute best cream you can source—preferably organic and from grass-fed cows. It makes all the difference. Since there's very little gelatin and just a whisper of sugar in the recipe, you really experience the richness and suppleness that only very good cream can provide. In winter, we serve panna cotta with a touch of *saba*, an Italian grape must syrup that lends just the right note of acidity and depth. But in season, ripe berries or other fruit make marvelous accompaniments to this simple dessert.

Really excellent ripe fruit can also be a flawless dessert served nearly all by itself, as evidenced by Melon in Lovage Syrup (page 303). One summer day, we made too much lovage syrup for the bar, so we poured it over ripe melon slices and served it at our family meal, to the delight of everyone at the table. The herbaceous syrup works especially well with the floral pungency of melon. And with a variety of different-hued melons, the plate is just beautiful. Make this dessert when melon season is at its height—it's worth waiting for the right time.

Although we don't often serve baked goods at Franny's, once we opened Bklyn Larder, there was no question that we needed to offer a regular but ever-changing roster of pastries, cakes, and other treats. Our pastry chef, Inga Sheaffer, stepped in with her ideas and enthusiasm, and now the Larder has a wide array of distinctive homemade goodies. Simple, subtly sweet cakes, such as moist Ricotta Pound Cake (page 309) and fragrant Almond Cake (page 317), can be dressed up with seasonal fruit, gelato, or sorbetto, or served elegantly plain, perhaps with a strong cup of tea.

Slightly more involved but well worth the effort, Inga's fruit crostatas (see pages 304 and 307) are all variations on one fantastic recipe. A flaky, buttery pastry crust barely contains the mound of soft, jam-like fruit that caramelizes in the oven. It's a recipe you can turn to again and again, filling the crostata with just about any variety of fruit you can get, letting the seasons be your guide. That's how we like to do most things at Franny's, from the beginning of the meal through its sweet ending.

Fior di Latte Gelato

With a name that translates as "flower of the milk," this gelato gives people the chance to experience just how remarkable high-quality dairy can be. We've had older folks tell us that this gelato takes them back to their childhood, and there is something about it that evokes flavors from our collective past. Even though many of us grew up with bland ultra-pasteurized milk, we seem to know intuitively how good milk should taste. This classic Italian gelato showcases that gentle yet compelling flavor, so be sure to start out with the best local dairy from pastured cows that you can find.

MAKES ABOUT 1 QUART

¾ cup sugar
1½ teaspoons xanthan gum
   (see Resources, page 357)

½ teaspoon kosher salt
2⅔ cups whole milk
⅔ cup heavy cream

In a medium heavy-bottomed saucepan, whisk together the sugar, xanthan gum, and salt. Slowly whisk in the milk and cream over medium heat and cook, whisking occasionally, until the sugar dissolves and the mixture thickens, 5 to 10 minutes. Transfer to a bowl.

Chill the mixture until it is completely cold, either set over an ice bath or in the refrigerator. (The gelato base can be refrigerated for up to 10 days.)

Churn the gelato in an ice-cream machine according to the manufacturer's instructions. Serve immediately, or transfer to a quart-sized freezer container for longer storage; the gelato can be frozen for up to 5 days. If necessary, soften the frozen gelato at room temperature for 20 minutes or in the refrigerator for 45 minutes before serving.

Andrew's Note: Xanthan gum is readily available in health food stores, and we call for it in all our gelati recipes here as a substitute for the professional gelato stabilizer that we use at Franny's. All ice creams and gelati need some form of stabilizer (often egg yolks) to promote a creamy texture and to keep them from developing ice crystals. We use PreGel Superneutro stabilizer. It does give a slightly better texture than the xanthan gum, but it's only available in large quantities sold wholesale. That said, if you do want to try it, you can order it online (see Resources, page 357). Substitute 1 teaspoon PreGel for every 1½ teaspoons xanthan gum.

Variation

Chocolate Chip Fior di Latte Gelato: Stir in 5 ounces bittersweet chocolate, chopped (⅔ cup), after the gelato has finished churning.

Strawberry Gelato

What could be more enticing on a hot summer day than a scoop of rosy strawberry gelato? We wait until berry season is in full swing—using sweet ripe berries that are red through and through makes a huge difference. After experimenting with a few different strawberry gelato techniques, we settled on one that calls for stirring a berry compote into the gelato base. Cooking the fruit with a little sugar accentuates its flavor, and also helps keep the berries from turning into chunks of red ice. Be sure to taste your strawberries—you might want to reduce the sugar if they're very sweet, or add more if they seem very tart. When we can get large quantities of great berries, we make extra compote and freeze it. Then we can make this gelato as long as our stash lasts, even when strawberry season is over. If you're a strawberry gelato fan, we suggest you do the same.

MAKES ABOUT 1 QUART

1 pound fresh strawberries, washed and hulled
½ cup plus 2½ tablespoons sugar, or to taste
½ teaspoon kosher salt, plus a pinch

1½ teaspoons xanthan gum (see Resources, page 357)
2⅔ cups whole milk
⅔ cup heavy cream

In a large bowl, combine the strawberries, 2½ tablespoons sugar, and pinch of salt. Cover with plastic wrap and refrigerate overnight.

Heat a large wide nonreactive pot over medium-high heat. Add the berries and any accumulated juices and cook until the berries are just starting to break down, about 7 minutes. Strain the mixture through a sieve set over a bowl.

Set the berries aside and return the juices to the pot. Bring to a simmer and simmer until syrupy. Do not let the syrup get too thick, or it may take on a slightly metallic, bitter taste.

Transfer the syrup to a food processor, add the berries, and pulse until the mixture comes together but is still somewhat chunky. Pour into a pint jar and let cool to room temperature, then cover with a tight-fitting lid and refrigerate. (The compote can be refrigerated for up to 3 days or frozen for up to 6 months.)

In a large heavy-bottomed saucepan, whisk together the remaining ½ cup sugar, the xanthan gum, and the remaining ½ teaspoon salt. Slowly whisk in the milk and cream over medium heat and cook, whisking occasionally, until the mixture thickens, 5 to 10 minutes. Transfer to a bowl.

Chill the mixture until it is completely cold, either over an ice bath or in the refrigerator. (The gelato base can be refrigerated for up to 10 days.)

Pour the gelato base into an ice-cream machine and add 1¼ cups of the strawberry compote (you might have a little compote left over; it's great on yogurt). Churn according to the manufacturer's instructions. Serve immediately, or transfer to a quart-sized freezer container for longer storage; the gelato can be frozen for up to 5 days. If necessary, soften the frozen gelato at room temperature for 20 minutes or in the refrigerator for 45 minutes before serving.

Mascarpone Honey Gelato

This rich gelato is extraordinary, and even more so when you seek out a distinctly flavored, interesting honey. We use much less xanthan gum in this gelato recipe than in the others—that's because the mascarpone imparts a dense silkiness and helps keep the cream from turning icy. If you're serving it right out of the machine, feel free to omit the xanthan gum altogether.

MAKES ABOUT 1 QUART

½ **cup sugar**
¼ **teaspoon xanthan gum** (see Resources, page 357)
½ **teaspoon kosher salt**

2 **cups whole milk**
1½ **cups** (12 ounces) **mascarpone**
3½ **tablespoons honey**
¼ **teaspoon vanilla extract**

In a large heavy-bottomed saucepan, whisk together the sugar, xanthan gum, and salt. Slowly whisk in the milk over medium heat and cook, whisking occasionally, until the mixture thickens, 5 to 10 minutes. Remove from the heat and whisk in the mascarpone and honey, then transfer to a bowl.

Chill the mixture until it is completely cold, either set over an ice bath or in the refrigerator. Once it is cold, whisk in the vanilla. (The gelato base can be refrigerated for up to 10 days.)

Churn the gelato in an ice-cream machine according to the manufacturer's instructions. Serve immediately, or transfer to a quart-sized freezer container for longer storage; the gelato can be frozen for up to 5 days. If necessary, soften the frozen gelato at room temperature for 20 minutes or in the refrigerator for 45 minutes before serving.

Pistachio Gelato

Delicate and sweet, pistachios are such special nuts that it's no surprise Italians feature them in so many desserts, particularly gelato. This recipe relies on the nuts exclusively for flavor, without the addition of pistachio extract (or green food coloring). What you get is a gelato with a subtle beige color flecked with green and a pure pistachio flavor.

MAKES ABOUT 1 QUART

4 ounces (1 cup) **pistachios**
½ cup plus 1 tablespoon sugar
1½ teaspoons xanthan gum (see Resources, page 357)

½ teaspoon kosher salt
2⅔ cups whole milk
⅔ cup heavy cream

Preheat the oven to 325°F. Spread the nuts on a rimmed baking sheet and toast until just fragrant, 3 to 5 minutes. You don't want the nuts to take on any color; you just want to bring out their flavor. Transfer to a food processor and blend to a paste.

In a large heavy-bottomed saucepan, whisk together the sugar, xanthan gum, and salt. Slowly whisk in the milk and cream over medium heat and cook, whisking occasionally, until the mixture thickens, 5 to 10 minutes. Remove from the heat and stir in the pistachio paste. Cover and let stand for 30 minutes.

Strain the mixture through a medium-fine sieve into a bowl (you want to use a medium sieve so that some of the little nut bits stay in the gelato). Chill until completely cold, either set over an ice bath or in the refrigerator. (The gelato base can be refrigerated for up to 10 days.)

Churn the gelato in an ice-cream machine according to the manufacturer's instructions. Serve immediately, or transfer to a quart-sized freezer container for longer storage; the gelato can be frozen for up to 5 days. If necessary, soften the frozen gelato at room temperature for 20 minutes or in the refrigerator for 45 minutes before serving.

DESSERTS

Caramel Gelato

This caramel gelato might be the most sophisticated flavor we make. It's rich and sweet, but with a sharp, complex edge to keep things interesting. Be sure to let the sugar caramelize until it's a deep ruddy color, like the red-brown of an Irish setter. Letting it get that dark lends it a touch of bitterness from the slightly burnt sugar, tempering its sweetness. A flourish of buttery crunchy praline stirred in at the end adds a satisfying textural element that puts things over the top.

MAKES ABOUT 1 QUART

FOR THE CARAMEL PRALINE
1 cup sugar
1 tablespoon unsalted butter
½ teaspoon kosher salt

FOR THE GELATO BASE
1 cup plus 2 tablespoons sugar
1½ teaspoons xanthan gum (see Resources, page 357)
½ teaspoon kosher salt
2⅔ cups whole milk
⅔ cup heavy cream
¼ teaspoon vanilla extract

To make the praline: Line a rimmed baking sheet with a Silpat or greased parchment paper. Sprinkle a little of the sugar in the bottom of a heavy skillet and set it over medium heat. As it begins to melt and caramelize, add a little more and melt it, swirling the pan occasionally; continue until all the sugar is melted and the caramel has turned a uniform reddish-brown. Stir in the butter and salt. Immediately scrape the mixture onto the Silpat-lined baking sheet and spread into an even layer. Cool completely.

Using a cleaver or a hammer, break the cooled praline into chunks. Transfer to a food processor and pulse until it is the size of corn kernels but is not completely ground. Toss the praline in a medium sieve to remove any ground candy dust. Set the praline aside.

To make the gelato base: In a large heavy-bottomed saucepan, whisk together 2 tablespoons of the sugar, the xanthan gum, and the salt; set aside.

In a large skillet, caramelize the remaining 1 cup sugar, using the same technique as for the praline. As soon as the caramel becomes reddish-brown, whisk in the milk and cream (beware of splattering). Whisk over medium heat until any bits of hardened caramel are completely melted and smooth.

Place the pan of sugar–xanthan gum over medium heat and slowly whisk in the hot caramel. Cook, whisking occasionally, until the mixture thickens, 5 to 10 minutes. Transfer to a bowl.

Chill the mixture until it is completely cold, either set over an ice bath or in the refrigerator. Once it is cold, whisk in the vanilla extract. (The gelato base can be refrigerated for up to 10 days.)

Churn the gelato in an ice-cream machine according to the manufacturer's instructions. Scrape into a bowl and stir in the praline. Serve immediately, or transfer to a quart-sized freezer container for longer storage; the gelato can be frozen for up to 5 days. If necessary, soften the frozen gelato at room temperature for 20 minutes or in the refrigerator for 45 minutes before serving.

Variation

Salted Caramel Gelato: Serve the gelato with a sprinkle of flaky sea salt, such as Maldon, on top.

Hazelnut Gelato

The profound nuttiness of this gelato, nubby-textured and dense, is achieved by roasting the hazelnuts all the way through in a low oven. There are no frills to this recipe; it's simply a great version of an Italian classic.

MAKES ABOUT 1 QUART

4 ounces (1 cup) **hazelnuts**
½ cup plus 1 tablespoon sugar
1½ teaspoons xanthan gum (see Resources, page 357)

½ teaspoon kosher salt
2⅔ cups whole milk
⅔ cup heavy cream

Preheat the oven to 325°F. Spread the hazelnuts on a rimmed baking sheet and toast until they are a rich dark brown, 15 to 20 minutes. Bundle the warm nuts in a dish towel and rub together to remove the papery skins. Transfer to a food processor and blend to a paste.

In a large heavy-bottomed saucepan, whisk together the sugar, xanthan gum, and salt. Slowly whisk in the milk and cream over medium heat and cook, whisking occasionally, until the mixture thickens, 5 to 10 minutes. Remove from the heat and stir in the hazelnut paste. Cover and let stand for 30 minutes.

Strain the mixture through a medium-fine sieve into a bowl (you want to use a medium sieve so that some of the little nut bits stay in the gelato base). Chill until completely cold, either set over an ice bath or in the refrigerator. (The gelato base can be refrigerated for up to 10 days.)

Churn the gelato in an ice-cream machine according to the manufacturer's instructions. Serve immediately, or transfer to a quart-sized freezer container for longer storage; the gelato can be frozen for up to 5 days. If necessary, soften the frozen gelato at room temperature for 20 minutes or in the refrigerator for 45 minutes before serving.

INGA SHEAFFER

BKLYN LARDER PASTRY CHEF

How did you get started in the food business?

My very first food job was actually at a food co-op. I was in high school and my mom joined the family up, and I worked all the shifts, bulk-bagging nutritional yeast.

First memorable meal?

I have a very strong memory of asking my parents how to make an omelet. I was five or six and I just really wanted to know what this omelet stuff was all about. I was always an eater. I was a food fan from a very early age. I remember coming home from school and reading my mom's battered old *Joy of Cooking.* Then I'd go and make béchamel. I was ten years old, and I was such a nerd about food.

Other than at Bklyn Larder, what is the best job you've ever had?

At Clear Flour in Brookline, Massachusetts. Throughout college, I worked as a barista at coffee shops. When I graduated, I wanted to pursue something more legit, so I decided that the next time my favorite local artisanal bakery was hiring, I'd apply. Before I started working there, I was a very serious home baker. At Clear Flour, I transitioned into a professional baking career.

Favorite dish on the menu, past or present?

I think my all-time favorite has to be the tomato, buffalo mozzarella, and basil pizza. It's just so perfect. But whenever the mushroom pizza is on the menu, I get that too. I just can't resist.

Almond Gelato

Almond grappa contributes bright floral notes to this exquisite gelato, which is smooth, creamy, and highly perfumed. It would be delicious on its own, if you don't feel like making the praline, but the swirl of homemade almond praline makes it truly singular. It's one of our most popular flavors, and if you make it, you'll see why.

MAKES ABOUT 1 QUART

FOR THE ALMOND PRALINE
⅔ **cup sugar**
1 tablespoon unsalted butter
Pinch of kosher salt
½ **cup toasted skin-on whole almonds**
¼ **teaspoon baking soda**

FOR THE GELATO BASE
½ **cup plus 1 tablespoon sugar**
1½ **teaspoons xanthan gum**
 (see Resources, page 357)
½ **teaspoon kosher salt**
2⅔ **cups whole milk**
⅔ **cup heavy cream**
⅛ **teaspoon pure almond extract**
1 tablespoon almond grappa,
 such as Nardini

To make the praline: Line a rimmed baking sheet with a Silpat or greased parchment paper. Sprinkle a little of the sugar in the bottom of a heavy skillet and set it over medium heat. As it begins to melt and caramelize, add a little more and melt it, swirling the pan occasionally; continue until all the sugar is melted and the caramel has turned a uniform reddish-brown. Turn off the heat and stir in the butter and salt. As soon as the butter is incorporated, stir in the almonds and baking soda. Immediately scrape the mixture onto the lined baking sheet and spread into an even layer. Cool completely.

Using a cleaver or a hammer, break the cooled praline into chunks. Transfer to a food processor and pulse until corn-kernel-sized pieces form but it is not completely ground. Set aside.

To make the gelato base: In a large heavy-bottomed saucepan, whisk together the sugar, xanthan gum, and salt. Slowly whisk in the milk and cream over medium heat and cook, whisking occasionally, until the mixture thickens, 5 to 10 minutes. Transfer to a bowl. Chill the mixture until it is completely cold, either set over an ice bath or in the refrigerator. Once it is cold, whisk in the almond extract. (The gelato base can be refrigerated for up to 10 days.)

Combine the gelato base and grappa in an ice-cream machine and churn according to the manufacturer's instructions. Scrape into a bowl and stir in the almond praline. Serve immediately, or transfer to a quart-sized freezer container for longer storage; the gelato can be frozen for up to 5 days. If necessary, soften the frozen gelato at room temperature for 20 minutes or in the refrigerator for 45 minutes before serving.

DESSERTS

Chocolate Hazelnut Gelato

Most of our gelati are smooth, but sometimes we want a little crunch, a little morsel to bite into. The homemade chocolate hazelnut candy stirred into this gelato satisfies that urge. Hazelnuts and chocolate are a time-honored duo in Italy, particularly in the north (gianduja, a harmonious blend of chocolate and hazelnuts, calls the region of Piemonte home), and with good reason—they are delicious together.

MAKES ABOUT 1 QUART

FOR THE CHOCOLATE HAZELNUT CANDY
2 ounces (½ cup) **hazelnuts**
2½ ounces milk chocolate, chopped (⅔ cup)

FOR THE GELATO BASE
4 ounces (1 cup) **hazelnuts**
½ **cup plus 1 tablespoon sugar**
1½ **teaspoons xanthan gum** (see Resources, page 357)

½ **teaspoon kosher salt**
2⅔ **cups whole milk**
⅔ **cup heavy cream**
2 **tablespoons good-quality unsweetened cocoa powder, such as Valhrona**
½ **ounce milk chocolate, chopped** (2 tablespoons)
½ **ounce bittersweet chocolate** (60%), **chopped** (2 tablespoons)

To make the candy: Preheat the oven to 325°F. Spread the nuts on a rimmed baking sheet and toast until golden, about 10 minutes. Bundle the warm nuts in a dish towel and rub together to remove the clinging papery skins.

Line a rimmed baking sheet with a Silpat or greased parchment paper. In the top of a double boiler or in a heatproof bowl set over a pot of simmering water, melt the chocolate, stirring occasionally until smooth (alternatively, you can melt the chocolate in a bowl in the microwave on low power, stirring every 10 seconds until smooth). Stir in the nuts. Spread the mixture into an even layer on the lined baking sheet. Refrigerate until completely firm, about 30 minutes.

Chop the candy into chocolate-chip-sized pieces and return to the refrigerator.

To make the gelato base: Preheat the oven to 325°F. Toast and skin the hazelnuts, using the technique described above. Transfer to a food processor and blend to a paste.

In a large heavy-bottomed saucepan, whisk together the sugar, xanthan gum, and salt.

Slowly whisk in the milk and cream over medium heat and cook, whisking occasionally, until the mixture thickens, 5 to 10 minutes. Remove from the heat and immediately whisk in the hazelnut paste, cocoa powder, and chopped chocolate until smooth. Cover and let stand for 30 minutes.

Strain the mixture through a fine-mesh sieve into a bowl. Chill until completely cold, either set over an ice bath or in the refrigerator. (The gelato base can be refrigerated for up to 10 days.)

Churn the gelato in an ice-cream machine according to the manufacturer's instructions. Scrape into a bowl and stir in the chocolate candy. Serve immediately, or transfer to a quart-sized freezer container for longer storage; the gelato can be frozen for up to 5 days. If necessary, soften the frozen gelato at room temperature for 20 minutes or in the refrigerator for 45 minutes before serving.

Espresso Gelato

Even people who don't like coffee often adore coffee ice cream. Assertive and aromatic, this sophisticated gelato has a toasty bitter edge thanks to the excellent espresso beans we use. Make sure to seek out a potent high-quality brand.

MAKES ABOUT 1 QUART

3 ounces (a generous cup) **good-quality coffee beans, such as Counter Culture Espresso La Forza**
½ cup plus 1 tablespoon sugar
1½ teaspoons xanthan gum (see Resources, page 357)

½ teaspoon kosher salt
2⅔ cups whole milk
⅔ cup heavy cream

Wrap half the coffee beans loosely in a dish towel. Roll a rolling pin back and forth across the beans to crack them.

In a large heavy-bottomed saucepan, whisk together the sugar, xanthan gum, and salt. Slowly whisk in the milk and cream over medium heat and cook, whisking occasionally, until the mixture thickens, 5 to 10 minutes. Remove from the heat and stir in all of the coffee beans. Cover and let stand for 30 minutes.

Strain the mixture through a fine-mesh sieve into a bowl. Chill until completely cold, either set over an ice bath or in the refrigerator. (The gelato base can be refrigerated for up to 10 days.)

Churn the gelato in an ice-cream machine according to the manufacturer's instructions. Serve immediately, or transfer to a quart-sized freezer container for longer storage; the gelato can be frozen for up to 5 days. If necessary, soften the frozen gelato at room temperature for 20 minutes or in the refrigerator for 45 minutes before serving.

Salted Peanut Gelato

For some reason, there aren't many peanut ice creams out there. There are plenty that incorporate peanuts as one of many elements, but here we feature them front and center, both steeped as a paste in the gelato base itself and then stirred in at the end. Well-toasted and perfectly salty, the roasted peanuts are savory and satisfying against the creamy gelato.

MAKES ABOUT 1 QUART

3½ ounces (⅔ cup) **raw peanuts**
½ cup plus 1 tablespoon sugar
1½ teaspoons xanthan gum
  (see Resources, page 357)

½ teaspoon kosher salt
2⅔ cups whole milk
⅔ cup heavy cream
⅔ cup salted roasted peanuts, chopped

Preheat the oven to 325°F. Spread the raw nuts on a rimmed baking sheet. Toast until they just start to speckle, about 10 minutes. Transfer to a food processor and blend to a paste.

In a large heavy-bottomed saucepan, whisk together the sugar, xanthan gum, and salt. Slowly whisk in the milk and cream over medium heat and cook, whisking occasionally, until the mixture thickens, 5 to 10 minutes. Remove from the heat and stir in the ground peanuts. Cover and let stand for 30 minutes.

Strain the mixture through a fine-mesh sieve into a bowl. Chill until completely cold, either set over an ice bath or in the refrigerator. (The gelato base can be refrigerated for up to 10 days.)

Churn the gelato in an ice-cream machine according to the manufacturer's instructions. Scrape into a bowl and stir in the roasted peanuts. Serve immediately, or transfer to a quart-sized freezer container for longer storage; the gelato can be frozen for up to 5 days. If necessary, soften the frozen gelato at room temperature for 20 minutes or in the refrigerator for 45 minutes before serving.

DESSERTS

Plum Sorbetto

Juicy summer-ripe plums make for a spicy, fruity sorbetto with a vibrant purple color. It's a refreshing finish to a meal on its own, or try it paired with a slice of Ricotta Pound Cake (page 309).

MAKES ABOUT 1 QUART

⅔ cup sugar
⅛ teaspoon xanthan gum (see Resources, page 357)
⅔ cup water

1½ pounds ripe plums, pitted and quartered
1 teaspoon fresh lemon juice, plus more if needed
⅛ teaspoon kosher salt

In a small heavy-bottomed saucepan, whisk together the sugar and xanthan gum. Slowly whisk in the water over medium heat and cook until the sugar is completely dissolved and the liquid is slightly thickened, 5 to 10 minutes. Remove from the heat.

Pass the plums through a food mill into a medium bowl (you should have about 2 cups fruit puree). Stir in the sugar syrup, lemon juice, and salt. The mixture should taste slightly too sweet, because freezing will dull the sweetness; add more lemon juice if necessary.

Chill the mixture until it is completely cold, either set over an ice bath or in the refrigerator. (The sorbetto base can be refrigerated for up to 10 days.)

Churn the sorbetto in an ice-cream machine according to the manufacturer's instructions. Serve immediately, or transfer to a quart-sized freezer container for longer storage; the sorbetto can be frozen for up to 5 days. If necessary, soften the frozen sorbetto at room temperature for 20 minutes or in the refrigerator for 45 minutes before serving.

Variation

Nectarine Sorbetto: Substitute 1¼ pounds pitted, halved ripe nectarines for the plums. Nectarines often need a bit more lemon juice than tart plums.

Chocolate Sorbetto

This intense, dark chocolate sorbetto is always a crowd-pleaser. It makes for a decadent-seeming finish to a meal, yet it isn't heavy or rich. Made without any cream or dairy, it also happens to be vegan, which means you can satisfy many different people with one dessert. We don't use any chocolate in the recipe—all of the flavor comes from cocoa powder, so be sure to use an excellent brand. Valrhona works particularly well here.

MAKES ABOUT 1 QUART

1¾ **cups sugar**
½ **teaspoon kosher salt**
⅛ **teaspoon xanthan gum** (see Resources, page 357)

3⅓ **cups water**
1⅓ **cups good-quality unsweetened cocoa powder, such as Valrhona**

In a large heavy-bottomed saucepan, whisk together the sugar, salt, and xanthan gum. Slowly whisk in the water over medium heat. Bring to a simmer and cook, whisking occasionally, until the sugar dissolves and the mixture thickens, 5 to 10 minutes. Remove from the heat and whisk in the cocoa powder until dissolved, then transfer to a bowl. Chill the mixture until it is completely cold, either set over an ice bath or in the refrigerator. (The sorbetto base can be refrigerated for up to 10 days.)

Churn the sorbetto in an ice-cream machine according to the manufacturer's instructions. Serve immediately, or transfer to a quart-sized freezer container for longer storage; the sorbetto can be frozen for up to 5 days. If necessary, soften the frozen sorbetto at room temperature for 20 minutes or in the refrigerator for 45 minutes before serving.

Lemon Sorbetto

If you've ever eaten at Franny's, you know we love lemons and their bright acidity; Andrew uses them liberally. And this traditional sorbetto gives you every reason to love lemons too. Almost like a frozen lemonade but with a perfectly smooth, almost creamy texture, this fantastic dessert is sunny and zesty—an ideal palate cleanser or light ending to dinner.

MAKES A SCANT 1 QUART

1½ **cups sugar**
⅛ **teaspoon xanthan gum** (see Resources, page 357)

1½ **cups water**
1 **cup fresh lemon juice** (from 5 to 6 lemons)

In a large heavy-bottomed saucepan, whisk together the sugar and xanthan gum. Slowly whisk in the water over medium heat. Bring to a simmer and cook, whisking occasionally, until the sugar dissolves and the mixture thickens, 5 to 10 minutes. Remove from the heat and whisk in the lemon juice. Transfer to a bowl.

Chill the mixture until it is completely cold, either set over an ice bath or in the refrigerator. (The sorbetto base can be refrigerated for up to 10 days.)

Churn the sorbetto in an ice-cream machine according to the manufacturer's instructions. Serve immediately, or transfer to a quart-sized freezer container for longer storage; the sorbetto can be frozen for up to 5 days. If necessary, soften the frozen sorbetto at room temperature for 20 minutes or in the refrigerator for 45 minutes before serving.

Melon in Lovage Syrup

Lovage is one of our favorite herbs. It's fresh and a little grassy, but with a pronounced sweetness. Fleshy, fragrant melons at the peak of their season need very little help—it's hard to improve upon their ambrosial qualities. But a dash of lovage syrup does just that, adding a layer of wild celery flavor. If you can find them, buy an assortment of different melons, and let them ripen on the counter until they're intensely aromatic. Sliced, tossed with the syrup and chilled, then arranged on a platter, they make a gorgeous, unusual dessert that comes together in minutes.

SERVES 4

About 1¼ pounds ripe summer melon (preferably a mix of varieties and colors), **rind removed, seeded, and sliced ¼ inch thick**

1 cup Lovage Syrup (page 356)
2 tablespoons thinly sliced mint leaves

In a large bowl, toss the melon with the lovage syrup. Marinate, refrigerated, for at least 3 hours, and up to 36 hours.

Toss the marinated melon with the mint leaves. Divide among four plates and serve immediately.

Summer Fruit Crostata

These pretty, rustic fruit crostatas make great dinner-party fare, and the recipe is versatile enough to suit whatever ripe fruit is in season. The pastry dough bakes up golden, flaky, and incredibly buttery, and it isn't terribly difficult to make. Our pastry chef, Inga Sheaffer, perfected this dough in her tiny Brooklyn apartment kitchen before she started making it at Bklyn Larder, so have confidence that you'll be able to master it in your own home. Use this basic crostata recipe as a template for any summer fruit you can get, from the first raspberries of June to the last of September's plums.

This recipe makes six small crostatas. You can make the pastry in advance and it will keep for up to 3 days. Although you could serve one per person, they are really meant for sharing, and each one feeds two people comfortably—especially if you serve them with a scoop of gelato on top. We recommend Fior di Latte Gelato (page 284). You won't regret it.

MAKES SIX 6-INCH CROSTATAS; SERVES 6 OR 12

FOR THE CROSTATA DOUGH
½ **cup** (4 ounces) **water**
¾ **teaspoon fine sea salt**
½ **pound** (2 sticks) **unsalted butter,**
  cubed and chilled
2⅓ **cups** (11.5 ounces) **all-purpose flour**

FOR THE FILLING
1 pound 2 ounces (about 3 cups) **fresh fruit,**
  such as pitted ripe peaches or nectarines,
  cut into eighths; pitted ripe plums, cut
  into sixths; or raspberries, blackberries,
  or blueberries

½ **cup** (4 ounces) **sugar**
3 tablespoons (.85 ounce) **cornstarch**
  (2 tablespoons/.55 ounce if using blueberries)
1½ teaspoons finely grated lemon zest
  (optional; see method)
1 tablespoon (.5 ounce) **fresh lemon juice**
  (optional; see method)
Large pinch of kosher salt
2 large egg yolks, beaten with
  2 tablespoons (1 ounce) **heavy cream,**
  for egg wash
1 tablespoon (.5 ounce) **sugar**

To make the dough: In a small bowl, combine the water and sea salt. Place the butter in a separate bowl. Put both bowls in the freezer for 10 minutes.

In the bowl of a food processor, pulse together the flour and cold butter about 5 times, or until the mixture has some large chunks and some small. Pulse in the water until the dough just comes together but is not smooth.

Dump the dough onto a lightly floured work surface and shape into a ball. Lightly flour a rolling pin. Pat the dough into a rectangle. Roll the dough out to 7½ by 10½ inches. With a short end toward you, using a dough scraper, fold the

top third down, then fold the bottom third over (like you're folding a letter to put in an envelope) and rotate ¼ turn clockwise. Reroll. Repeat 3 times, lightly flouring the work surface as needed. Wrap the dough tightly in plastic wrap and refrigerate overnight, and up to 3 days.

Divide the dough into 6 equal pieces and flatten into disks. Chill for 15 minutes. On a lightly floured surface, roll each one into a 6-inch round slightly less than ⅛ inch thick. Transfer the rounds to a baking sheet, cover with plastic, and chill for at least 10 minutes. (The dough can be refrigerated for 24 hours.)

continued

Preheat the oven to 375°F.

To make the filling: In a large bowl, toss together the fruit, sugar, cornstarch, lemon zest, lemon juice (if using nectarines, plums, or blackberries, omit the lemon zest and juice, as they are naturally more acidic), and salt.

Spoon about ½ cup of the filling onto the center of each dough round, leaving a 1-inch border of dough all around. Fold the edges of the dough up over the filling to partially cover it. Chill the crostatas for 15 minutes. Brush the crush of each crostata with the egg wash. Sprinkle the dough with the remaining sugar.

Bake, rotating the pan halfway through baking, until the crust is golden brown and the fruit is bubbling, 40 to 50 minutes. Transfer to a wire rack to cool slightly and serve warm, or let cool completely and serve at room temperature. The crostatas can be rewarmed in a 350°F oven for about 10 minutes before serving.

Apple Crostata

When autumn's apples and pears hit the farmers' market and the last of summer's stone fruit and berries fades away, we switch over to this crostata recipe. The dough is the same as for the summer fruit crostatas, but instead of piling it high with juicy raw summer fruit, Inga sautées apples in butter or poaches pears in spiced syrup until tender. Then she adds a cinnamon-scented crumb topping for a homey crunch. You could serve these warm from the oven with a scoop of gelato, but a little dollop of crème fraîche is really all they need.

MAKES SIX 6-INCH CROSTATAS; SERVES 6 TO 12

FOR THE CRUMB TOPPING
1 cup (5 ounces) **all-purpose flour**
½ cup (3.8 ounces) **packed light brown sugar**
½ teaspoon ground cinnamon
Pinch of kosher salt
Pinch of baking powder
8 tablespoons (1 stick/4 ounces) **unsalted butter, cool but not cold**
⅓ cup (1.5 ounces) **chopped pecans** (optional)

FOR THE FILLING
4 tablespoons (2 ounces) **unsalted butter**
½ cup (3.8 ounces) **packed light brown sugar**
1 vanilla bean, split, seeds scraped out and reserved

½ teaspoon finely grated lemon zest
1 teaspoon fresh lemon juice
2 pounds tart apples, such as Granny Smith, peeled, cored, and sliced ¼ inch thick (about 3 cups)
Large pinch of kosher salt

Crostata Dough (page 304), **rolled into 6 rounds and chilled**
2 large egg yolks, beaten with 2 tablespoons (1 ounce) **heavy cream, for egg wash**
1 tablespoon (.5 ounce) **sugar**

To make the crumb topping: In a medium bowl, combine the flour, brown sugar, cinnamon, salt, and baking powder. Using a pastry cutter or a fork, cut in the butter until the mixture forms coarse crumbs. Toss in the pecans, if using. Cover with plastic wrap and chill until ready to use. (The topping can be refrigerated for up to 2 days.)

To make the filling: In a large skillet, melt the butter over medium heat. Add the brown sugar, vanilla seeds, lemon zest, and juice. Stir in the apples and cook until the apples are tender but not mushy and the juices have thickened slightly, 7 to 10 minutes. Transfer to a bowl to cool, then toss with the salt.

Preheat the oven to 375°F. Spoon about ½ cup of the filling onto the center of each dough round, leaving a 1-inch border of dough all around. Mound about 2 heaping tablespoons of the crumb mixture on top of each portion of apples. Fold the edges of the dough up around the filling to partially cover it. Chill the crostatas for 15 minutes. Brush the crust of each crostata with the egg wash. Sprinkle with the sugar.

Bake, rotating the pan halfway through baking, until the crust is golden brown and the fruit is bubbling, 40 to 50 minutes. Transfer to a wire rack to cool slightly and serve warm, or let cool completely and serve at room temperature. The crostatas can be rewarmed in a 350°F oven for about 10 minutes before serving.

Ricotta Pound Cake

Fresh ricotta adds a round milky flavor to this delicious pound cake, which is pure, moist, and not too sweet. When baked in a loaf pan, it'll sink a bit in the center; if you're looking for something more uniform, bake it in a 9-inch round cake pan instead (it will take 45 to 50 minutes). Either way, it's a perfectly simple cake to enjoy on its own, with fresh or stewed fruit, or with Plum Sorbetto (page 299).

SERVES 8

FOR THE CAKE
1½ cups (7 ounces) **cake flour**
2½ teaspoons baking powder
1 teaspoon kosher salt
12 tablespoons (1½ sticks/6 ounces)
  unsalted butter, at room temperature
1½ cups (10.5 ounces) **Vanilla Sugar** (page 356) **or sugar**
3 large eggs
1 teaspoon vanilla extract
1½ cups (14 ounces) **fresh ricotta**

FOR THE GLAZE
¼ cup (1.7 ounces) **Vanilla Sugar** (page 356) **or sugar**
½ vanilla bean, split, seeds scraped out, seeds and bean reserved
¼ cup (2 ounces) **water**

To make the cake: Preheat the oven to 350°F, with a rack in the middle position. Grease and flour a 9-by-5-inch loaf pan.

Sift together the flour, baking powder, and salt into a large bowl.

In the bowl of a stand mixer fitted with the paddle attachment, beat together the butter and vanilla sugar on low speed until fluffy, about 2 minutes. Beat in the eggs one at a time, mixing well after each addition. Beat in the vanilla extract. Slowly beat in the ricotta, then the dry ingredients on low speed. This cake benefits from gently mixing.

Pour the batter into the pan and smooth the top with a spatula. Bake for 15 minutes. Reduce the temperature to 325°F and bake for about 20 minutes more, until the cake is golden and a toothpick inserted in the center comes out clean. Cool in the pan on a wire rack for 15 minutes.

While the cake is cooling, make the glaze: In a small saucepan, combine the sugar, vanilla bean and seeds, and water, bring to a simmer, and simmer until the sugar dissolves and the glaze is beginning to thicken, about 5 minutes. Remove from the heat.

Unmold the cake and return it to the wire rack, right side up. Set the rack over a rimmed baking sheet. Pour the glaze over the top of the cake, allowing it to run down the sides. Cool completely.

DESSERTS

Vanilla Panna Cotta

When panna cotta (literally, "cooked cream") is right, it's perfect in its simplicity and purity, tasting of little more than fresh cream with just a hint of sugar and vanilla. The maybe-not-so-secret tip here is using excellent-quality local cream and keeping all other ingredients to a bare minimum—a dash of vanilla, a pinch of salt, and just enough sugar. It's a defining menu item at Franny's, as important to our identity as our Brooklyn cocktail (see page 337) or our clam pizza (see page 263). It's one of the things that we always recommend to people eating with us for the first time.

We serve these unmolded, but if you prefer, they can be eaten right out of the ramekins. Either way, accompanied by a touch of *saba* (grape must syrup) or some ripe figs, or even all by itself, panna cotta is the ultimate in dairy indulgence.

SERVES 6

3 cups (24.3 ounces) **heavy cream**
6 tablespoons (2.6 ounces) **sugar**
½ **vanilla bean split, seeds scraped out and reserved**
⅛ **teaspoon kosher salt**

2 sheets gelatin or 2 teaspoons powdered gelatin
Saba (see Resources, page 357) **or fresh fruit for serving**

In a large heavy-bottomed pot, bring the cream, sugar, vanilla seeds, and salt to a simmer over medium-low heat, stirring frequently to prevent scorching.

While the cream mixture is warming, soften the gelatin sheets, if using, in a bowl of ice water for about 2 minutes (any longer, and the sheets might dissolve). Remove from the water, squeeze out any extra water, and set aside; or, if using powdered gelatin, put it in a small bowl with a tablespoon of cold water and allow it to soften for 5 minutes.

When the cream mixture comes to a simmer, remove from the heat and whisk in the gelatin sheets or the powdered gelatin mixture until dissolved. Pour the mixture into a bowl, set it in a bowl of ice water, and chill, stirring often with a spatula, until very cold, about 5 minutes.

Ladle the cream mixture into six 4-ounce ramekins. Cover with plastic wrap and refrigerate for at least 6 hours, and up to 1 week. To unmold, run a paring knife around the inside of each ramekin and release the panna cotta onto serving plates (or serve in the ramekins). Top with a drizzle of *saba* or some fresh fruit.

DESSERTS

Tangerine Cake

This cake is a marvelous way to highlight winter citrus. An intensely perfumed pound cake with a velvety crumb, it's topped with a zesty glaze to keep it moist.

SERVES 10 TO 12

FOR THE CAKE
2 cups (9.2 ounces) **cake flour**
1¼ teaspoons **baking powder**
¾ teaspoon **kosher salt**
1 cup (7 ounces) **sugar**
Grated zest of 1½ tangerines (1½ teaspoons)
Grated zest of ½ lemon (¼ teaspoon)
11 tablespoons (5.5 ounces) **unsalted butter, at room temperature**
1½ teaspoons vanilla extract

4 large eggs, at room temperature
¼ cup (2 ounces) **fresh tangerine juice** (from about 1½ tangerines)
2 teaspoons fresh lemon juice

FOR THE GLAZE
½ cup plus 2 teaspoons (3.8 ounces) **sugar**
⅓ cup (2.6 ounces) **fresh tangerine juice** (from about 2 tangerines)
2 teaspoons fresh lemon juice

To make the cake: Preheat the oven to 325°F, with a rack in the middle position. Butter and flour a 9-by-5-inch loaf pan and line the bottom with parchment paper. Butter the paper.

Sift together the flour, baking powder, and salt into a large bowl.

In the bowl of a stand mixer, combine the sugar with the tangerine and lemon zests and mix well with your fingertips, rubbing the zest and sugar together until the mixture is uniform in color. Fit the mixer with the paddle attachment and cream the butter and sugar together on medium-high speed until light and fluffy, about 4 minutes, stopping the mixer to scrape the bowl halfway through. Scrape the bowl, then add the vanilla and mix to combine. Add the eggs one at a time, mixing well after each addition. Mix in the tangerine and lemon juices. Add the dry ingredients on low speed, ¼ cup at a time, mixing until well combined.

Pour the batter into the pan and smooth the top with a spatula. Bake for 1 hour, or until the top of the cake is firm to the touch and a toothpick inserted in the center comes out clean. A few small crumbs on the toothpick are okay, but large moist crumbs mean the cake is not done. Cool the cake in the pan on a rack for about 15 minutes, then invert onto a wire rack set over a rimmed baking sheet. Peel off the parchment paper.

While the cake is cooling, make the glaze: In a small saucepan, combine the sugar and juices and bring to a boil over medium heat. Reduce the heat and simmer, stirring frequently, until the sugar is fully dissolved. Remove from the heat and set aside.

Brush the bottom of the cake several times with the glaze, then turn right side up and glaze the top and sides. Let the glaze set for at least 30 minutes before slicing the cake.

Olive Oil Cake

It might be hard for Americans to imagine a cake made with olive oil instead of butter, but in Italy, olive oil cake is a common treat. Intense, high-quality olive oil is so good and savory in a cake. Our version is moist and delicious, with a tart lemon glaze covering the top. And olive oil cake is a great recipe for folks who don't eat dairy.

Use the best olive oil you can get, preferably something herbal and fruity rather than peppery and spicy.

SERVES 8

FOR THE CAKE
1¾ cups plus 2 tablespoons (6.5 ounces)
  cake flour
1 teaspoon baking powder
½ teaspoon salt
1 cup (7 ounces) **sugar**
Grated zest of 4 lemons
1¼ cups (9.5 ounces) **olive oil**
4 large eggs, at room temperature
1½ teaspoons vanilla extract

FOR THE GLAZE
1½ cups (6 ounces) **confectioners' sugar**
3 tablespoons (1.5 ounces) **fresh lemon
  juice, plus more if needed**

To make the cake: Preheat the oven to 325°F, with a rack in the middle position. Grease and flour a 9-inch round cake pan and line the bottom with parchment paper. Grease the paper.

Sift together the cake flour, baking powder, and salt into a large bowl.

In the bowl of a stand mixer, combine the sugar and lemon zest and mix well with your fingertips, rubbing the mixture together until well blended. Fit the mixer with the paddle attachment, add the oil to the sugar mixture, and beat on medium speed for 1 minute. Add the eggs one at a time, mixing well after each addition. Beat in the vanilla. Add the dry ingredients in 3 additions, beating on low speed and scraping the sides and bottom of the bowl after each batch, until just combined.

Pour the batter into the prepared pan. Bake for 45 to 50 minutes, until the top springs back when lightly pressed. Cool the cake in the pan on a rack for 15 minutes, then remove from the pan, peel off the parchment paper, and allow to cool completely on the rack.

To make the glaze: In a medium bowl, whisk together the confectioners' sugar and lemon juice to make a thick but pourable glaze; add more lemon juice if needed.

Set the cake, on the rack, over a rimmed baking sheet. Pour the glaze on top of the cake, letting it run down the sides. Let the glaze set for at least 30 minutes before slicing the cake.

Pistachio Cake

Inga Sheaffer, our pastry chef, convinced us she was right for the job by baking us this fabulous, slightly exotic cake. And since it's now our best-selling dessert at Bklyn Larder, it's clear that everyone thinks this cake is as special as we do. Loaded with pistachios, it has a light, melt-in-your-mouth texture when eaten within a few hours of pulling it from the oven. After a day or two, all the nut oil distributes throughout, compacting the crumb and making it delightfully dense and moist. We love it both ways, and so it is a great keeping cake. The center of the cake rises and then sinks when it is baked, but piling the indentation high with candied pistachios hides the dip. It's a stunning, very festive presentation. Make this for a party and be prepared to share the recipe—everyone will want it.

SERVES 12

FOR THE CAKE
1 cup plus 2 tablespoons (5.5 ounces) **all-purpose flour**
1½ teaspoons baking powder
¾ teaspoon kosher salt
1½ cups plus 2 tablespoons (11.6 ounces) **sugar**
1 vanilla bean, split, seeds scraped out and reserved
Grated zest of 1 lemon
¾ pound (3 sticks) **unsalted butter, at room temperature**

6 large eggs, at room temperature
1¼ cups (6.3 ounces) **pistachios, finely ground**
1 cup (5.3 ounces) **blanched almonds, finely ground**

FOR THE TOPPING
¼ cup (1.75 ounces) **sugar**
⅔ cup (3.3 ounces) **pistachios**
Grated zest and juice of 1 lemon

To make the cake: Preheat the oven to 325°F, with a rack in the middle position. Grease and flour a 9-by-5-inch loaf pan and line the bottom with parchment paper.

In a small bowl, whisk together the flour, baking powder, and salt.

In the bowl of a stand mixer, combine the sugar, vanilla seeds, and lemon zest and mix with your fingertips until well combined. Fit the mixer with the paddle attachment, add the butter to the sugar mixture, and beat together on medium speed until fluffy, about 3 minutes. Beat in the eggs one at a time, mixing well after each addition. Beat in the pistachios and almonds. Add the flour in 2 additions, beating on low speed until just combined.

Scrape the batter into the prepared pan. Bake for 65 to 75 minutes, until the cake is golden brown and a toothpick inserted in the center comes out clean. Cool the cake in the pan for 15 minutes, then turn out onto a wire rack set over a rimmed baking sheet. Cool completely.

To make the topping: In a small saucepan, combine the sugar, pistachios, and lemon zest and juice and bring to a boil over medium heat. Cook until the syrup thickens slightly, 1 to 2 minutes.

Pour the topping over the cake, nestling the pistachios into the trough in the top of the cake.

Almond Cake

We serve this cake, golden, soft-textured, and lush with fragrant almonds, very simply with just a dollop of lightly whipped cream, though it'd be easy to dress up with a scoop of gelato or sorbetto, or some fresh fruit. It was inspired by a recipe by Gale Gand, but we omitted her addition of ginger in favor of a touch of vanilla. For such an elegant, well-textured cake, this recipe is surprisingly simple.

SERVES 8

1 cup plus 2 tablespoons (5.5 ounces) **all-purpose flour**
2 teaspoons baking powder
½ teaspoon kosher salt
¾ cup plus 1 tablespoon (8 ounces) **almond paste**

1¼ cups (8.75 ounces) **Vanilla Sugar** (page 356) **or sugar mixed with the scrapings of 1 vanilla bean**
10 ounces (2½ sticks) **unsalted butter, at room temperature**
5 large eggs, at room temperature
Confectioners' sugar for dusting

Preheat the oven to 325°F, with a rack in the middle position. Grease and flour a 9-inch springform or cake pan and line the bottom with parchment paper.

In a small bowl, whisk together the flour, baking powder, and salt.

In a food processor, pulse the almond paste and vanilla sugar until well combined.

In the bowl of a stand mixer fitted with the paddle attachment, cream the butter on medium speed until light and fluffy, about 2 minutes. Add the almond-sugar mixture and mix on high speed until well incorporated. Add 2 of the eggs, mixing well to incorporate and scraping the sides of the bowl with a rubber spatula. Add 2 more eggs, mixing well and scraping the bowl, then add the last egg. Add the dry ingredients in 2 additions, mixing on low speed just until combined—do not overmix.

Scrape the batter into the pan and smooth the top with a rubber spatula. Bake for 1 hour, or until a cake tester or a toothpick inserted in the center of the cake comes out clean.

Cool the cake in the pan on a rack for 20 minutes, then release the sides and cool for 30 minutes longer.

Serve the cake warm, or wrap in plastic, while still slightly warm (the cake will keep for up to 2 days at room temperature). Dust the top of the cake with confectioners' sugar before serving.

COCKTAILS AND OTHER DRINKS

I started my restaurant career as a bartender. I'd spent five years immersed in the nonprofit world, but the company I was devoted to folded and I needed a new job. At the suggestion of my older brother, I signed up for a two-week bartending course, during which I was schooled in how to make pink squirrels and fuzzy navels but not in how to mix a proper martini. Fortunately, I got a job at a restaurant that taught me all about great cocktail basics. In the tiny, beautiful upstairs bar at Savoy (one of New York's most beloved restaurants until it closed in 2011), I mastered the classics, learned the importance of using high-quality spirits, and generally absorbed the foundation necessary to set up the bar at Franny's.

It was the late nineties when I was just starting out, and the cocktail scene was completely different from the way it is now. The exuberant culture of high-end mixology was still in its natal stages. I'm sure somewhere out there people were experimenting with historically accurate cocktails and making their own small-batch bitters, but there were no mixologists in arm garters and no designer ice cubes—and, quite frankly, there were a lot of badly made cocktails in very good restaurants.

Since then, of course, the whole bar scene has exploded in an incredible way. Where there used to be premade sour mix shot from a soda gun, you now see house-infused simple syrups. There is an ever-growing choice of artisanal high-end spirits, many of them distilled locally, using organic ingredients. Restaurants

319

are putting as much energy and thought into their cocktail lists as they do into their regular menus, which often means using the best seasonal herbs, fruits, and vegetables one can get. This just might be one of the best times in recent history to go for a drink—or make one yourself at home.

Whether ordering them at a bar or shaking up a batch for friends, people now get really excited about well-made cocktails, with good reason. Cocktails can be simple and clean or layered, structured, and complex; there are infinite ways to make and enjoy them. Cocktails can be yet another avenue toward getting the most pleasure possible out of a meal. In Italy, cocktails are almost always served with food—which can be anything from a bowl of potato chips at a local bar to an opulent spread of hors d'oeuvres at the Four Seasons Hotel in Milan. Small, savory bites both offset and complement cocktails, and the Italians embrace the tradition with grace.

Of course, it's one thing to serve a few bites of food with a favorite cocktail and something else entirely to pair specific dishes with particular cocktails, and that is another trend we've seen grow over the years. It's a fun thing to do as a convivial and special start to a dinner party, or just as a well-deserved reward after a long day. Mix up The Anisette (page 326) to sip alongside crisp pancetta crostini with fennel butter (see page 14), which echoes the licorice flavors. Or try a Greenmarket Gin and Tonic (page 330) with a crunchy dish of Sugar Snap Peas with Ricotta, Mint, and Lemon (page 128), or any other crudité-type dish you love.

Considering how the flavors in a cocktail might work well with an appetizer or even a whole meal can change the way you think about food and drink pairings, opening up a world that was formerly restricted to wine. And don't limit yourself to cocktails. Creative nonalcoholic drinks are also prime fodder for pairings, and offering them, either by themselves or alongside more traditional cocktails, can make the kids and guests who don't drink alcohol feel included.

The beauty of making your own soft drinks and sodas is that you can adjust the ingredients to suit your needs—your kids can enjoy special fizzy drinks without being bombarded with huge amounts of sugar and artificial ingredients. And homemade sodas appeal to grown-ups too, especially when they aren't too sweet. In particular, the Celery Soda (page 338) and the Lemon-Lime Bitter (page 341) are very sophisticated, and work either with a meal or as an aperitif beforehand.

The easiest way to create nonalcoholic drinks is to make infused simple syrups

and stir them into seltzer, lemonade, or iced tea. Seasonal ingredients work really well here, and you'll be able store the syrups in the fridge for weeks. Play with herbs such as rosemary, basil, lovage, verbena, and mint, mixing and matching them with each other, or with ripe fruit, citrus zest, or whole spices. These fragrant syrups are also terrific drizzled over a plate of sliced ripe summer melon or stone fruit for dessert. And, of course, they're great in cocktails too.

One thing to keep in mind when stirring a simple syrup—infused or plain—into a cocktail is to use a light hand. At Franny's, we favor Italian-style cocktails and aperitifs, which tend to be less sweet than their American counterparts. Most Italian drinks are based on bitter spirits known as *amari* ("bitter"), which give them an intense, complex flavor layered with herbs and spices. And bitter flavors are thought to aid in digestion, so they naturally partner well with food. Italians are obsessed with amari of all kinds. Every little region in Italy has an amaro, an herb and spice liqueur, or a grappa to call its own, and as demand for them grows, they're becoming more and more available in the United States. A little research online can yield all sorts of sources if you can't find any in your hometown.

Even better, try making your own amari and grappas. This will definitely be an investment of time, especially for amari, which take at least nine months for the flavors to marry and mature. And they also take planning: you'll have to track down all the necessary botanicals, probably by ordering them online (see Resources, page 357). The fruit grappas are easier. The most important thing is to use very ripe fruit and seasonal citrus so the flavors will be intense and perfumed. Also, there's no question that if you start out with a good base spirit (such as Jacopo Poli grappa), you'll get a better result in the end. We strongly suggest that for the amari and grappas, you stick to the recipes here at least for the first time you make them. They've been tweaked and perfected over the course of many years. Because some of the ingredients are a bit hard to find, and there's a good amount of waiting time involved in the maceration, you want to make sure you end up with something wonderful. The upside is that once you've procured the ingredients, the processes for making grappas and amari are fairly uncomplicated and don't require any special equipment.

On the other hand, while the tools you will want for crafting cocktails are few (and relatively inexpensive), they're pretty necessary. A Boston shaker, a cocktail strainer, a bar spoon, a muddler, and a good jigger with multiple measurements will all serve you well. Invest in a bit of good-quality bar gear, and it will reward you with lovely cocktails for years to come.

In all of our cocktail recipes, we specify the precise spirits that we think make the individual drink what it is. In some cases (as with the amari), there's no substitute; in others, there are. When we call for Junipero gin, we're doing so because we want its assertive piney, herbal qualities. Detailing the recipes this way allows you to re-create them at home exactly as if you'd ordered one at Franny's. That said, there are a lot of good gins, for example, on the market—so use our spirit choices as a guide, but don't feel hemmed in by them. Cocktails are ripe for experimenting with in your own kitchen. Make these cocktails yours and, above all, enjoy them. That's the point.

Prosecco Cocktail

This clever take on a Prosecco cocktail raises the bar—you're not using just a simple citrus-peel garnish here. The Angostura-poached orange peel is warm, condensed, and exotic, while the Nardini Tagliatella adds a touch of cherry-perfumed sweetness. As with our other Prosecco-based cocktails, we recommend using a dry, crisp sparkling wine so as not to overcomplicate the complex flavors.

SERVES 1

3 Cara Cara or navel oranges
1 cup water
⅔ cup sugar

⅓ cup Angostura bitters
1 ounce Nardini Tagliatella Liqueur
Prosecco

Use a vegetable peeler to remove the zest from the oranges in 2-inch strips, including as little of the white pith as possible.

In a medium saucepan, combine the zest, water, sugar, and Angostura bitters and bring to a boil over medium-high heat. Reduce the heat to low and cook, uncovered, until the zest is completely tender, about 45 minutes (the liquid should be thick enough to coat the back of a spoon). Remove from the heat and let cool, then chill. You'll have extra orange peel; either make more drinks or store for up to 2 months in the fridge, covered in the syrup.

Pour the Tagliatella into a champagne flute. Top off with Prosecco and garnish with a piece of poached orange peel.

Twice Bitter

Fernet Branca is easily one of the most bitter amari available, and we created this cocktail as an homage to its intense flavor. Chinotto, a remarkably herbaceous bitter orange soda produced by San Pellegrino, doesn't tame the Fernet's bitterness—in fact, it contributes to it. Together they make for a cocktail that's refreshing, earthy, and unapologetically bitter.

SERVES 1

1½ ounces Fernet Branca
2 ounces Chinotto soda

½ ounce fresh lime juice
A lime wheel

Fill a highball glass with ice. Add the Fernet Branca, Chinotto, and lime juice. Toss into a cocktail shaker, then pour back into the highball glass. Repeat once more to combine. Garnish with the lime wheel.

Rhubarb Bridge

I was determined to incorporate rhubarb into our bar, and this beautiful pink drink (pictured opposite) was one of the first cocktails I created at Franny's. I've always liked cocktails that lean toward tart, bitter flavors. However, rhubarb's lovely sourness varies from stalk to stalk, so it's important to adjust the sweetness according to your taste.

SERVES 1

1 pound rhubarb, trimmed and cut into 1-inch pieces
1 ounce Ketel One vodka

½ ounce Aperol
¼ to ½ ounce Simple Syrup (page 355), **or more to taste**

In a food processor, puree the rhubarb until smooth. Pour the puree into a strainer lined with a double layer of cheesecloth and set over a bowl. Gather the ends of the cheesecloth together and very firmly wring out the rhubarb to release all the juice from the solids. Discard the solids.

Let the juice sit in the refrigerator for at least 6 hours, then strain off red juice that has separated out on top and discard the green juice in the bottom of the bowl. It will keep for 3 days.

Fill a cocktail shaker two-thirds full with ice cubes. Add 1½ ounces of the rhubarb juice, the vodka, Aperol, and simple syrup and shake well. Strain into a chilled cocktail glass.

Prosecco and Wild Celery

Andrew and I grew up drinking Dr. Brown's Cel-Ray soda, a sweet celery-flavored soda you find in old-style New York delicatessens. So when we learned that farmer Bill Maxwell grew gorgeous lovage all summer long, we couldn't wait to make it into a condensed, wild-celery-flavored syrup for our own homemade version (see page 338). Adding a dash of that same syrup to a flute filled with Prosecco was a natural progression. Be sure to use a very dry Prosecco here (we use the ethereal Bisson Prosecco)—it would be a shame to distract from the lovage with a fruity wine.

SERVES 1

¼ to ½ ounce Lovage Syrup (page 356)
Prosecco
A lovage leaf

Pour the lovage syrup into a champagne flute. Top off with Prosecco and garnish with the lovage leaf.

Sparkling Mint

Based on the heady classic Sicilian iced tea, this refreshing, summery drink (pictured opposite) is a great use for a surplus of fresh mint. It's a bittersweet cocktail, full of effervescent complexity.

SERVES 1

5 mint leaves
1¼ ounces Cynar
½ ounce fresh lime juice

½ ounce Mint Syrup (page 355)
Prosecco

In a cocktail shaker, muddle 4 of the mint leaves with a few ice cubes. Add enough ice to fill the shaker two-thirds full, and stir in the Cynar, lime juice, and mint syrup. Pour into a chilled highball glass. Top off with Prosecco and garnish with the remaining mint leaf.

The Anisette

Years ago, we'd ordered too much Meletti anisette (which is similar to sambuca but less viscous and less sweet). So I challenged our bartender at the time, Todd Woodward (known to everyone as "Woody"), to make a cocktail that featured the spirit. This is the refined creation he came up with. When mint is in season, we use Mint Syrup (page 355) instead of plain simple syrup to add a fresh, herbaceous flavor.

SERVES 1

1½ ounces Bulldog gin
½ ounce anisette
¾ ounce fresh lime juice

¼ ounce Simple Syrup (page 355)
Fennel fronds or a lime wheel for garnish

Fill a cocktail shaker two-thirds full with ice cubes. Add the gin, anisette, lime juice, and simple syrup and shake well. Strain into a chilled cocktail glass. Garnish with fennel fronds (or a lime wheel).

Ramp Gibson

The classic Gibson, basically a dirty gin martini made with pickled onions instead of olives, relies on limp, purchased cocktail onions to define its personality. But I have yet to find a commercially available pickled cocktail onion that I like. Homemade pickled ramps, on the other hand, are a treat. Both sweet and pungent, they're also absolutely beautiful draped in a cocktail glass (see opposite).

SERVES 1

2½ ounces Bulldog gin
½ ounce dry vermouth

1 Pickled Ramp (page 353),
   with ¼ teaspoon of its liquid

Fill a cocktail shaker two-thirds full with ice cubes. Add the gin, vermouth, and ramp pickling liquid and shake well. Strain into a chilled cocktail glass. Garnish with the pickled ramp.

Lime Greyhound

The classic Greyhound is given an Italian twist with the addition of Campari, and the Campari gives it a brilliant pop of ruddy orange. With all the tart citrus involved, this is one refreshing cocktail.

SERVES 1

1½ ounces Ketel One vodka
½ ounce Campari
½ ounce fresh lime juice

1½ ounces fresh grapefruit juice
A lime wheel

Fill a highball glass with ice. Add the vodka, Campari, lime juice, and grapefruit juice. Toss into a cocktail shaker, then pour back into the highball glass. Repeat once more to combine. Garnish with the lime wheel.

Quince and Gin

Our quince grappa is so fragrant and delicious, I couldn't help but blend it with a little gin to create an elegantly simple cocktail. But sip this slowly—quince grappa and gin may be pretty, but they're powerfully strong.

SERVES 1

1¾ ounces **Quince Grappa** (page 346)
1¼ ounces **Junipero gin**

Fill a cocktail shaker two-thirds full with ice cubes. Add the grappa and gin and stir gently with a bar spoon. Strain into a chilled cocktail glass.

Greenmarket Gin and Tonic

An homage to the greenmarket, this cocktail (pictured opposite) is a way to feature all those pretty little vegetables that are so irresistible in the early summer. Baby carrots of every hue, sweet sugar snap peas, peppery radishes, and thinly sliced fragrant cucumber make for a festive gin and tonic garnish. Use as many veggies as you can get your hands on.

SERVES 1

1½ ounces **Junipero gin**
¼ ounce **Luxardo Triple Sec**
¼ ounce **fresh lime juice**

Club soda
Greenmarket vegetables for garnish
  (see the headnote)

Fill a highball glass with ice. Add the gin, Triple Sec, and lime juice and stir gently with a bar spoon. Top off with club soda and garnish with the vegetables.

Sweet Olive

Our former bartender Woody once took a trip to Venice and came back inspired to make this cocktail (pictured opposite). He'd had a version of it and fallen in love with all the elements—sweetness, saltiness, and a touch of bitterness. It's marvelously complex and very Italian.

SERVES 1

1 ounce Meletti amaro
¼ ounce (just shy) **Aperol**
Dash of olive juice

Prosecco
3 small green cocktail olives (or 1 large)
An orange wedge

Pour the amaro, Aperol, and olive juice into a champagne flute. Top off with Prosecco. Garnish with the olives and orange wedge.

Cynar Orange

On its own, Cynar makes for a terrific aperitif, at once syrupy-sweet and bitter. Here we play up its citrusy notes, mixing it with Triple Sec, tart lime juice, and orange bitters. A generous splash of club soda brings everything together.

SERVES 1

1½ ounces Cynar
¼ ounce Luxardo Triple Sec
¼ ounce fresh lime juice

2 dashes orange bitters
Club soda
An orange wedge

Fill a highball glass with ice. Add the Cynar, Triple Sec, lime juice, and orange bitters and stir gently with a bar spoon. Top off with club soda, give it another gentle stir, and garnish with the orange wedge.

L'Eva

This cocktail, created by former Franny's bartender Matthew Walters, is full of warm flavors reminiscent of cider. The infused bourbon is absolutely amazing, and very easy to make. You don't have to peel or core the apples—you can even leave the stems on if they are still attached—it all just adds more flavor to the mix. When removing the lemon zest, try and peel away just the yellow zest, avoiding the bitter white pith. Rinsing the cocktail glass with a touch of fresh lemon juice keeps things bright, and the dried apple ring garnish is a fun finish.

SERVES 1

2½ pounds crabapples, cut into
  6 wedges each
1 Gala or Honeycrisp apple, thinly sliced
About 2 cups Bulleit bourbon
2 lemons

½ ounce Montenegro amaro
½ teaspoon Honey Syrup (page 356)
Fresh lemon juice
A dried apple slice or ring (optional)

To make the apple-infused bourbon: Pack the apples into a large lidded jar. Cover with bourbon. Use a vegetable peeler to remove the lemon zest in strips and add to the jar. Seal tightly and let stand upside down for 5 days. Strain the bourbon, discarding the apples and zest.

Fill a cocktail shaker two-thirds full with ice cubes. Add 2½ ounces of the bourbon, the amaro, and the honey syrup and stir gently with a bar spoon. Give a chilled cocktail glass a light rinse with lemon juice, then strain the contents of the shaker into the glass. Garnish with a dried apple ring, if desired.

Arlecchino

This cocktail is an excellent way to savor the beauty of good-quality Italian amarena cherries. Search them out—they're nothing at all like the strange fluorescent red things we're familiar with in the States. Italian maraschino or amarena cherries are much more complex and interesting, and they aren't full of preservatives. They're a great addition to desserts, and the syrup is fabulous stirred into cocktails. Try Fabbri amarena cherries or Luxardo maraschino cherries—both are top-notch (see Resources, page 357). Marty McLoughlin, another of our great former bartenders, created this cocktail.

SERVES 1

1 ounce Bulldog gin
1 ounce Nardini Tagliatella Liqueur
½ ounce fresh lime juice
¼ ounce Simple Syrup (page 355)
½ teaspoon cherry syrup, from amarena cherry jar

Dash of orange bitters
1 jarred Italian amarena or maraschino cherry

Fill a cocktail shaker two-thirds full with ice cubes. Add the gin, Tagliatella, lime juice, simple syrup, cherry syrup, and orange bitters and shake well. Strain into a chilled cocktail glass. Garnish with the cherry.

Calabrian Ransom

This unusual and delicious cocktail, created by Matthew Walters, combines sweet amaro del capo from Calabria and rich Ransom Old Tom gin—the ingredients themselves suggested the name. Gin and amari are always great partners in a glass, and here a touch of honey and lemon pulls everything together beautifully.

SERVES 1

1½ ounces **Ransom Old Tom gin**
¾ ounce **amaro del capo**
½ ounce **Honey Syrup** (page 356)

¼ ounce **fresh lemon juice**
A lemon twist

Fill a cocktail shaker two-thirds full with ice cubes. Add the gin, amaro, honey syrup, and lemon juice and stir gently with a bar spoon. Strain into a rocks glass filled with ice cubes. Garnish with the lemon twist.

Brooklyn

When we first opened, I was determined to have a signature cocktail, and this nod to the borough we call home has been it ever since. I researched various recipes for the classic Brooklyn cocktail (pictured opposite), then tweaked it to lighten and freshen it up. For many folks, this is a whole new way to enjoy bourbon.

SERVES 1

1½ ounces **Maker's Mark bourbon**
¾ ounce **sweet vermouth**
½ ounce **fresh lemon juice**

¼ ounce **Simple Syrup** (page 355)
A lemon twist

Fill a cocktail shaker two-thirds full with ice cubes. Add the bourbon, sweet vermouth, lemon juice, and simple syrup and shake well. Strain into a chilled cocktail glass. Garnish with the lemon twist.

Marsala Cocktail

This urbane cocktail features the nutty and mature flavors of Marsala, which we find perfect for the colder months of the year. The almond grappa and gin contribute clean layers, and the finish of a salt-cured olive is almost gilding the lily. But who doesn't love things sweet and salty?

SERVES 1

1¾ ounces dry Marsala
½ ounce Junipero gin
¼ ounce Nardini almond grappa
¼ ounce fresh lemon juice

2 dashes Peychaud's bitters
1 sal secco or other good-quality black
  salt-cured olive

Fill a cocktail shaker two-thirds full with ice cubes. Add the Marsala, gin, grappa, and lemon juice and shake well. Strain into a chilled cocktail glass. Finish with the biiters and garnish with the olive.

Celery Soda

This bright, summery soft drink tastes profoundly of celery, and it isn't too sweet. Everyone who tries it loves it, though few guess that the secret ingredient is lovage.

SERVES 1

1 ounce Lovage Syrup (page 356)
¾ ounce fresh lime juice
2 dashes celery bitters

Club soda
A lovage leaf

Fill a water glass with ice. Add the lovage syrup, lime juice, and celery bitters, and top off with club soda. Toss into a cocktail shaker, then pour back into the glass. Repeat once more to combine. Garnish with the lovage leaf.

Grape Soda

Homemade grape soda is a real pleasure. This tastes like all the grape sodas from our childhood were supposed to taste but didn't. Concord grapes are an ultra-special seasonal treat, and our method for "juicing" them results in almost a puree-like texture that adds a lot of body to the soda. Make this on a hot summer day and delight whomever you serve it to.

SERVES 1

1 pound Concord grapes, stems removed
¾ ounce Simple Syrup (page 355),
 or more to taste
Club soda

In a food processor, puree the grapes until smooth. Set a strainer or sieve with holes just small enough to filter out the seeds over a large bowl and pour in the puree. With a large spoon, press the juice and as much of the solids as possible through the strainer. Discard the remaining seeds and solids. (You will have more grape juice than you need; it can be stored in the refrigerator for up to 5 days.)

Fill a water glass with ice. Add 2 ounces of the grape juice and the simple syrup, and top off with club soda. Toss into a cocktail shaker, then pour back into the glass. Repeat once more to combine. Taste and stir in more simple syrup if needed.

JILLIAN LAVINKA
FRANNY'S BARTENDER

How did you get started in the food business?

I really earned my restaurant stripes as a hostess at The Cheesecake Factory in Denver while I was in grad school for acting. It was awful.

Has your relationship to pizza changed since you started working at Franny's?

Oh, yeah. Before working at Franny's, I wouldn't have called pizza one of my favorite foods. But pizza has taken on a completely new meaning to me. I eat pizza more than I ever did before, and actually crave it. But it's really just Franny's pizza that I crave.

Favorite dish on the menu, past or present?

I used to have a running shift every Friday night, and at the end, I'd order a white pie and have the kitchen put pickled hot peppers on it. I'm in love with the pickled peppers at Franny's. That's the way the white pie is now served, and I think it's just perfect. I love the way the acid and heat of the peppers evens out the fattiness of the cheese.

Favorite cocktail?

The Arlecchino. I love the Nardini Tagliatella by itself with ice or in this cocktail. It's sweet without being cloying and goes down almost too easily.

Favorite secret midshift snack?

It's not really a secret, but sometimes I'll get an intense chocolate craving in the middle of a shift and have to zip out and grab some at the deli. But I check in with everyone to see if they want anything—keeping the sugar flowing helps with morale.

Lemon-Lime Bitter

This very grown-up soda doesn't rely on seasonal ingredients, so you can make it year-round. Tart, bitter, and effervescent, it's an ideal aperitif when something nonalcoholic is called for.

SERVES 1

1 lime wedge
1 ounce fresh lemon juice
½ ounce **Simple Syrup** (page 355)

3 dashes Angostura bitters
2 dashes orange bitters
Club soda

Squeeze the lime wedge into a water glass filled with ice, then add the lime wedge, lemon juice, simple syrup, Angostura bitters, and orange bitters. Top off with club soda. Toss into a cocktail shaker, then back into the water glass. Repeat once more to combine.

Red Currant Vermouth

Clusters of ruby-red currants are brief visitors at the farmers' market. The juicy little globes are so sweet and delicate, there's little you need to do here other than crush them a bit and pour good white vermouth over them. The alcohol does the work, extracting their sweet-tart juice. The resulting infusion is beautifully red, fruity, and light.

MAKES ABOUT 1 QUART

4 pints red currants, stem-on, rinsed
One 1-liter bottle Martini & Rossi bianco
  vermouth

In a medium bowl, slightly crush 2 pints of the currants with a fork.

Pour the crushed currants and juices into a large lidded jar and add the remaining 2 pints whole red currants and the vermouth. Seal tightly and refrigerate for 3 days.

Strain the vermouth through a fine sieve into a large bowl. With the back of a large spoon, crush the currants until most of their remaining liquid is released into the vermouth. Store the vermouth in the refrigerator; it will keep for 2 months.

Amaro #4

We use so many different kinds of amari in our cocktails at Franny's that eventually I got the idea to start making our own. When I expressed this desire to Nekisia Davis, our manager at the time, she dove in headfirst, researching and digging up what little information there was. We made nine different batches of amari, using an array of different aromatics. This one, which we call simply #4, has always been one of the best sellers. It's light, citrusy, and approachable while still retaining a solid bitter finish. It's not hard to make once you get all the ingredients, though it does need to macerate for nearly a year. You can find all the unusual herbs and other botanicals at Starwest Botanicals (see Resources, page 357).

MAKES ABOUT 2½ QUARTS

48 ounces (6 cups) **Martini & Rossi bianco vermouth**
16 ounces (2 cups) **dry vermouth, such as Noilly Pratt**
1½ cups sugar
21 ounces (2½ cups plus 2 tablespoons) **grain alcohol or vodka**
3 tablespoons dried organic chamomile flowers
6 fresh lemon verbena leaves, or 2 tablespoons dried lemon verbena or lemon balm

2 thyme sprigs (approximately 3 inches long)
1 eucalyptus leaf
1 tablespoon dried gentian root
1 tablespoon dried rhubarb root (not powder)
1 tablespoon dried sweet orange peel
1 tablespoon dried life everlasting flowers
1½ teaspoons quassia
1 teaspoon rue
1 teaspoon anise hyssop
Zest and pith from 1 navel orange, removed with a peeler

In a large sealable glass container or jar, combine both vermouths and the sugar. Cover and shake to mix. Set aside for 5 days. In another glass container, combine all the other ingredients; set aside.

After 5 days, strain the grain alcohol into another jar, and add the herbs and flowers to the jar with the vermouth. Reserve the infused grain alcohol. Let the vermouth steep for 1 week.

After 1 week, strain the vermouth into a tight-lidded jar. Add the grain alcohol. Let sit in a cool, dark area for at least 6 months before tasting. The amaro generally needs 8 to 11 months to age; it's ready when it tastes full, rich, and round. Store at room temperature.

Serve in small glasses.

Amaro #6

Piney and woodsy, with notes of cedar and toasted nuts, our Amaro #6 has a more earthy and assertive character than #4.

MAKES ABOUT 2½ QUARTS

48 ounces (6 cups) **Martini & Rossi bianco vermouth**
16 ounces (2 cups) **dry vermouth, such as Noilly Pratt**
1½ cups sugar
1 Meyer lemon
21 ounces (2½ cups plus 2 tablespoons) **grain alcohol or vodka**
12 basil leaves
8 sage leaves
5 tablespoons dried rosebuds

1 tablespoon dried gentian root
1 tablespoon juniper berries
1 tablespoon powdered wild cherry bark
1 tablespoon dried rhubarb root (not powder)
1 tablespoon quassia
1 tablespoon dried lavender flowers
1 tablespoon life everlasting flowers
1 tablespoon dried hibiscus flowers
2 whole star anise

In a large sealable glass container or jar, combine both vermouths and the sugar and shake to mix. Set aside for 5 days to marry the flavors of the vermouths.

Meanwhile, using a vegetable peeler, remove the zest from the lemon in long strips. Quarter the fruit. In a large glass container, combine the lemon zest and quarters with all the remaining ingredients. Set aside for 5 days.

After 5 days, strain the grain alcohol into another jar, and add the herbs, flowers, and anise to the jar with the vermouth. Reserve the infused grain alcohol. Let the vermouth steep for 1 week.

After 1 week, strain the vermouth into a tight-lidded jar. Add the grain alcohol. Let sit in a cool, dark area for at least 6 months before tasting. The amaro generally needs 8 to 11 months to age; it's ready when it tastes full, rich, and round. Store at room temperature.

Serve in small glasses.

Blood Orange Grappa

If you've ever had dinner in a restaurant in Southern Italy, chances are you've been offered a little glass of homemade limoncello, maybe even made from the lemons growing in the garden. This bright-tasting, pale pink grappa evokes those citrus flavors, albeit using blood orange instead of lemons. We've cut the sugar as well, so the tangy flavor of the citrus is front and center, not muted by sweetness. Serve chilled after a rich winter meal.

MAKES ABOUT 5 CUPS

4¼ pounds blood oranges (about 8)
½ cup sugar
⅛ teaspoon kosher salt

One 750-ml bottle best-quality grappa, such as Jacopo Poli
1 cup fresh blood orange juice

Using a vegetable peeler, remove the zest from the oranges in long strips; reserve. Remove the pith with a paring knife or your fingers and reserve. Cut each orange into eighths.

In the bowl of a food processor, combine the pith, sugar, and salt and process until the pith is finely chopped.

Pack the pith into the bottom of a 1-gallon glass jar. Top with the reserved zest. Place the fruit on top of the zest, taking care to leave the fruit as intact as possible. Pour in the grappa. Cover tightly. Let the grappa stand at room temperature for 4 days.

Strain the grappa into another glass jar; use your hands to squeeze all the excess liquid from the pith and fruit (discard the pith, peels, and fruit). Stir in the blood orange juice. Store in the fridge for up to 1 month. Serve chilled.

Plum Grappa

Fruity and only slightly sweet, this summery grappa has a hint of almond flavor from the cracked plum pits, which we infuse into the alcohol along with the fruit.

MAKES ABOUT 1½ QUARTS

3 pounds Italian, black, or Dinosaur plums
2 pounds yellow, purple, or red sugar plums
¼ cup sugar

1 liter (34 ounces) **best-quality grappa, such as Jacopo Poli**

Pit the plums; reserve the pits. Cut the fruit into wedges. Using your hands or a potato masher, mash half the fruit in a bowl. In a large bowl, combine the mashed and unmashed fruit and toss with the sugar.

Place the pits under a dish towel (preferably an old one, since the pits sometimes catch on the fabric) and, using a wooden rolling pin or a mallet, crack them open. The kernels inside should be exposed.

Pour the grappa into a large sealable glass container. Add the plums, pits, and any loose kernels. Press the fruit into the grappa with a wooden spoon. Cover and let stand at room temperature for 3 days.

Strain the grappa through a fine-mesh sieve into a bowl, then strain again through a sieve lined with a linen dish towel, so that the grappa won't be too thick. Store in the fridge for up to 1 month. Serve chilled.

Variation

White Peach Grappa: Substitute 3½ pounds white peaches for the plums and increase the sugar to ⅓ cup.

Sour Cherry Grappa

This bright red grappa tastes like sour cherries in liquid form. It's sublime.

MAKES ABOUT 2 QUARTS

5 pints (3½ pounds) **sour cherries, rinsed but not stemmed**
1 pint (8 ounces) **sweet cherries**
½ cup sugar

⅛ teaspoon kosher salt
1 liter (34 ounces) **best-quality grappa, such as Jacopo Poli**

In a large bowl, combine the cherries, sugar, and salt. Using your hands, smash about half of the cherries (do not remove any stems or pits). Transfer all the fruit to a tight-lidded glass jar and cover with the grappa. Seal the jar and shake vigorously for 1 minute. Let stand in a cool place for 3 days.

After 3 days, transfer the mixture to a large bowl. Using your hands, smash the rest of the fruit into the grappa.

Strain the grappa through a fine-mesh sieve into a clean bowl, then ladle into glass jars or other airtight containers and store in the refrigerator for up to one month. The grappa will separate into a cloudy layer on the bottom and a clear layer on top. Pour the clear part off to serve, chilled.

Quince Grappa

Make this in autumn when quinces are at their peak.

MAKES ABOUT 1½ QUARTS

3½ pounds quinces
¼ cup sugar

1 liter (34 ounces) **best-quality grappa, such as Jacopo Poli**

Wash the quinces well to remove the fuzz. Dice the quinces, place on a rimmed baking sheet, and sprinkle with the sugar. Sprinkle with enough grappa to moisten the sugar. Cover with plastic and let sit for 15 minutes, or until the quinces start to release their liquid.

Pulse the quinces in a food processor until they break down to a rough puree. Transfer to a tight-lidded jar and cover with the remaining grappa. Seal the jar and shake vigorously for 1 minute. Let stand in a cool place for 3 days.

After 3 days, line a fine-mesh sieve with a linen dish towel and set over a bowl. Strain the grappa into the bowl and refrigerate overnight. Set the sieve over another bowl, put a weight on the quinces, and refrigerate overnight to drain the remaining grappa from the quinces. The next day, add the liquid from the drained quinces to the rest of the grappa. Store in the fridge for up to 1 month.

Preserved Meyer Lemons

MAKES 10 TO 12 PRESERVED LEMONS

10 to 12 Meyer lemons (about 2 pounds)
1¾ cups kosher salt
2 tablespoons sugar

Scrub 5 of the lemons under cold running water. Cut them lengthwise into quarters from the bottom up to but not through the top; they should remain attached at the stem end.

Transfer the lemons to a large jar with a tight-fitting lid, or use two small jars. Juice 5 more lemons and stir the salt and sugar into the juice. Pour the juice into the jar—it should come halfway up the lemons; if not, juice more lemons as needed. Screw the lid on the jar tightly. Let stand at room temperature for 1 week, turning the jar over once a day.

Put the lemons in the refrigerator and turn once a week for 6 weeks after that. The lemons will keep, tightly covered, in the refrigerator for at least a year.

Basic Tomato Sauce

MAKES 2 CUPS

¼ cup extra-virgin olive oil
½ yellow onion, chopped
1 garlic clove, thinly sliced
½ teaspoon kosher salt, plus more to taste

Freshly cracked black pepper
One 28-ounce can San Marzano or other good-quality plum tomatoes

In a medium saucepan, heat the oil over medium-low heat. Add the onion, garlic, salt, and a few grinds of pepper and cook, covered, until the vegetables are very soft, 5 to 7 minutes.

Pour in the tomatoes and their liquid, bring to a simmer, and simmer until the sauce thickens and the oil separates and rises to the surface, about 25 minutes.

Run the sauce through a food mill fitted with the large disk (or puree in a food processor). Season with additional salt and pepper as needed. The sauce will keep, in an airtight container, in the refrigerator for 1 week or in the freezer for 3 months.

Shrimp Stock

5 tablespoons extra-virgin olive oil
1¼ pounds shrimp shells and heads
3 tablespoons dry vermouth
2 onions, coarsely chopped
3 celery stalks, coarsely chopped
8 garlic cloves, coarsely chopped

⅓ cup chopped flat-leaf parsley
1½ teaspoons fennel seeds
1 bay leaf
1 dried chili
1½ teaspoons tomato paste
8 cups water

In a large pot, warm 1½ tablespoons of the olive oil over medium-high heat. Add half the shrimp shells and heads and sear them, stirring, until fragrant and toasty and golden in places, about 5 minutes. Transfer to a large bowl. Repeat with 1½ tablespoons more olive oil and the remaining shells and heads. Before removing the second batch of shells, pour the vermouth into the pot and deglaze, scraping up the browned bits from the bottom of the pot. Transfer the second batch of shells to the bowl.

Add the remaining 2 tablespoons olive oil to the pot. Stir in the onions, celery, garlic, parsley, fennel seeds, bay leaf, and chili and cook over medium heat, stirring occasionally, until the vegetables are soft and translucent, about 10 minutes. Stir in the tomato paste and increase the heat to medium high. Cook, stirring occasionally, until the tomato paste browns a bit.

Return the shrimp shells and heads to the pot, pour in the water, and bring to a simmer. Cook gently for 1 hour.

Strain the stock through a fine-mesh sieve, pressing on the solids with the back of a spoon to extract as much flavor as possible. Let cool. The stock will keep, in an airtight container, in the refrigerator for 1 week or in the freezer for 3 months.

Fennel Conserva

MAKES ABOUT 3 CUPS

3 large fennel bulbs
2 cups extra-virgin olive oil
3 cloves **Garlic Confit** (page 354),
  finely chopped
1 teaspoon fennel seeds
½ teaspoon chili flakes

1 teaspoon kosher salt
Freshly cracked black pepper
1 tablespoon **Garlic Confit oil** (page 354)
Finely grated zest of ½ orange (½ teaspoon)
1 teaspoon Strega or Pernod

Cut off the fennel fronds and roughly chop ¼ cup. Reserve 3 tablespoons of the chopped fronds for the Roasted Fennel, page 145. Remove the stems; reserve the bulbs for the Roasted Fennel. Trim away any rough ends and very thinly slice the stems crosswise, about ⅛ inch thick. (You should have about 2 cups sliced stems.)

In a small saucepan, warm the oil over medium-low heat. Add the fennel stems and cook gently over low heat for 25 minutes.

Stir in the garlic, fennel seeds, chili flakes, salt, and pepper to taste and continue to simmer until the stems are meltingly tender, with no bite remaining, 15 to 20 minutes longer.

Stir in the confit oil, the remaining 1 tablespoon fennel fronds, the orange zest, and the Strega. Remove the pan from the heat and let stand for at least 10 minutes to infuse. The conserva will keep, in a tightly covered jar, in the refrigerator for 2 weeks.

Andrew's Note: Fennel Conserva is a great addition to a piece of roasted fish. Or spoon onto grilled bread for a crostini.

PANTRY/BASICS

Pickled Hot Peppers

MAKES ABOUT 1 CUP

8 ounces mixed hot peppers, such as Hungarian hot wax, Anaheim, cayenne, jalapeño, serrano, cherry, and/or banana peppers, cored and seeded
1 cup white wine vinegar
½ cup moscato vinegar (see Resources, page 357)

¼ cup sugar
1 tablespoon kosher salt
1 ounce small hot peppers, such as habanero, Scotch bonnet, Granada, ghost, Brazilian bird, or Thai bird, seeded

In a medium saucepan, combine the peppers, vinegars, sugar, and salt and bring to a simmer.

Place the small hot peppers in a bowl. Pour the hot mixture over the peppers. Cool to room temperature, then transfer to an airtight container and refrigerate for 1 week.

Remove the peppers and finely chop, then return them to their pickling brine. The peppers will keep, tightly covered, in the refrigerator for 6 months or longer.

Pickled Fennel Stem

MAKES 1½ CUPS

1¼ cups white wine vinegar
3 tablespoons sugar
2 teaspoons kosher salt
1 small sprig rosemary

1 small chile de árbol
Zest of 1 small orange
2 cups thickly sliced fennel stem

In a small saucepan, combine the vinegar, 1¼ cups water, the sugar, salt, rosemary, and chili. Bring to a boil; remove from heat and strain.

Place the orange zest and fennel in a bowl. Pour the hot brine into the bowl. Cover with plastic wrap and refrigerate for at least 24 hours before using. Refrigerate in an airtight container for up to 3 months.

Pickled Ramps

MAKES 2 CUPS

1 pound late-season ramps with well-
  developed bulbs
½ cup white wine vinegar
¼ cup moscato vinegar (see Resources,
  page 357)

5 teaspoons sugar
1½ teaspoons kosher salt

Trim the hairy roots from the ramps. Separate the bulbs from the greens; reserve the greens for another use. Rinse the bulbs under warm running water and pat dry.

In a small saucepan, combine the vinegars, sugar, and salt and bring to a simmer. Stir in the ramps,

reduce the heat to low, and return the liquid to a simmer.

Let stand, stirring occasionally, until cool.

Transfer the ramps and liquid to an airtight container; the pickles will keep in the refrigerator for up to 3 months.

Homemade Bread Crumbs

YIELD DEPENDS UPON HOW MUCH BREAD YOU USE

1 loaf or the saved ends from several
  loaves of good bread, preferably
  a few days old

Preheat the oven to 300°F. Cut the bread into 1-inch-thick slices and arrange in a single layer on a baking sheet. Bake for 20 minutes, or until completely dried. The time will vary depending on the type of bread and how dried out it was to begin with; after 20 minutes, check the slices for any signs of "give," and if they yield in any way, return to the oven for another 10 minutes. Let cool.

In a food processor or blender, pulse the bread until pulverized to crumbs. Store in an airtight container at room temperature for up to 3 months.

Garlic Confit

1 head garlic, cloves separated and peeled
Extra-virgin olive oil to cover (about 1 cup)

Place the garlic cloves in a small skillet and pour in just enough olive oil to cover the garlic. Place the pan over low heat and cook the garlic until tender and pale golden, 30 to 35 minutes. Let cool completely.

Transfer the garlic and oil to a jar with a tight-fitting lid. The confit will keep in the refrigerator for 2 weeks.

Homemade Mayonnaise

MAKES ABOUT 1 CUP

1 large egg yolk, at room temperature
Juice of ½ lemon
¼ teaspoon kosher salt

½ cup grapeseed or canola oil
¼ cup extra-virgin olive oil

In a large bowl, whisk together the egg yolk, lemon juice, and salt. Whisking constantly, slowly drizzle in the grapeseed or canola oil in a thin, steady stream, whisking until the oil is completely incorporated and the mayonnaise begins to thicken, then repeat with the olive oil. Store in the fridge, in an airtight container, for up to 3 days.

Simple Syrup

MAKES ABOUT 1½ CUPS

1 cup sugar
1 cup water

In a small saucepan, combine the sugar and water and bring to a boil, stirring until the sugar dissolves. Let cool. Store in the fridge, in a tightly sealed jar, for up to 3 months.

Mint Syrup

MAKES ABOUT 1½ CUPS

1 cup sugar
1 cup water
½ cup mint leaves

In a small saucepan, combine the sugar and water and bring to a boil, stirring until the sugar dissolves. Turn off the heat, add the mint leaves, and let infuse for 3 hours.

Strain the syrup; discard the mint. Store in the fridge, in a tightly sealed jar, for up to 3 months.

Lovage Syrup

MAKES ABOUT 1½ CUPS

1 cup sugar
1 cup water
½ cup lovage leaves

In a small saucepan, combine the sugar and water and bring to a boil, stirring until the sugar dissolves. Turn off the heat, add the lovage leaves, and let infuse for 3 hours.

Strain the syrup; discard the lovage. Store in the fridge, in a tightly sealed jar, for up to 3 months.

Honey Syrup

MAKES ABOUT 1 CUP

½ cup honey
½ cup water

In a small saucepan, combine the honey and water and bring to a boil, stirring until the honey dissolves. Remove from the heat. Store in the fridge, in a tightly sealed jar, for up to 3 months.

Vanilla Sugar

In an airtight container, bury 1 scraped vanilla bean in 2 pounds of sugar. Let stand for at least 1 week before using. The sugar will keep for about 1 year.

RESOURCES

Italian Pantry Items

Salt-packed capers from Pantellaria, moscato vinegar, aged balsamic vinegar, Tutto Calabria Calabrian chilies packed in oil, *saba,* colatura di alici, pasta, dried cannellini and Controne beans, high-quality anchovies, bottarga, excellent olive oils, San Marzano tomatoes, amarena and maraschino cherries

www.bklynlarder.com
www.buonitalia.com
www.gustiamo.com

Note: For a cheater's moscato vinegar substitute, whisk together ½ cup apple cider vinegar, 2½ teaspoons honey, and ¼ teaspoon balsamic vinegar.

Xanthan Gum
www.nowfoods.com

PreGel Neutro Ice-Cream Stabilizer
www.chefswarehouse.com

Dried Herbs and Spices

Lucknow fennel seeds, fennel pollen, bay leaves, chiles de árbol, Controne chili, vanilla beans, and more

www.bklynlarder.com
www.kalustyans.com
www.madecasse.com
www.manicaretti.com
www.thespicehouse.com

Heritage Meats

www.heritagefoodsusa.com
www.nimanranch.com

Curing Supplies

Cure #1 pink salt, hog casings, meat injection pump (aka brining needle), and sausage stuffers

www.butcher-packer.com
www.sausagemaker.com

Amari Supplies

Obscure botanicals, herbs, and dried flowers

www.starwest-botanicals.com

Flours

Premium flours, including durum, "00" pasta flour, and all-purpose

www.kingarthurflour.com

Spirits and Liqueurs

For grappas, amari, and liqueurs

www.wine-searcher.com

ACKNOWLEDGMENTS

This cookbook brings together our favorite recipes from the past eight years at Franny's. We hope it provides inspiration.

Amazing people have been with us along the way, including all the Franny's staff, both past and present, who have helped us create an exciting and happy place to eat and work. You have all held the perfect combination of graciousness and true passion for good food. Thank you, thank you.

Specifically, we want to thank our incredible chefs, Danny Amend and John Adler; our prep cook, Roberto Guzman; our great friend Brandon Gillis; our brilliant general manager, Martin Gobbee; our agent, Janis Donnaud; our editor, Judy Pray, and everyone at Artisan; our recipe testers, Sarah Huck, Olga Massov, Rebecca Klus, and Sunny Michelson; Bklyn Larder pastry chef Inga Sheaffer; our crazy talented photographer, John von Pamer; our stylist, Cindy DiPrima; Melissa Clark, who sat through hours and hours of our stories and translated them beautifully; all of the farmers who provide our ingredients, most especially Bill Maxwell; Alice Waters; our accountant/father/financial guru, Hoby Shapiro; all of our "regulars" who have created a strong community for us on Flatbush Avenue; and, lastly, both our moms, whose help every step of the way has been invaluable.

INDEX

INDEX

363

INDEX